Life's

The Road to Heaven, Leads Through Hell

Joshua 1:9

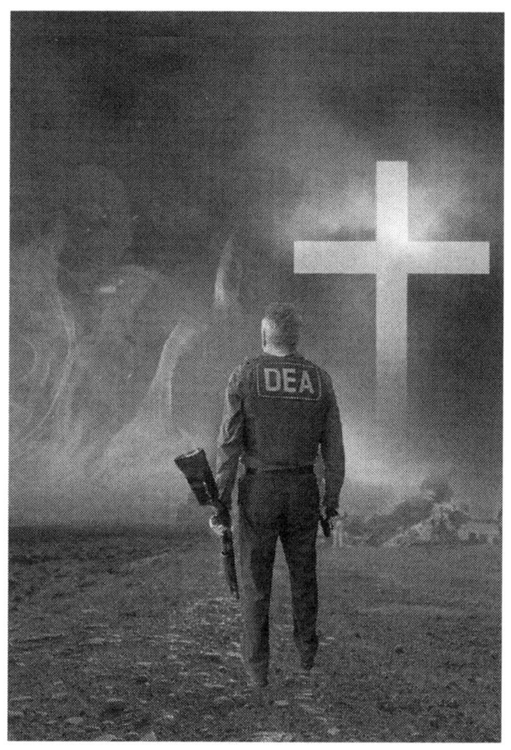

Inspired by Factual Events

Of

Larry Ray Hardin, Retired DEA, Author

Dianne DeMille, PhD, Writer

While this book is not endorsed by DEA, it has been reviewed by the DEA Publication Review Board to ensure that no classified or law enforcement sensitive material is released pursuant to DEA and DOJ policy.

April 2023
Dianne's Consultant Services
Anaheim, CA

Paperback ISBN: 979-8-9865623-5-3
eBook ISBN: 979-8-9865623-6-0

Acknowledgment

God Hath not Given us a Spirit of Fear

I have written this fourth book *Life's a Journey Between Heaven & Hell* after I almost decided to abandon the project. However, I'm fortunate and blessed to be surrounded by a committed, brave, talented, and intelligent writer, editor, and publisher who inspired me to continue what I started.

This book and the others, *Path of the Devil-2nd Edition*, *Fighting My Greatest Enemy-Myself*, and *Home is Never the Same*, would not have been published without her. So, this is my "Thank You," to Dianne DeMille, who is my writer, publisher, and editor. She has been my great friend who believed in my books; continually challenging me to be a better writer and a better person.

This book could not have been written without the assistance of my former co-workers, informants, and dedicated men and women within the law enforcement and medical communities that are not afraid to speak out. Many good law enforcement officials take their constitutional oaths and responsibilities to the American people to heart, just as many good people within the medical community believe in the Hippocratic Oath. "Do No Harm."

I want to thank Tim Snodgrass and Dianne DeMille, Ph.D., for their hard work editing and proofreading these true-to-life stories. They dedicated a lot of their time to the book and hopefully helped me bring the truth to the public in *Life's a Journey Between Heaven and Hell* and why *The Road to Heaven, Leads Through Hell.*

I have seen the evil that men do, and I have seen their crimes. I have witnessed the tragic effects of drug addiction within our communities. I want to thank God for the families at Plum Creek Baptist Church and neighbors on Plum Creek Road for helping me stay true to my faith and teaching me that the lust for power and money is evil.

"For God hath not given us a spirit of fear; but of power, and of love, and of a sound mind."
(Second Timothy 1:7, King James Version)

Foreword

I was at the airport in Venice Italy, waiting for the bus that would take me to the cruise ship I would be traveling on for the next two weeks. As I waited patiently to board the bus, I happened to turn around and looked at the people in line behind me. The face of the man immediately behind me seemed impossibly familiar. After staring back at the face for just long enough to be awkward, I turned around and told myself that it couldn't be who I thought it was. That is when I heard the unmistakable Kentucky accent.

"Larry," I asked turning around to look at the man once more.

He stared back quizzically, pausing to look me in the eyes when recognition suddenly dawned.

"You son of a gun," he fired back with a hearty grin.

I first met Larry Ray Hardin while I was working as an IT (Information Technology) Specialist for the DEA in San Diego. Larry was outgoing, friendly, and generous. He was well known for bringing back mason jars of "Apple Pie Moonshine," to share with friends whenever he came back from Kentucky. What I found most likeable about Larry was his sense of humor. Tensions could run high within the office at times, and it was always enjoyable to interact with someone that knew how to laugh and didn't take themselves too Seriously. Larry was one of a handful of people that I would stop to chat or joke with whenever our paths happened to cross.

I had not seen Larry since he had retired, 11 years earlier. After coming across a series of YouTube videos that he had created we had exchanged a couple of messages on social media, expressing hopes for meeting up over lunch at some point in the future. The intended lunch at some point in the future had suddenly become an impromptu two-week cruise down the Adriatic coast and into the southern Mediterranean.

During the cruise, I would frequently have dinner with Larry and his wife. At times we would all wander into ports together with other passengers we befriended during the journey. The truly revealing moments, were the late afternoon chats we would have in the ships crow's nest, a lounge area at the front of the ship, high above the ocean waves. It was during these chats that I would come to know who Larry was, what he had experienced, and what drove him.

Although the settings and roles that we have played in life differ, the path was remarkably similar. Like Larry, I had grown up in poverty. Church had come to play a big role during my adolescent years and provided me with a compass that guided away from the dark paths that could have easily been taken during those formative years. I even joined the Navy as a Spanish linguist after a bad relationship left me wondering what I was going to do with my life, and a desire to go far away.

Several months later I found myself in Panama at a time when tensions ran hot with Operation Just Cause on the Horizon. It was at a time when I was young, had no concept of my own mortality, and felt a deep urge to wonder and explore. Although I generally felt quite safe wandering through Panama, it could turn dangerous very quickly if you were in the wrong place at the wrong time. I found myself staring the barrel of a gun on more than one occasion as my misadventures led me into dangerous situations. Those misadventures also enabled me to get the kind of close look at what was happening that most Americans never saw. The stories that I was watching on the news clips from back home distorted what was really happening. There was also no getting around the fact that the monster named Noriega, was one of our own creations.

The similarities in our lives did not end there. Larry and I both married beautiful Spanish-speaking women while stationed overseas in the Navy, with whom we are still married after many years. Finally, we both unexpectedly found ourselves working for the DEA. We had worked together for many years, but it was only during these two weeks that I would really come to know Larry Ray Hardin.

Larry is a modern-day crusader, and it was only fitting that I learned to know him better in settings such as the isle of Malta (one of our port calls) where crusading knights had once fought so bravely. I have often said that the road to heaven leads through hell. That is a truth that I imagine those ancient knights would understand quite well, as does Larry. He has walked through the darkness, but steadfastly remained on a path towards the light.

It is my heartfelt belief that to achieve any heavenly state we must be tested. We are guaranteed to fail some of the tests which we are given. It's ok to make mistakes as long as we find the strength to get back up and continue traveling the road. We become stronger as we overcome defeat, and ultimately, we find the strength to reach our destination.

The Larry Ray Hardin that you will see in much of this book is a younger, angrier version than the one I came to know in San Diego. What makes Larry's journey great is not just that he refused to be lured in by corruption as he walked the path through hell. What makes it great is that he learned from his failures along the way, replaced anger with wisdom, and continued to walk the road to heaven.

Author's Note

The Law of the Lord

The stories you are about to read are true. They are based on transformative moments in the life of DEA Special Agent Larry Ray

Hardin that challenged and ultimately strengthened his faith. They deal with the deceit he faced within the law enforcement community, judicial system, military, and from government officials and politicians. As a boy growing up in Kentucky, these are people Larry Ray had learned to trust, and he was forever changed by the harsh realities he observed firsthand.

These stories are also about the victims of careless and unethical behavior within the medical community and pharmaceutical industry. Millions of people turn to those industries for help each year, and some will walk away to prescription drugs such as OxyContin, Vicodin, and other narcotic pain medications. Larry Ray would come to know those victims personally, not only the victims of illegal drugs but those who became dependent on prescription drugs.

Larry Ray has reflected deeply on the Incidents, flow of events, and heart-to-heart discussions he experienced while working as a Special Agent. Using notes, memory, and interviews with previous co-workers in law enforcement, the military, and the medical community, he has reconstructed those events in the pages of this book. He has also reached out to concerned citizens and past informants for their unique perspectives. Although the stories you are about to read are true, the names of individuals in law enforcement, informants, and medical community sources have been changed to protect their safety and privacy.

Larry Ray will never forget the young and old individuals he has arrested over the years. Nor will he forget the lives he has seen destroyed by addiction to narcotics and pain medication. He arrested several nurses for manufacturing and distributing methamphetamine. He was even shocked and disappointed to see respected individuals within the medical community that lost their DEA prescription licenses for over-prescribing narcotic pills and capsules to patients.

Following his retirement from the DEA, Larry Ray became a Hospice Volunteer. While visiting Hospice patients nearing their end of life, he would be deeply saddened by some of the things they said.

"Why can't the doctors help me to live?"

"I trust the Doctors to help me to get better."

"Please give me more pain medication. Why me?"

He sadly wondered; why some patients continue begging for more narcotic medications?

"Blessed is the man that walketh not in the counsel of the ungodly, nor standeth in the way of sinners, nor sitteth in the seat of the scornful."

(Psalm 1:1, King James Version)

About the Author

For Whatever Things Were Written

I signed an agreement with DEA to wait five years after retirement before writing about my experiences as a Special Agent with front-line experience in narcotics trafficking investigations. Shortly after those five years ended, I resolved to commit those experiences to write. With the help of two Private Investigators (PIs) and Dianne DeMille (Ph.D., Educator), I wrote my first book: Path of the Devil: Camino del Diablo. The book examines corruption in law enforcement at the Port-of-Entries (POE) along the Southwest United States (U.S.) and Mexico border. It is now a Second Edition, Revised.

Readers shared their belief that the PIs and I were "fighting the devil" and expressed deep concerns for our safety and our lives.

My second book, "Fighting My Greatest Enemy: Myself," shares my spiritual journey with Christ Jesus while working in the DEA.

My third book, "Home is Never the Same," discusses my life as an innocent Country boy in the backwoods of Kentucky and how I became a man in a world of evil. This was a time of deep soul searching as I looked for the truth and asked myself, "Where is God, His son Jesus Christ."

These books are available in Podcasts, Kindle, and Audio in Spanish and English. To ensure authenticity, I have personally provided most of the narration for the Audio.

What I learned from working "Street Narcotics" for almost 24 years in DEA is incredible. Throughout the years, I have lost good friends in the law enforcement community: DEA Agent Richie Fass, DEA Agent Frank Moreno, Yuma PD (Police Department) Lieutenant

Danny, Elkins, DPS (DPS) Sergeant Michael Crowe, Spain Guardia Civil Julio Gomez Franco, and my trusted informant, Angelito.

Some of them were even killed by corrupt cops while working narcotics. They all believed in the promises made by our political leaders and thought that the United States could win the war on drugs.

At times I have even asked myself, could some of them have been killed because of my work targeting corruption in law enforcement and the drug Cartel on the Southwest U.S. and Mexico border?

Trust is essential to law enforcement operations, and sometimes it wasn't easy to know whom I could trust. I personally dealt with mistakes made by wicked men who wore the badge. They were involved in some of the narcotic cases we investigated, especially along the Southwest border with Mexico. I had to be very cautious about dealing with the local law enforcement near the Mexico border. I had to scrutinize anything I was told, even from law enforcement and the medical community. I constantly had to ask myself what a lie was and what the truth was.

Looking back on the cases I worked on and the time I spent "working the streets," it was incredible to witness the filth of crime and corruption. A lot of the corruption was not only in Mexico but here in the United States. I consciously decided not to follow the mistakes of wicked men lusting for money, sex, and power over life and death.

To stay alive, I had to focus on what I knew in my heart was right; tell the truth and remain faithful to God, family, home, and my brothers and sisters in the law enforcement community.

"For whatever things were written afore time were written for our learning, that we through patience and comfort of the scriptures might have hope."

(Romans 15-4, King James Version)

Introduction

What doth the Lord require of Thee

Larry Ray was raised as a country boy surrounded by rural Kentucky's dark woods and shallow creeks. Growing up in a farming community, he learned to live a moral, purpose-driven life and not fear death. He was guided by his daddy's firm hand and Momma's daily prayers. Each day Momma asked God to keep Larry Ray safe from the wickedness of this world. Larry Ray quickly understood not to be selfish and truthful, to keep promises, not to cheat, to forgive, and not to hurt others for the lust of evil.

As a backwoods boy, Larry Ray listened to the spoken words of his parents, family, relatives, neighbors, and Plum Creek Baptist church that Jesus Christ lives in our spirit.

Larry Ray sometimes quietly wandered near the rocky edges of the creeks, ponds, and lakes in the backwoods hollers of Kentucky. He would listen to the gentle breeze that danced through the rainbow color tree leaves as he explored. As he picked his way along the tree-lined creeks, he would ponder the things he had been taught. Honesty and devotion were Larry Ray's values, the best way to live.

In Larry Ray's Christmas book, "Home Is Never the Same," he shares how ten family members lived together crowded in a wooden three-room house. It did not even have running water or even a bathroom. Water had to be brought in from an outside well, and the toilet was in a small shed outside. The four brothers and four sisters were squeezed into one bedroom: the boys in one feather bed and the girls in another. The parents lived in the living room.

The old house was built next to a rocky creek with a small ledge creating a four-foot waterfall. The waterfall was his brothers and sisters' shower in the hot, humid summers. Despite all these hardships, Larry Ray was happy, oblivious to his poverty.

What is hardship? Is it not having running water?

A bathroom inside the home. Is it to have a wooden and coal-burning stove to keep warm and have hot water? How about an outhouse toilet and sulfurous well water? Does it matter if the home is next to a creek and in a holler?

Larry Ray began his career as a Special Agent in the Drug Enforcement Administration (DEA) with trust in God, HIS son Jesus Christ that had been instilled in him as a child in Kentucky. He had learned to live a life of integrity and not to lust for power, adultery, and money, as he discusses in his other books, *Path of the Devil/Camino del Diablo & Path of the Devil - 2nd Ed Revised, Fighting My Greatest Enemy: Myself*, and *Home is Never the Same.*

"He has shewed thee, O man, what is good; and what doth the Lord require of thee."

(Micah 6:8, King James Version)

Prologue

The most dangerous moments I encountered while working narcotics were the temptation of money and sex. We sometimes found large amounts of money that needed to be carefully accounted for and turned in. This required a lot of integrity. I made it through the temptation with the blessing of my faith, and I worked hard not to be corrupted. In a world of corruption and seduction, I could hold on to my faith and stay true to the values I had been taught as a boy. I put many people in jail who did not share those values. Looking back on how I dealt with some of the corruption I encountered in law enforcement, I think it was about knowing how to stay away from dishonesty, focusing on the truth, being thankful for what I had, and enjoying every moment in life.

Some of the poor "mules" we encountered were very uneducated. They turned to crime to make a living, buy food for their families, and pay bills. The poor drug traffickers who were arrested had to rely on Public Defenders, the worst lawyers paid for by taxpayers.

I do not have any regrets about what happened with the investigative cases. Some cases were easy to adjudicate. Some were difficult. There was greed on both sides of the fence and government officials that would abuse their authority. It is amazing what money can do to people in the world of illegal drugs and prescribed narcotics.

I never got promoted in DEA. I wanted to become a group supervisor, maybe a manager (Special Agent in Charge), which was as far as I could go in the agency. I had the personality and integrity to lead. I needed connections with senior leadership in DEA, who shared my values and integrity.

I needed clarification about what I should do next with my life. I learned that corruption was deeper in law enforcement and politics than ever imagined. What I learned from working narcotics on the streets for almost 24 years is incredible. On the streets, I had to stay focused, trying to do what I knew in my heart was right. That was the struggle of working narcotics, in the shade of evil, and the path of the devil. I decided not to follow the path of evil. I resolved to find "the light in a battle with darkness."

Trust in the Lord with all your heart. There you can find the light.

DEA gave me a promising career. I am in good health. I have an enjoyable retirement with a great pension. I made it. The following pages show that my real triumph was keeping my faith in our Lord Jesus, not with my wife or family, but with confidence in God. I stayed focused on that. That was my biggest challenge to face the evil sickness of men.

I had to stay focused, doing what I knew was right in my heart. In a battle with darkness, I chose to embrace the light, or as I would say, *Life's a Journey Between Heaven and Hell.* That was my struggle as I worked narcotics and dealt with the evil men in control.

"No man can serve two masters: for either he will hate the one and love the other; or else he holds to the one and despise the other."
(Matthew 6:24, King James Version)

Chapter 1

A Wise Son Maketh a Glad Father

Daddy placed the heavy shotgun in my hands. Then he lifted it up to my left shoulder. "It's too heavy. I can't hold the big gun," I fearfully said.

I was only six years old, but Daddy insisted. "Boy, here, take the shotgun!" He paused as he waited for me to do as he had said, "Now point at the empty coffee can standing on top of the rock pile."

I stared at him as I struggled with my fear. "But Momma says guns can hurt you." I timidly blurted out.

Daddy yelled loudly, "Point the gun at the coffee can. Squeeze the trigger!"

"What trigger? Where's the can?" I asked.

Suddenly, I heard a loud noise like a thunderstorm and saw a flash of lightning at the end of the gun. The gun flew out of my hands, knocking me backward and landing on the ground with a thump. I found myself unable to move or say anything. "Did the flash of lighting hit me on the head?" I thought.

Daddy jerked me up off the ground. I stood there staring, unable to say a word.

He knocked the dirt off my butt. "Boy, are you okay?" he asked.

In the distance, I could see my brother running like Daddy's rabbit dog to the outhouse. For a moment, I feared that I had shot him in the butt.

I heard Daddy's voice again saying, "How does it feel to shoot a single-barrel 12-gauge shotgun?"

"Did I hit the coffee can?" I asked.

"No, you didn't hit the can. But you sure did send the rocks jumping off the ground."

After shooting Daddy's shotgun that cold, early morning, I felt like Daniel Boone. I begged Momma for a gun.

"You can hurt or kill your brothers and sisters. Lawrence Raymond, you're not getting a gun," Momma yelled.

"A wise son maketh a glad father: but a foolish son is the heaviness of his mother."

(Proverbs 10:1, King James Version)

Chapter 2

A Merry Heart Doeth Good Like a Medicine

Suddenly, the rotten wooden rafter broke, falling on the ground beside me.

"Daddy, are you okay?" I fearfully asked, "You have blood on your chest."

Not knowing what to do, I screamed for Momma, "Daddy's fell. He hurt his chest. There's blood everywhere. We're here in the bacco (tobacco). Hurry, Momma!"

Momma was running out the kitchen door with a white bed sheet in her hands before I could call out to her again.

"Junior, are you okay? Did you break any bones?" asked Momma. She looked at my father and suddenly realized what had happened. "Lawrence Raymond, get some water!" she shouted. She knelt beside Daddy, staring at the wound, as I ran to get the water. His chest was covered in blood.

When I returned, Momma slowly cleaned the blood off Daddy's chest with a torn bed sheet.

"Go get the jar with white cream. It's next to the kitchen sink," she ordered. I wasn't sure if she was talking about the pig lard, but I quickly darted off to do as she directed, then returned to the barn. She gently rubbed white cream on Daddy's chest. Then she wrapped him around the chest several times with the torn bed sheet.

After a few minutes, Daddy finally stood up on his feet. "Junior. Don't climb back up in that old barn."

"I think you broken your ribs," stated Momma as she inspected Daddy.

He grinned like a possum as he slowly started climbing up into the barn like a cat, searching for a bird's nest.

"Daddy, you're not going to fall again, are you?"

Momma sighed as she turned to walk back to the house. "You hard-headed man."

Several days later, I saw my sister, aged 5, lying down on the dirt, shaking like a wet dog that Daddy had thrown in the creek.

"What kind of game are you playing?" I asked. Then I noticed that she was spitting up watery vomit."

Before I could scream, Momma was there, quickly picking my sister up off the ground.

"She's not breathing!" yelled Momma as she slapped her on the face and back. Nothing happened. She shook her body several times until her breath returned. Suddenly Momma saw an empty bleach bottle on the ground.

"Did she swallow bleach?" she screamed. Clutching my sister in her arms, Momma ran back into the house. That evening when Daddy came home from work, Momma told him what had happened.

"A merry heart doeth good like a medicine: but a broken spirit drieth the bones."

(Proverbs 17:22, King James Version)

Chapter 3

Teacheth My Hands to War, and My Fingers to Fight

"You can't go to school, Lawrence Raymond. We are too far back in the hollers," explained my momma. "Walking alone in the early morning from the house to the school bus is too dangerous. You would have to walk back to the house when it's getting dark."

"You can go to school once we move to the city. You and your brother can start the first grade together," she offered.

Finally, after that first year in the old two-room broken-down wooden farmhouse next to the creek, Daddy moved the family to the big city. I was age seven and in the first grade.

I always got in trouble with the Nuns at the Catholic school for fighting with the other kids. The Nuns slapped me across the hands with a long wooden ruler while pulling my ear lobe.

As I was screaming, I thought; the Nuns were hitting me on my hands and pulling my ear lobe. "Why's my brother grinning like a possum eating roadkill?"

At home, I tried explaining to Momma why the Nuns whipped me.

"The bad kids are laughing because of my potato sandwich. The nuns are standing next to me. I couldn't fight them in the lunchroom... I had to wait to fight some kids on the playground."

Did the Nuns whip me because I beat up the bad kids?

"Blessed be the LORD my strength, which teacheth my hands to war, and my fingers to fight."

(Psalms 144:1, King James Version).

Chapter 4

Rejoice Evermore

Chasing my younger brother, I picked up an empty glass beer bottle in my right hand. I was about to put it in the trash can when I tripped on the sidewalk, falling on the bottle.

After breaking the beer bottle in my hand, I was amazed by all the blood coming from my hand. The hanging skin looked like a strip of bacon. Maybe I needed to tell Daddy what happened.

With my right-hand dripping blood on the brick sidewalk, I asked my brother, "Do you think I should tell Daddy what happened?"

"I don't know if you want to tell Daddy you had a beer bottle in your hand. He might think I knocked you down, causing you to cut your hand," he suggested.

"You're right. He might whip us for fighting with a beer bottle." I agreed.

I remember a pretty young woman in a white coat at the hospital. She was freckle-faced and had red hair.

"I'm supposed to take care of your hand," she said.

Immediately, I knew she was a doctor. I noticed she was wearing a weird silver necklace. I stared at her pretty, rose-colored freckles.

"What kind of necklace is around your neck?" I asked.

"It's a Stethoscope to listen to heartbeats and the lungs," she said, flashing a pretty "Snow White" smile.

Then she stuck a long needle in my cut hand. "It won't hurt," she promised.

"It hurts!" I screamed.

Daddy shot me a look. I stopped myself from crying, but continued staring at Snow White.

"Are you going to listen to my heart and lungs with that necklace around your neck?" I asked.

Growing up as a young boy, I learned from my family and relatives to trust anyone wearing a white coat or having a Stethoscope wrapped around their neck. I admired how beautiful Snow White looked in her white coat. What a beautiful doctor, I thought.

Do I have to trust Snow White with the long needle? I wondered.

She did have a pretty smile. Her teeth were Whiter than first snow. Maybe that's why I thought of *Snow White. Perhaps I could be one of her dwarfs.*

Then, an older man wearing thick black frame eyeglasses entered the room. He had a Stethoscope in his pocket, not around his neck. Like *Snow White*, he wore a white coat, but I could not help but notice that it was spotted with blood. I thought, *he looked like Dracula without the two long front pointed teeth. He hasn't smiled yet, and the blood on his coat looks like he killed a pig.* He scared me.

"Is the boy ready for cleaning and closing?" *Dracula* asked Snow White.

I wondered what he was talking about.

Dracula started pouring water on my cut hand. *Ouch*! It burned.

"Boy, you're getting stitches in the hand," said *Dracula.*

Looking at Daddy, I asked, "What's stitches?"

Then *Dracula* began sewing up the cut with white thread and a crooked needle, like Momma sewing up a torn bed sheet. *Why did Momma use a straight needle when sewing up holes in my shirts? I wondered, Dracula's using a crooked needle.*

A different man wearing a white shirt, white pants, and white shoes wrapped my hand with white bandages. Later, another woman dressed like an "Angle fruit cake" in a white dress, a small white cap on her head, and a "necklace" (Stethoscope) quickly stuck another long straight needle in my left arm.

Thank you, baby Jesus, I thought; she wasn't using a crooked needle. Looking around the room, I wondered, *what happened to Snow*

White with the shining teeth. Did Dracula scare her too? Where's Dracula?

> *"Rejoice evermore."*
> *(1 Thessalonians 5:16, King James Version)*

Chapter 5

Blessed are Those Who Mourn

"Lawrence Raymond, tell the neighbor I want to see her after she washes the clothes," said Momma.

"Who?" I asked.

"The next-door neighbor," she replied.

"Okay. I go now and tell the neighbor what you said, Momma."

At the neighbor's house, I walked to the open front door.

"Hello, lady. Are you home?" I shouted. "Momma wants you to see her after you finished washing clothes."

"I'm here washing clothes. Wait, I can't hear you. I be there in a minute," she replied.

As I stood waiting for the neighbor to come to the front door, I saw a white baby crib next to a large window in the living room. A lot of nasty green flies were hovering over the crib.

That's odd, I thought. Momma said our next-door neighbor had a new baby. Why are there a lot of nasty green flies flying over the baby's crib?

I approached the crib to swap the flies away from the crib. Then, I saw flies on the baby's back. The baby was laying down on its belly, its tiny hands stretched out on each side. I stared at the baby for a moment.

Why are their nasty flies on top of the baby? Why's the baby's hands so dark looking? I wondered out loud.

"Hey, Larry Ray. What did your mom say?" Then she paused, "Where are all these flies coming from?"

"Momma wants you to…." I began to say.

Suddenly she grabbed the baby and screamed. She continued screaming and crying while she held the baby in her arms.

"Get your momma!"

I ran out of the house shouting for Momma.

"Lawrence Raymond. What's wrong? What happened? Who's that screaming?" said Momma with obvious concern as I reached the house.

"Momma," I said, "I think something happened to the lady's baby.

"You watch your brothers and sisters," she said as she ran off towards the neighbor's house.

While standing outside in the front yard, I could hear the lady screaming and crying inside her home. Then I saw a police car and ambulance stopping in front of the neighbor's house. A policeman and two men from the ambulance ran inside the lady's house. They left soon after with the lady, who was holding the baby in her arms.

Momma came back crying.

"What happen to the baby, Momma?" I asked.

When Daddy arrived home from work, Momma met him in the front yard. Momma started crying again as she told Daddy what had happened to the neighbor's baby. Later that night, Momma asked me to pray for the baby and the neighbor's family.

While praying, I whispered to God, "What happened to the baby? Why did the baby die? Why couldn't you save the baby from dying?"

"Blessed are those who mourn: for they shall be comforted."
(Matthew 5:4, King James Version)

Chapter 6

As the One Dieth, So Dieth the Other

On a cold early morning at home, I heard something scratching at the back door. I went to investigate and slowly opened the door. To my surprise, a little hairy white puppy was wagging its tail, trying to get into the house. That's odd, I thought; where did the dirty white puppy come from? Was it lost? What would Momma do if I sneaked the puppy into the house? I gripped the white puppy's front leg, dragging it into the house.

"It's a snowball puppy," one of my sisters shouted out gleefully.

"What's a snowball puppy?" asked Momma before stepping into the room to see the furry little visitor. "You girls, take snowball puppy to the bathtub; give it a bath before you play with it," she said.

A few days later, I saw a bald old man with a long red nose and black eyes. The nose was pointed, and he had no teeth in his mouth. He was yelling at Snowball to stop barking at him.

What happened, I thought, Why's Snowball barking at the toothless baldheaded old man? Did Snowball see the evil devil in the old man?

A few nights later, Snowball was scratching my bed. "Snowball, are you scared of the old man?" I whispered. "Get in bed with me. He can't hurt you. I will protect you."

When I got up the next morning, Momma was concerned.

"Lawrence Raymond, Snowball's sick," she said.

"How do you know he's sick? What's wrong, Momma?" I asked.

"Before you boys go to school, take Snowball to the doctor near the animal stockyard in the red wagon. Here's the direction. Take $5 to give to the doctor."

I wrapped Snowball in an old blue blanket he loved and laid him down in the red wagon. I was worried. *Why's Snowball not moving his legs and wagging his tail?* I thought.

At the doctor's office, a man in a white coat gently lifted Snowball out of the red wagon. With Snowball lying in his arms, he disappeared into another room. After a few minutes, he returned with Snowball. The doctor laid Snowball back in the wagon.

"Take this note to your mom," he said.

"Is he going to be okay?" I asked.

"Give your mom the note," said the doctor.

I handed the $5 to the Dr. "Momma wants you to have the $5."

"No. Give it back to your mom."

On the way home, I noticed Snowball was trying to breathe. He was crying.

"Snowball, are you okay? Why're you crying?

At home, Momma started to cry as she read the doctor's note.

"Snowball has been poisoned. He's dying."

My brothers and sisters started to cry too. We joined with Momma to ask God not to let our puppy die. I could not cry at first. I knew who gave Snowball the poison. It was the nasty old man with the devil inside of him.

Later that night, Snowball was at my bed scratching the bed frame. I looked to see Snowball's wet eyeballs. What happened? What's wrong with his eyes? I thought. Is he suffering? Before I could rub Snowball on the head, he looked down at the floor. Slowly he walked to his cardboard bed. He slowly crawled into the cardboard box. I watched him fall on the wooden floor, then struggle to get back up. Momma came over and gently started to pet Snowball.

"What's wrong, Momma?" I asked.

She was crying, "He's not breathing anymore. Snowball's gone to heaven."

I asked myself; did Snowball come to me to say goodbye? Is that why his eyes were wet with tears?

Later that morning, my family took Snowball out to the hollers to bury him in the woods. After a few miles, Daddy stopped in a wooden area. He took Snowball out from the car's trunk. I followed Daddy as he carried Snowball in his arms, wrapped in the old blue blanket. He gently laid Snowball next to an old elm tree. I did not want to leave him lying on the cold, wet ground.

Daddy and I returned from the woods. As we approached the car, I saw everyone still crying for Snowball. I could not shake the feeling that I had failed to protect him from the old man. I had already learned about death from Momma when the next-door neighbor's baby died, but Snowball's death was different.

"For that which befalleth the sons of men befalleth beasts; even one thing befalleth them: as the one dieth, so dieth the other; yea, they have all one breath; so that a man hath no preeminence above a beast: for all is vanity."

(Ecclesiastes 3:19-20, King James Version)

Chapter 7

For Where Your Treasure Is

Under an old elm tree, I was dreaming about all the Big Red soft drinks and the bags of salted peanuts I could buy. I loved putting peanuts inside my Big Red soda drink. I learned that from the older boys that lived on Plum Creek Road. They would do that when they went down to RT's grocery store.

Early in the morning, my aunt and I went to work all day in the bacco (tobacco) field next to the creek. We chopped ragweed and cleared it away from the leaves of the plants. It was in mid-July, and the weather was hot and humid. Bees were flying about in the fields and would sting our arms. It was my first paying job; I was only eight years old.

"Larry Ray, go over there and sit down in the shade of that old elm tree. You need to cool down. Here take some water," said my aunt.

Later that evening, at RT's grocery store, RT's wife asked, "Do you want your $5?"

I replied, "Yes, I do."

"Then come over here. I want you to kiss me on the cheek, and I'll give you the $5." I glanced up at Daddy to see if it was okay to kiss her.

After kissing her on the cheek, I took my $5 and ran out of the country grocery store's front door like a dog chasing a black cat.

The next day, Daddy took me to the surplus clothing store. He said, "Larry Ray, get a pair of blue jeans and a short brown sleeve shirt. Then follow me to the cashier."

The cashier had long, greasy brown hair hanging over his shoulders. His face was hidden behind a reddish bird.

He looks like a savage caveman that just ate a juicy red fox, I thought.

"Give him your money," said Daddy. To my shock and surprise, he was not kidding.

If I gave the old fox the $5, I couldn't buy the Big Red soft drink or the salted honey-roasted peanuts. I sadly thought about everything I had to do to earn that money. Not only did I have to work in the fields, but I had to kiss the old lady too.

The cashier reached his hand out, pulling the $5 bill out of my tight little hand. He looked down at me and handed me a few coins.

"Here's what's left from the $5," he said. "The clothes are in the brown paper bag,"

I felt terribly disappointed as I stared at the coins that remained from my $5. Then I looked back up at the cashier. *I know why you have a dirty red beard,* I thought. *You're a redneck.*

Later, Daddy stopped at a vegetable market. With the few coins in my pocket, I hoped to have enough money to buy a Big Red soda. Maybe even a bag of peanuts. I followed Daddy into the market and watched him grab a Pabst Blue Ribbon beer and fishing worms. I saw peanuts next to the beer and looking around, I also saw the Big Red.

"How much is the Big Red? How about peanuts?" I asked.

Wow! I had enough coins for a Big Red and a bag of honey-roasted salted peanuts. At age 8, I learned the value of money from that experience.

"For where your treasure is, there will your heart be also."
(Matthew 6:21, King James Version)

Chapter 8

With Good by The Fruit of His Mouth

Grandpa grabbed a long hooter (udder) under one of the black spotted Jersey milk cows. He jerked up and down on the cow's fat hooter, squeezing it hard. Then Grandpa aimed that fat hooter at my face, squirting warm milk. Oh boy! It tasted so sweet.

I was laughing at myself while Grandpa jerked on the cows' fat hooters. As Grandpa milked the cows, they started pooping and peeing on the floor. Grandpa finished jerking the cow's hooters for milk, and they slowly walked out of the milk barn.

"Okay. You boys can start cleaning it off the walls and floors," he said. "After you fill up the wheel barrel with the poop, push it outside of the barn and dump it in the poop pile."

From early morning to late evening, my brother and I shoveled cow poop out of the barn twice a day. After cleaning the milk barn, my brother and I would have poop on our faces down to our shoes. Grandpa would say, "Clean up that splatter manure off your faces and mouths. Get it off your hair too."

I loved the taste of the sweet, warm cows' milk in my mouth. Why I enjoyed the smell of the steamy cow pies (poop) was a mystery to me.

Sitting at the kitchen table each morning, I enjoyed eating Grandma's cooked hog sausage, hog bacon, hog sausage gravy, and chicken eggs. My favorite was the brown biscuits she cooked inside a wood-burning stove. I would push poop out of the barn all day to eat Grandma's cooking.

Late one night, I could not sleep and grabbed her cold hard milk biscuits from the kitchen table. Then I spread cow butter and some homemade blackberry jam on it. While I was enjoying the biscuits, I longed for a glass of fresh warm hooters milk.

Several years later, I was helping an old farmer chase a skinny Jersey steer. I tripped on a rock, landing like a dead bird, face down in some watery green cow pie poop. I slowly stood up, flicking the warm cow poop from my mouth and nose. I was amazed that the warm poop didn't smell.

"Heck!" I exclaimed as I spat some of the green poop pie on the ground.

The old farmer laughed, "Don't worry about the cow pie in your mouth; it's green alfalfa grass pie from the hay field," he said. "The cows eat grass, some corn, but not meat. Does it taste like spinach?"

It did taste like sweet green spinach.

Later, my grandparents were killing a few old chickens that had quit laying eggs. I watched Grandpa as he jerked some old hens by their necks near the woodpile, not far from the stinking outhouse toilet. After Grandpa jerked their necks, the headless hens ran in circles. Grandma started pulling the feathers off the headless hens as I watched in horror.

"Boy, grab the chicken heads out of the dirt," shouted Grandpa. "Take the heads behind the outhouse, not behind the chicken house."

"No. I'm not picking up those chicken heads," I stubbornly responded. *It's time for me to go horseback riding*, I thought as I turned my back to Grandpa. Suddenly, something hard smacked me on the butt, and I glanced down at the dirt, seeing a chicken head. Looking up at Grandpa, I noticed he had another chicken head in his hand, ready to throw.

"Boy! You better stop running from me. Come here and pick up those heads."

Later that night, Grandma cooked fried chicken for supper. I sure did love eating her fried chicken.

After dinner, I saw my overfed uncle pumping well water into a silver ten-gallon bucket for drinking. Suddenly, he spitted bacco juice from his toothless mouth. It landed near the well water, splattering red, watery juice next to the water bucket. I wondered if some of the bacco juice made it into the water bucket. The thought disgusted me, but I decided I wanted some chew too.

"Hey, give me a piece of your bacco in your shirt pocket. Not from your month." I added, "I want some chew."

Before I could say it again, he spit bacco juice in my right eye.

"Ouch!" I exclaimed. That bacco juice burned my eye. Glancing up with my left eye, I saw him grinning like an old grey-haired coon (raccoon).

"It's burning my eye. It hurts." I explained.

"Throw some drinking water on it. It'll be okay after a while."

Grandpa had thrown a chicken head at me, straight as an arrow. Uncle spit in my right eye without wasting any bacco juice. *What else could happen today?*

Most days on the farm were not so eventful. At the end of the day, I would run down to the creek or pond and jump headfirst into the water. I never had swimming clothes. Heck! I did not wear underwear either. I learned from Grandpa and Daddy that only women wear underwear.

"You can hurt or kill your brothers and sisters. Lawrence Raymond, you're not getting a gun," Momma yelled.

"A man will be satisfied with good by the fruit of his Mouth: and the recompence of a man's hands will be rendered unto him."

(Proverbs 12:14, King James Version)

Chapter 9

A Broken Spirit Drieth the Bones

"Hey, uncle!" I shouted. "I can't pull the pitchfork out of my rubber boot."

"What happened?" yelled my uncle.

"I can't pull the pitchfork out of the boot. I think it went right through the toe," I shouted.

Uncle quickly climbed the latter up into the silo like a red fox squirrel looking for a Hickory nut and looked to see what had happened.

"Are you okay, Larry Ray? What happened to you?"

"The pitchfork's stuck in my boot. I can't pull it out. I think it's stuck in the big toe," I replied.

"Why would you do something like that?" he asked.

Crawling, he slowly squeezed into the small silo door and rose to his feet. Looking at the pitchfork, he took a moment to spit out a big wad of chew next to the unmoving boot.

"Don't move your right foot," he said.

Before I could say a thing, he grabbed the pitchfork, and quickly jerked it out of my booted foot. He removed the boot from my foot and then the bloody sock. I could see a hole in my big toe. "I think it went straight through it," I said, stating the obvious.

Grandpa and my brother were waiting down on the barn floor. My Uncle shouted down to them,

"That pitchfork went right through Larry Ray's big toe."

Suddenly he threw me over his left shoulder. He slowly carried me down the silo ladder where Grandpa and brother were waiting.

"Boy, how did you stick yourself in the big toe?" asked Grandpa.

"Dad, we need to take him to see the doc up the road," said my uncle.

We went to go see the doc, and he examined my foot.

"The boy has a hole in his big toe," he announced.

What a surprise, I thought sarcastically.

After cleaning out the hole in the big toe using rubbing alcohol and iodine, he wrapped the toe in a white cloth.

"Now, boy, drop your pants," said the old doc.

Oops! I don't wear underwear like Daddy and Grandpa, I thought.

I couldn't understand why he wanted me to drop my blue jean pants down to my ankles. Did he think I poked a hole in my butt with that pitchfork? Is he looking for something else? He's wearing a white coat. I must trust him.

"Now lean over against that small table." Instructed the doc.

I glanced over the top of my right shoulder and saw the old doc sticking a long, pointed needle in my butt. Bracing myself for the pain that I expected as the needle pierced my skin, I was pleasantly surprised to find that I didn't feel a thing.

"Now you can pull your pants up."

Grandpa gave the doc $5.

"That boy's going to have a scar on that big toe for the rest of his life," he stated.

A few years later, I hurt my right-hand playing basketball. Another old doc said that I had broken my hand and wrapped it tightly with a bandage. The next day, I was playing basketball with my brothers and our buddies.

Reflecting on the various scars and wounds I had acquired over the course of my life, I wondered why some of them healed differently than others. For instance, I noticed that my big right toe looked very crooked.

Many years later, I decided to see a Podiatrist. After he conducted an examination and did x-rays of the foot, the doc sat down with me to discuss his findings.

"I see a scar on your big toe," he said. "Was it fractured? How long has the toe been bent like this?"

"Since I was a boy," I replied.

"Well, someone did not set the big toe in its right position."

"Can you look at my right hand? Do you think the middle finger bone's been broken?" I asked.

He took a moment to examine the finger and feel the bone.

"You have the same problem that you have with your toe. No one fixed the bone in your hand. Does it hurt?"

"Sometimes, when I shake someone's hand real hard," I replied.

We depended on the town doctors for serious problems like stitches and broken bones. I wondered why the old doc never said my big toe was broken or why the other doc never fixed the bone in the hand. Back home, Momma and Daddy would take care of the cuts and burned skin. Grandma would help, too; I remember her putting iodine on the deep-down cuts. After she cleaned them, she would cover them with white cloth torn from some worn-out clothes. Sometimes she would put a copper wheat penny and some hog bacon grease over the cut skin.

"You can hurt or kill your brothers and sisters. Lawrence Raymond, you're not getting a gun," Momma yelled.

"A merry heart doeth good like a medicine."
(Proverbs 17:22, King James Version)

Chapter 10

Thou Shalt Not Bear False Witness

Am I dying like Snowball? I can't die now. I must find the boy that shot me in the belly. Where's the boy? Those thoughts went through my head while I was lying down in the street, overcome with pain.

A few hours before, I was running like someone had stolen a Three Musketeer candy bar from a candy store. I was trying to catch a dark-skinned boy who shot me in the belly with his BB gun. Finally, I saw him running across the street like an alley cat chasing a rat. I was closing in on him when something hit me in the right leg. Stumbling forward, I fell into the street.

I felt disoriented and wondered why I was rolling in the street. *Oops! I forgot to look for traffic*, I thought. I remembered the boy and glanced up to see if I could see him. He was gone. *That boy must be running home like a scared dog with his tail between his legs.*

I was suddenly startled to see a man squatting over me. He looked like a Munchkin from The Wizard of Oz and filled me with a sense of fear and foreboding. Breathing heavily, I struggled to come to terms with the apparent nightmare I found myself in.

"Boy, are you okay? You bounced like a rubber ball on the street pavement for several feet. I thought you were a goner."

Recovering from my disorientation, I looked up at him and noticed a white pickup truck. He's not a Munchkin, I thought. He must be the driver of the white pickup truck. I'm the one who got hurt. Why are his hands and head trembling?

It looked like the driver was about to cry. He was as afraid as I was.

"Are you okay?" he asked, his hands trembling. He tried to help me stand up, and I could see he looked sick.

Why's he so sick looking, I thought. Is he going to puke on me?

Without the driver's help, I jumped up from the street. "Ouch!" I screamed. It felt like my right leg had been stung by a red wasp. "My right leg hurts."

My cries of pain were making the driver increasingly nervous.

"Where're you going, boy?" he asked.

"I'm going home. I lost the boy who shot me in the belly," I snapped.

That boy lives somewhere close to me. I'll see him again, I thought.

I hopped back home on the left leg and crawled to the bathroom. The right leg was still in pain.

"Lawrence Raymond, what happen to you? Are you fighting those neighbor boys again?" Momma asked.

"No, Momma. I think a red wasp stung me in the right leg," I lied.

Later that evening, Daddy asked me why I was hopping around the house.

"I'm okay, Daddy." I felt awful lying to Daddy and Momma.

That night I prayed that Daddy and Momma would not find out I lied to them. If they found out I had not told them that a pickup truck had run over me, Daddy would whip me with his leather belt, and Momma would yell.

The next day at school, I had what I thought was a very bright idea. I could fake like a dead possum, drop down on the playground and pretend that the boy with the BB gun hurt my leg at school. My brother would tell Daddy and Momma some boy ran into me and hurt my leg. *What could go wrong?*

Without hesitating, I fell on the school playground. "Ouch! My leg hurts. It's hurting. I can't move my leg."

Hearing my fake cries of anguish, my brother came running to my side.

"What happen to you?"

"Ouch! That fat dark-skinned boy ran into me, hitting my leg. He knocked me down to the ground. Ouch! It hurts," I cried.

"What, boy? Can you get up?" he asked with obvious concern.

"I can't get up from the ground. The leg won't move," I yelled in exaggerated distress.

A tall Catholic nun heard the commotion and quickly made her way to where I was laying on the playground.

"Are you okay, Larry Ray? What happened to you?"

"A fat dark-skinned boy was running. He knocked me down on the ground and hurt my right leg. I can't stand up on my leg."

"Did you say a fat dark-skinned boy? Where is he?" she asked.

My brother leaned over knowingly and whispered into my ear.

"You're lying about the boy."

I stared into his eyes, glaring. "Don't you say anything to the nun, or I'll bust you in the stomach later," I threatened.

The tall nun looked at my brother.

"What happened to Larry Ray?"

My heart skipped a beat as I waited for his reply.

"It's a girl that knocked him down, not a boy," he stated.

I looked away from him, praying he would close his big mouth. Please don't say anything about a girl knocking me to the ground, I pleaded to myself.

"Your brother is saying it's a big dark-skinned boy. You and your brother know very well that no children look like that at this school."

I was furious; my brother needs to shut up. I fumed that he needs to let me do the lying when talking to the nun. Did she know we were lying?

"We are calling your daddy. He will come to pick you up and take you to the hospital," she stated in a very "matter of fact" tone.

After lying on the school playground for a while, I saw Daddy walk onto the playground. He went over to talk with the tall nun. My brother saw him too. He took off like a scared little pussy cat running into the school building.

Daddy took me to the hospital, where they ushered me into an examination room. I was laying on a small bed when two older girls wearing white coats stepped into the room.

"Who're you? Are you doctors?"

They laughed.

A man wearing a long white coat came into the room as well. He was talking with Daddy, and I listened like a hoot owl to what the man was saying.

"Your boy injured his right leg on the school playground. He needs to stay off the leg for a few days. No school for a week. No playing outside." He paused for a moment, considering the facts. "Are you sure the boy hurt his leg at school?"

Daddy glanced at me suspiciously but said nothing.

At home, I laid back on the couch for about a week. When I was hungry or thirsty, I begged my sisters to bring me soup, beans, and water. My brother would not bring me anything to eat, not even a glass of water. He knew I lied about the boy pushing me down at school. He could not say anything to Daddy and Momma about me lying because Daddy would know he lied also. If that happened, Daddy would whip us both with his leather belt while we were in bed naked.

"Thou shalt not bear false witness against thy neighbor."
(Exodus 20:16, King James Version)

Chapter 11

Thou Shalt Not Steal

Several days earlier, Daddy had moved the family into an old three-room house on Plum Creek Road. The house did not have indoor heating, bathrooms, or running water. It did have electricity.

It saddened me that Daddy had moved us out of the city and into the boonies, where there were only hollers and creeks. It was blue cold outside, which made the move more challenging. At least the sulfurous-smelling water from the outdoor well was not so bad in the cold winter months. The well wasn't the only stinky thing next to the house; there was also a foul-smelling outhouse. The smells were especially difficult to take when I had a nasty head cold.

One cold morning, I woke up early and remembered that I had forgotten to get firewood for Daddy. I poked my brother in the belly and whispered, "Come on, we've got to get up and go over to the uncle's porch to get some firewood. If I don't, Daddy's going to whip me." He used the wood to start the stove and warm the house.

My other two brothers stayed in the feather bed, unsympathetic to my dilemma.

"If you don't help to get some wood, I'm going to beat you up outside," I whispered.

We quietly tiptoed out of the backdoor like two mice, and it occurred to me that the easiest way to get the wood was to take it off our uncle's porch. I had taken wood off our uncle's porch several times and had never been caught. As I approached his house, I saw smoke coming out of the chimney.

"Brother, Uncle's up moving around the house. Keep your eyes on the front door and the windows. If you see his hairy face looking out the window, make a whistle like a quail," I instructed.

It was cold and dark, but no lights were on inside our uncle's house. I'm amazed that old uncle has no idea I'm about to grab some of his wood, I thought as I crawled up to his porch.

Slowly creeping onto the porch like a chipmunk searching for hickory nuts hidden in the firewood, I grabbed some wood and left. Quiet as a field mouse, I thought, that groundhog of an uncle is sound asleep like a baby.

As we returned home, I noticed Daddy looking for some firewood to put in the wood stove.

"Daddy. Here's the wood," I said.

Later that morning, I went outside to feed the pigs when the sun was up. I heard our uncle shouting out to Daddy.

"Hey, Junior. I saw Larry Ray crawling on his hands and knees up on my porch before sunrise. He took some firewood off the porch without asking me. I also saw your other boy hiding behind the elm tree. Did he know there were no leaves on the tree?"

"I was about to shoot my shotgun over that boy's head when he snuck up on the porch," he went on to say. "That boy would have broken his neck trying to get off the porch with no firewood. That other boy behind the tree would be running home screaming like one of your baby pigs."

I was shocked to hear the uncle telling Daddy he saw me taking his firewood off the porch.

Why didn't my brother whistle, I thought. Why didn't he see our uncle peeping behind the window curtain? I was more upset than a wet dog.

"Larry Ray, where are you? Come here right now!" yelled Daddy. Uncle just stood there chewing his bacco and spitting while he waited for what would happen next.

With his leather belt, Daddy whipped me on the legs for taking his brother's firewood. After the whipping, I made sure there was always firewood in the house.

Later that day, I saw my brother outside in the front yard. I was still angry that he had failed to warn me that the uncle was looking out his window, so I chased after him.

"Stand there. Don't move. I'm going to hit you in the arm," I told him when he finally quit running.

"Why me?" he demanded.

"Because you didn't tell me the uncle was looking out his window."

The weather grew warmer as winter turned to summer, and the sulfurous well water started to stink like rotten eggs. It was so bad I had to squeeze my nose to swallow the water.

The old doc (Doctor) had once said that "Sulfurous water is healthy to drink. Sulfurous water is good for bad breath, too, and you will not have rotten teeth either." I was amazed that nobody in my family ever had bad breath or rotten teeth. Maybe sulfurous water really is good for your health.

The smell from the outhouse also grew worse. One evening Momma was outside walking by the boys' bedroom window and saw someone "peeing in the wind."

"Stop that peeing out the window. I'm telling your daddy," She shouted.

"Momma, it's not me!" I protested.

After Daddy's whipping, I started using the smelly pee pot under the bed. I used the woods behind the stinky outhouse during the summer to poop and pee. Sometimes I would even use the outhouse, even when it was cold or rainy. When it was warm, I also used the nearby creeks and ponds to wash up, making sure my butt was clean. I hated a smelly butt in bed.

"Thou shalt not steal."
(Exodus 20:15, King James Version)

Chapter 12

Ye Serpents, Ye Generation of Vipers

"Do you see the big black snake under the water?" I asked my brother as we stood next to the creek. "He's in front of you. If you move your feet, it might jump out of the water at you." We paused, watching it cautiously.

"Wow! That big snake's looking right at us!" I whispered.

Slowly, I reached down to pick up a small rock and threw it into the water behind the snake. The snake whipped around and swam toward the sound of the rock hitting the water. Suddenly the snake came to a stop. Popping his head out of the water, he began to look around, and his eyes fixed on us.

"Don't move," I told my brother. "The devil snake's looking for us."

The snake's head began to rise about two feet out of the water, supported by its long neck. Its forked red tongue flicked through the air, sensing the movement around it. Large black eyes darted right to left. It was searching for something to bite.

Unable to identify a threat that it could dig its fangs into, the snake's head slowly went back under the water.

I picked up a bigger rock and threw it in front of the snake. "Let's run, brother. Let's get out of here," I yelled.

A few days later, my two younger brothers and I were out in the woods searching for something to do. I found a large vine hanging down from an oak tree. Grabbing the vine, I started to swing back and forth, yelling like Tarzan.

"It's my turn to swing on the vine," complained one of my brothers.

"No. It's my turn complained my youngest brother to no avail.

My youngest brother and I stood there watching as our other brother grabbed the vine with both hands and swung out from the oak tree. As he was swinging on the vine, a black snake, about four feet long, leaped out from a small poison ivy bush near the tree. It grabbed our brother's left leg. He hooted and hollered joyfully as he swung on the vine, blissfully unaware of the snake that clung to the leg of his blue jeans with its fangs.

"Hey, you're dragging a big fat snake with you on your pants leg. The snake's on your left leg. Look! Look!" shouted our little brother.

Our little brother was laughing so hard at the spectacle that he almost started to cry. I thought he lost his marbles; did he think our little brother was lying about the snake hanging on his pants leg? He just kept laughing, screaming like Tarzan as he swung back and forth on the vine.

He has no idea, I thought, if he sees the black snake hanging onto his pants, he's going to wet and poop all over himself.

At long last, our brother paused his revelry long enough to glance down at his pants leg. After a long minute, he finally realized it was a snake. Screaming for help, he leaped off the vine like a squirrel with the snake still stuck in his pants leg. Running around the oak tree, he tried desperately to shake the snake off his pants leg.

I was laughing as our little brother yelled, "The poison snake won't let go of your leg. You got to shake your leg hard."

Finally, the snake fell off his pants. I looked closely at the black snake's tail. Daddy said a poisonous snake has a blunt tail, but this snake's tail was pointed. The snake's not poison, I thought, it must be a cow sucker. The cow sucker quickly disappeared into the tall grass behind the oak tree.

"Raise up my pant leg now. I want to see if the snake has bitten me on the leg," screamed my brother.

Suddenly, a funny thought came to my mind.

"It's a cow sucker. It's not poison," I whispered to my little brother, urging him to play along.

"I'm pulling up your pants leg. I need to see if the poison snake bitten you," I told my other brother with feigned urgency.

"Can you see any snake bites on my skin?" he screamed.

Our little brother leaned over my shoulder, "Oh my God. Yes. There's a devil snake bite," he exclaimed.

"I can see little teeth bites right here, below your knee," I explained. "Lay down on the ground and don't move unless you want to die."

He stood unbudging, so I pushed him on the ground.

"Lay still on the ground. Don't move your leg," I insisted.

"Why?" he insisted.

"Shut up and don't move. I need to cut the devil snake bite to suck out the poison. If I don't suck out the poison, you're going to die like Snowball." He remained motionless.

"Little brother's going to hold your leg," I explained. "I don't want to cut too deep in your skin. So don't move."

I slowly reached in my left pocket, pulling out my Marlow' Buck Knife.'

"Don't move. I'm going to cut you now."

I slowly touched the knife's blade to the skin of his leg, near the fake snake bite.

"Now don't you move your leg," I commanded.

Suddenly he kicked me in the stomach like a baby calf. I fell backward and hit the ground with a thump. He also kicked out at our little brother and jumped to his feet.

Like a spotted bullfrog, he hopped away and ran off like a dog with tin cans tied to its tail.

"I'm going to die. Help me, Momma," he cried as he ran to the house.

"Don't run so fast. The devil's poison will kill you for sure. You're going to die before eating supper," shouted our little brother.

It was awesome, a great life. Playing in the creeks and the woods was better than visiting the zoo in the city. I enjoyed country life with my brothers and sisters.

"Ye serpents, ye generation of vipers, how can ye escape the damnation of hell?"

(Matthew 23:33, King James Version)

Chapter 13

Destruction Shall Be to the Workers of Iniquity

Suddenly, an evil thought came to me.

"Hey, hold the firecracker in your right hand. When the school bus starts moving, and the old man isn't watching us, I'm going to light it," I whispered to my brother.

"Now don't forget, throw it under the seat behind you, not to the front. You need to throw it fast from your hand. It could blow your fingers off. Daddy would kill me if you lost a finger," I admonished him.

Every morning during the school months, the yellow school bus stopped at the old house to pick up the Hardin kids (seven of us). Momma was so happy to see us go to school. She was finally alone with our baby brother in the old three-room house.

The yellow school bus was an opportunity for me to socialize and fight with kids living on Plum Creek Road. I was screaming and yelling like everyone else if I was not fighting with the kids on the school bus.

If there was any mischief or bad behavior on the school bus, the old grey-haired bus driver would immediately focus on my brothers and sisters, especially me. I don't know why the old bus driver singled us out.

"Lawrence Raymond, we're a good boy," Momma always said. "You take care of your brothers and sisters. Don't let anyone mistreat them."

The old bus driver decided to have me sit behind him one day. I guessed he wanted to watch me from the big mirror that hung down over his grey-haired head. I could not figure out why he watched me so carefully when the other kids on the bus screamed and yelled at each other, too. Well, maybe I was fighting too much with the kids on the bus.

I sat behind the old bus driver for about a week while he continued watching me in his big mirror. Did he believe that I would do something stupid on the bus to get a whipping at school and at home?

One day, my brother was sitting with me behind the bus driver. Two older boys gave me a small red firecracker and a match, smiling silently as they did so. The old bus driver didn't see a thing. He had failed to watch me in his big mirror. *I never had a firecracker*, I thought. *When I get home, I could scare my sisters or the hogs.*

Then I looked up to see if the old man was watching me in his mirror and considered the alternative. How can the old man watch the other kids and me and drive the school bus at the same time, I thought. The old man has no idea what I plan to do in the next few minutes.

We traveled a few miles on Plum Creek Road as I considered my plan. As we came closer to the old house, I turned to my brother and whispered the plan.

"Now, brother, remember when I light the firecracker, you don't throw it under the old man's seat. You need to throw it towards the back, not in front of you." I repeated this to him several times to make sure he understood, "Throw the firecracker under the seat behind us."

I lit the firecracker, but my brother continued to hold on to it.

"Brother, don't hang on to the firecracker. It's burning. Throw it now under the seat behind you now. If you don't, it will blow your hand off," I insisted.

Instead of throwing the firecracker behind him under the seat, he threw it under the old man's seat.

"Not towards the front," I groaned as the firecracker landed under the driver's seat. Suddenly there was a loud explosion, like the blast from my 20-gauge shotgun. It numbed my ears. The old bus driver hit the brakes, and the bus came squealing to a stop. Some of the kids lurched forward and were flying toward the front of the bus like little sparrows.

Pandemonium ensued as the other kids started to scream and shout. Slowly, the old bus driver rose from his seat, and all went silent. His head and hands were shaking like a scarecrow as he paused with heavy breaths to reign in his temper. His gaze fixed on me, and I looked at my brother. Meekly, my brother reached down to the floor to pick up the burnt match.

"What happened?" He had the gall to ask.

That was stupid, I thought; you shouldn't have picked up the burnt match. The old man's going to throw you off the bus.

The old bus driver saw my brother with the match in his hand and came to the obvious conclusion.

"It wasn't me. I swear it wasn't me," protested my brother with the match in his hand.

It was too late. The old bus driver grabbed my brother's hair and jerked him up from the seat, saying,

"It wasn't me! I swear. Ask Larry Ray," he cried, screaming for his life.

"Shut up!" I silently mouthed.

With tears in his eyes, my brother begged the old bus driver to stop pulling his hair. I watched without saying a word.

I hope he doesn't say it was me that gave him the firecracker, was all I could think as I stood there. He needs to keep his mouth shut. I'll beat him up if he says it was me.

The old man pushed my brother back into the seat and paused.

"Get off the bus now!" he shouted at last.

Lucky for him, the yellow school bus had stopped in front of our old house. My brother was screaming as he leaped off the bus. I slowly walked off the bus behind him.

I did not mention what happened on the school bus to Daddy and Momma; neither did our little brothers or sisters. No one said a thing about anyone throwing a firecracker under the old bus driver's seat. Daddy and Momma would be furious if they learned what really happened on the bus. I would beat up anyone that said anything; only our little brother would be spared.

The next day, the two older boys that gave me the firecracker and match told me my brother was screaming like a baby.

"Where is he?" I asked.

"He's in the Principal's office," they said, laughing. "The principal must be using the wooden paddle."

"He will never mention that I gave him the match and firecracker," I insisted.

After the whipping stopped, he ran out of the principal's office, grinning like he had just eaten Momma's homemade blackberry pie without telling her.

"The principal whipped me on the butt ten times with a wooden paddle," he said. "Heck! Daddy whips a lot harder than the principal."

I was proud of him. He had gone to the principal's office, gotten a whipping (10 hits on the butt), and remained silent. If only he hadn't picked up that burnt match from the bus floor, it could have been me getting a whipping.

Later, my red-headed sister told Daddy what happened on the school bus.

"Did Larry Ray give it to you? Did he tell you to throw the firecracker under the bus driver's seat?" he asked my brother accusingly.

My brother was a trooper and never told Daddy that I gave him the firecracker and the match. He told him that one of the older boys had given it to him. For the remainder of the school year, my brother and I took our place of honor behind the old grey-headed bus driver. I was proud of my brother for not squealing to the principal and Daddy that I gave him the firecracker and match.

"It is a joy to the just to do judgment: but destruction shall be to the workers of iniquity."

(Proverbs 21:15, King James Version)

Chapter 14

The Dead Know Nothing

It was a cold November morning, about 4:30 am, when I heard Daddy rousted me from my sleep.

"Get out of bed and get your mom's wash water," he demanded.

I had forgotten to get Momma's sulfurous well water before I went to bed that night. She was washing bed sheets this morning.

"Get out of bed," he boomed for a second time.

He did not have to; my brother and I were already running to the backdoor with two empty buckets. The sun had still not risen, and it was dark and cold. When I grabbed the handle we used to pump water from the well, it was almost frozen with ice. If the pump was frozen, I realized Momma would have to warm up water from the wood stove. We would then have to pour the water onto the pump's handle to de-ice it. Now I wondered if I had forgotten to get the firewood as well.

I tried to stay warm as best I could. I didn't have gloves on, so I used one bare hand to push up and down on the icy handle. Some of the buttons were missing from my oversized brown jacket, and I was using the other hand to keep it wrapped around my chest.

My brother stood behind me, shivering, waiting for a bucket of water.

"Hurry up, Larry Ray. I'm cold and scared. I might see one of Momma's ghosts."

I had managed to pump the first bucket full of water. As I attempted to fill the second one, I heard a blood-curdling scream in my right ear. Spinning around to see what had happened, I turned to look at my brother's ashen face. He screamed again as if the black snake was hanging on his pants leg. Dropping the bucket of water, he took off running as fast as he could. He threw caution to the wind as he ran, slipping on the frozen dirt.

"Daddy!" he screamed.

"Get off the frozen dirt! What's wrong with you?" I yelled, perplexed.

I could not understand what he was running from. What happened? It was then that I heard a noise behind me, like someone crying. Slowly, I turned around, and there it was…A white ghost was standing on top of the coal pile.

Stunned to see a real ghost, I could not move my feet to run. It was headless but screamed and moaned in the dark morning gloom. Its arms waved high in the air as it called out to me.

"I'm going to get you!" echoed its voice in the cold morning darkness of the hollers.

It couldn't be Momma's headless ghost stories were true!

I had to run from the screaming ghost, but I stood there paralyzed with fright. Finally, with an effort of will, I forced my unresponsive feet to move. Dropping the partially filled bucket, I reluctantly followed my brother into the dark. In my haste, I slipped, falling on the water he spilled. I lay there on the cold, wet, frozen ground screaming for Daddy to help me.

The screaming, headless ghost was flying towards me. It had taken my brother, and it was going to take me. Deep into the hollers, it would carry me, and I would never see my family again.

In those terrifying thoughts, I found the strength to leap onto my feet once again. I flew the final few feet to the house, slipping and sliding as I ran.

"Daddy!" I screamed, my hands flailing in the air.

Then I heard Momma laughing. I turned around to see if the headless ghost had followed me. Where the ghost had been just moments before, there was Daddy taking off a white sheet.

After that night, I never believed in ghosts again. Not even the ones from Momma's headless ghost stories.

"For the living know that they will die; But the dead know nothing. And they have no more reward."
(Ecclesiastes 9:5, King James Version)

Chapter 15

He Will Wipe Away Every Tear From Their Eyes

"Junior, you have a Beagle dog. Since Lassie died, I don't think the kids want another dog right now. But why a dog like this one? He looks mean," Momma protested as she looked at Daddy's new German Shepherd.

"I got this German Shepherd to protect the kids. The Beagle's my rabbit dog," he explained.

"What's his name?" I interjected excitedly.

"His name's Pepper," replied Daddy.

My brothers, sisters, and I started petting Pepper. Of course, Daddy's hunting dog also wanted to be petted.

One morning, my brother and I were sword fighting with a couple of sticks we had found outside. I poked him in the stomach with the stick sword, and he fell to the ground, pretending to have fallen in battle.

"Get up!" I demanded, "I'll poke you again."

"You killed me. I can't get up," he insisted.

Suddenly, I heard someone yelling off in the distance. "Hey, it's me. Tell your black dog not to bite me."

I looked up, and I saw my friend Bubba in the distance.

"Is that really you, Bubba," I asked, waving. "Don't worry. Pepper's not going to bite you. But don't run from him."

Bubba would come to the house to play with us boys. But he also liked to see my sisters, especially the redheaded sister.

On one occasion, the redheaded sister said, "Bubba's mean to me." Later, I punched him in the arm.

"Why did you hit me in the arm?" he asked.

"Because you were mean to my sister."

"Which one?" he had asked.

Now, as he approached the house, Bubba waved his hand at the redheaded sister. Pepper suddenly jumped up next to her. His ears were pointed straight up, focused like a hunting bird dog on Bubba.

"Walk slowly up to her," I instructed him. "If Pepper stares at you, don't be scared. Whatever you do, don't run from him."

Pepper continued to stare intently at Bubba.

"You need to walk slowly. He's staring at you," I insisted.

As focused as I was on Pepper, I failed to notice the less-than-friendly look my sister was giving Bubba.

"Get him!" she suddenly commanded.

Why did she say that to Pepper, I thought.

Pepper slowly approached Bubba like a wolf about to jump on his next meal.

"Don't run. Don't run," I urgently whispered.

Bubba stared at Pepper's snarling mouth, seeing the long, pointed, white teeth.

I saw the horror on Bubba's face. It looked just like the expression on my brother's face when he saw the headless ghost on the coal pile.

"Don't run!" I loudly insisted.

Pepper leaped at him.

"Pepper, stop!" I screamed, too late.

Bubba panicked. He screamed like a pig stuck in the mud as he turned and bolted from Pepper as fast as he could run.

"Don't run from him!" I pleaded. "Pepper, stop! Stop Pepper!"

Bubba leaped on the road like a scared rabbit running from Daddy's Beagle dog. I guess he thought he could outrun Pepper. Running like a wild rabbit on Plum Creek Road, he quickly glanced over his left shoulder to see if Pepper was closing in behind him. Looking over his shoulder again, he saw Pepper about to chew his butt. He started running a lot faster on the road than a wild Turkey being chased by a red fox. Pepper quickly closed the distance between them and dug his teeth into Bubba's butt.

Bubba screamed like a hungry baby crying for milk while Pepper grabbed onto his butt like a chew toy. Bubba continued to try and run, dragging Pepper down the road with him.

What are you doing? I thought. You can't outrun Pepper.

Bubba continued to scream like a baby pig getting his "mountain oysters" cut off by Grandpa while I pleaded for Pepper to stop. Finally, he let go and trotted back dutifully to my redheaded sister. Bubba continued running down Plum Creek Road, screaming for help. Soon, his screams faded to silence as he vanished into the distance. He lived about three miles down the road, and I'm sure he ran home without stopping to see what happened to his butt.

I shot my redhead sister an angry glance. I was going to yell at her for making Pepper chase Bubba. One look at Pepper standing next to her convinced me not to.

To my surprise, she just stood there laughing, patting Pepper on the back, as though nothing had happened.

Later in the afternoon, Bubba's dad came to our home with Sheriff Buckwheat. When they saw Pepper lying in the front yard, they decided not to walk up to the house.

"Have your daddy meet us on the road," they insisted.

The Sheriff was our neighbor and lived about four miles from us on Plum Creek Road. I believe he gave Daddy a traffic ticket for reckless driving once. Despite the reckless driving incident, the Sheriff and Daddy became good friends for many years.

Bubba's dad was clearly upset with Daddy that Pepper had bit his son on the butt.

"I had to take my boy to the doc's office uptown," stated Bubba's dad angrily. "The doc (Doctor) stitched up the bite holes in the skin. He then gave the boy rabies shots in the stomach. The boy won't be able to sit down for several days."

Standing beside Daddy, I saw Pepper staring at Bubba's dad and the Sheriff. They were staring back at Pepper with a hint of fear in their eyes.

Do they think Pepper will bite them on the butt too, I thought. I hope they don't run from Pepper. I also hope my redhead sister doesn't tell Pepper to get them.

My redheaded sister was standing next to the other sisters and brothers, watching.

"The Sheriff's going to lock you up. You're going to jail," my brother told her.

"Yes, you're going to jail," concluded my other sisters.

She started to cry and ran back into the house.

"Do you have papers showing the dog had rabbi's shots?" asked the Sheriff.

"Yes. Here're the papers," said Daddy as he handed them to the Sheriff. The Sheriff took the papers and quietly looked them over.

"I'm sorry it happened," said Daddy, explaining that Pepper was a smart dog and protected the children from anyone who came to our home.

"The Doctor charged $5 to clean up the boy's torn skin. The rabies shots are included," stated the Sherriff.

"Can I pay later?" asked Daddy.

Later in the afternoon, Bubba walked to our house to show what Pepper did to his butt.

"Where's your dog?" he asked nervously.

"He's tired up to the Elm tree in front of the house. Don't you see him?" I replied.

As he looked around, he saw my redheaded sister standing there.

"Hello," he said awkwardly.

Dispensing with the awkward moment, my brother impatiently interjected, "Okay. Let's see Pepper's teeth bites?"

Bubba dropped his pants showing Pepper's teeth marks.

"You don't have to worry about Pepper anymore," said my brother. "He won't do it again after he chewed on your skinny butt. Did you pee and poop in your pants when he was chewing on your butt?"

Dispensing with curiosity and turning to play, I gave Bubba a wooden stick sword. He shouted as I poked him in the stomach.

"Ouch!" he exclaimed. "My stomach hurts. Old man Doc gave me rabies shots in the stomach. The needle was over five inches long."

Several days later, when I was returning home from grocery shopping, I saw the owner of our home standing in the front yard talking to Daddy.

"Hey, Junior, your black dog tried to kill one of my hogs."

"Okay. Show me the hog."

After seeing the hog, Daddy looked at me.

"Go find Pepper," he said.

I asked my brothers and sisters to find Pepper.

"Pepper, Pepper. Where are you?" they yelled.

Something had happened; Pepper always got excited when we returned home, but he wouldn't come.

We started looking for him, but I couldn't find him. At last, I heard my sister calling.

"Here's Pepper. He's under the house," she said.

I called Pepper several times, prompting him to come out. He slowly came out from under the old house with dirt on his face. Looking closely, I saw that dried blood was mixed in with the dirt. I knew he had done something wrong, But I couldn't believe he would try to kill the old man's hog.

After finding Pepper, I ran to see what Daddy and the old man were doing at the hog pen. I saw a hog's back leg chewed down, almost to the bone. The meat on the hog's leg was gone. He was alive but slowly dying from loss of blood.

"Junior, you need to get rid of that dog," stated the old man. "Next time, he'll kill all my hogs."

"Okay, I'll take care of it. I'll pay you for the hog," Daddy responded.

Daddy and I slowly walked back to our house without talking. I tried to convince myself, Pepper did not do this to the hog, even if he had dried blood on his face. But what could I say to Daddy? We returned to the house, and he looked at Pepper's face covered in dried blood.

"Put a rope around his neck," he said.

Pepper stared at me as I put the rope around his neck for the final time. *Did Pepper know he did something wrong at the hog pen, I wondered?*

"You hold on to the rope. I don't want him to run from me when I come back," said Daddy as he turned to get something from the house.

Pepper's going to die for what he did to the hog, I thought as I stood there holding the rope. I looked into his sad eyes. They looked like Snowball's eyes before he died. Daddy returned with my Christmas gift, the 20-gauge shotgun in his hand. Once I saw the shotgun in his hand, I knew Pepper was going to die. Daddy took the rope from my hands. Pepper slowly followed him for several feet and turned to look at us, especially my redheaded sister, for one last time.

"I'm sorry, I love you. Goodbye," he seemed to say.

Then they turned to disappear into the dark woods, somewhere in the hollers.

I remember Daddy giving me a single-barrel 20-gauge shotgun for Christmas when I was 12. I was so happy. Now my Christmas gift would kill Pepper. *Why did Pepper try to kill the old man's hog*? I thought, with a deep sense of sadness, *he was going to die for what he did.*

Seeing Pepper alive for the last time, I thought about what Grandpa once said at the woodpile.

"When a dog kills a farm animal, tasting blood, he'll kill other animals again, or it could be one of us."

I kept staring into the dark woods, praying Daddy would change his mind about killing Pepper. I desperately hoped he would bring him back home. After a few minutes, I heard a loud noise from the shotgun. I continued praying that he did not kill Pepper. When Daddy returned alone, without Pepper and without the rope, I knew he hadn't changed his mind. He killed him.

"Where's Pepper?" I asked, though I already knew the answer.

"Pepper's gone," he said. Then he handed the shotgun back to me. Daddy never mentioned Pepper again.

I could not cry for what Pepper did to that hog, but I cried for Pepper. I will always miss him.

Later in life, working with DEA, I remembered Grandpa's words when I tried to understand why a human being can kill. If you do not stop a man from killing, he will kill again. I gradually learned on the streets that evil human beings were much the same as animals. They will hurt and kill again unless justice is quick.

"Wicked men do not understand God's Justice."

Once while I was on the job for less than a year searching for dopers on the streets, I saw a homeless man.

"Do you fear living on the filthy streets," I asked.

"What man has been waiting for on earth is righteousness and justice; it can be found only in God's kingdom," he oddly replied.

Before Daddy died and one year after Momma died, I asked him about Pepper. He paused and looked out into the distance before replying.

"I tied Pepper to a cedar tree, then he looked up at me..." Suddenly, Daddy paused. He looked down to the floor, not saying another word.

"He will wipe away every tear from their eyes, and death shall be no more, neither shall there be mourning, nor crying, nor pain anymore, for the former things have passed away."

(Revelation 21:4, King James Version)

Chapter 16

Look Not Every Man on His Own Things

When I turned 16, Momma gave me her old black 4-door Chevy.

"You got to get your license before driving up to town," she advised me.

"Momma, I know how to drive. I been driving my uncle's car ever since I was 8 years old on the farm," I assured her.

After getting my driver's license, Grandpa would ask me to take him to the old doc for his medical checkups.

"Larry Ray, take me to see the doc," he would say.

I took Grandpa to see the doc, thinking everything had gone fine. Later that evening, Daddy approached me with some concerns.

"Larry Ray, Dad said you scared him when the car almost ran off the road."

"When did that happen?" I asked.

"When you were taking him to see the Doc."

"Oh. I thought Grandpa was talking about me driving across the one-lane bridge before getting to the town. I did drive off the edge of the road. But I made it back up on the road."

I paused to reflect on the drive into town. There had been an incident, but I couldn't remember driving off the road; well, not exactly.

"That's strange, Daddy. Grandpa didn't say anything about running off the road after he yelled at me not to hit the bridge."

"Your Grandpa said before he got to the doc's office, you almost ran over a stop sign, nearly hit a groundhog crossing over the bridge, and almost hit a pickup truck driving in front of you," explained Daddy. "I told your grandpa, 'Dad, the boy just started driving."

When Grandpa heard that I was just learning to drive, he seemed shocked.

"That boy's learning how to drive now!" he said.

After a few days, Grandpa asked me to take his pigs to the stockyard.

"I need to sell my pigs. You can drive the pickup. But boy, you can't drive off the road with the pigs."

I was surprised that he was asking me. Poor Grandpa was worried that I'd hurt his pigs. Why couldn't he find someone else to take him with the pigs to town?

I drove Grandpa's old pickup truck about 30 miles an hour on the country road to the animal stockyard. His pickup truck was loaded with screaming pigs.

"Grandpa. Why are the pigs screaming so much?" I asked.

"Well, Larry Ray, you need to slow down. Try not driving off the road. You might hurt my pigs. That's why they are screaming. You need to keep your eyes on the road."

I could tell that Grandpa was worried I might hurt his five screaming pigs. Any doubts about that were erased when Momma spoke with me after we returned home.

"Lawrence Raymond, you need to learn how to drive on the right side of the road. Your Grandpa's scared of your driving."

"Grandma didn't seem to worry about how I drove her to the doc's office. She even had her far-sighted reading glasses on," I responded defensively.

Grandpa continued to ask me to take him to the doc's office despite his fear of my driving. Sometimes he would ask me to take him to the stockyards to sell his pigs. Perhaps if Grandpa was so afraid of my driving, I shouldn't have been looking around while driving.

"Look not every man on his own things, but every man also on the things of others. Let this mind be in you, which was also in Christ Jesus."

(Philippians 2:4-5, King James Version)

Chapter 17

Who Deceives the Whole World

My uncle had dug about two feet into the grave when I noticed the white marble tombstone. It was lying flat on the ground next to the hoe. The inscription on the tombstone was faded, and I couldn't read what it said. I resumed where my uncle had left off and started to dig. Suddenly, I heard Grandpa's booming voice across the family cemetery.

"Stop digging. Leave the grave alone," he shouted.

On Thanksgiving Day, Grandpa had a family reunion to kill about five to eight hogs. One of my uncles would shoot a 22 long-rifle bullet into the hog's skull. Daddy immediately cut the hog's throat to drain out the blood.

Once the blood was drained from the hog's body, my other uncle would use a tractor to drag the hog to a hot tub of water. We left the hog soaking in hot water for a few minutes then the aunts, cousins, and I would scrape the hog hairs off with a small knife.

After removing the hog's hair, the hog would be hoisted up high, where Daddy would cut the meat into large sections. The uncles would then distribute the large areas of the hog meat to other family members to cut into smaller sections for ham, sausages, pork chops, and ribs. All the fat from the hog would be made into cooking lard.

Later in the evening, after milking cows and cleaning cow poop from the barn, my brother and I followed Grandpa and one of the uncles into the hollers with two coonhound dogs. While the dogs chased a raccoon, possum, fox, or some other animal through the woods, creeks, and fields, Grandpa would stop and look for a place to sit. He would find a tree log or whatever he could find and sit down while the dogs hunted, placing his old gas lantern beside him. Then he would reach into his small white tobacco pouch, and using any paper he could find, he would roll up a cigarette.

As he puffed the cigarette, he told us about the evil ghosts wandering through the hollers. Maybe he would even mention the Robinson's family 19th-century graveyard on the farm.

When we returned to Grandpa and Grandma's house after an evening of hunting, my brother and I ate some of Grandma's cold hard biscuits and homemade blackberry jam. After finishing my late-night snack, I jumped in the chicken feather bed before my brother and uncle got there.

I was falling asleep when my uncle whispered, "You want to hear some ghost stories about the graveyard?" "Nope! Not now," I assured him.

He continued to tell them anyways until, after a few ghost stories, he drifted off to sleep. Interestingly, he left his oil lamp burning all night beside the bed. Perhaps he feared his own ghost stories. As I tried to drift back to sleep, I heard strange noises, like someone walking around upstairs in the old log house. I didn't think much of it and eventually went to sleep.

The next day my uncle was using a shovel to dig up dirt from an unknown grave. I laughed as I watched my overfed uncle throwing dirt out of the grave and sending it flying into the air like a baby groundhog. I wondered if he was looking for bones and artifacts.

"Hey uncle, are you going to find some stuff in the grave?"

My uncle stopped digging, and I looked up from the grave to see Grandpa walking toward me. Suspecting that I was in trouble, I took off running. I knew he had a good throwing arm, and I remembered when he hit me in the back with a chicken head. Looking over my shoulder, I saw Grandpa pushing dirt back into the grave with the hoe. He was mad at me for the rest of the day.

Later that night in bed, I heard someone slowly coming downstairs, walking as if they were tiptoeing. The chicken feather bed was under the stairs, and I thought my aunt was probably going to the kitchen to get a drink from the water bucket. *Maybe she wanted to eat something off the kitchen table, but why is she tiptoeing down the stairs?* I wondered.

As I listened to the noise on the stairs, I sensed someone walking up to the bed. I pretended to be asleep as I experienced the growing sensation that my body was on fire. The heat was not burning my skin. The heat was burning me inside my body.

What's happing to me? I silently prayed. I'm burning inside. What's happening to me?

An inner voice told me not to open my eyes as the presence by the bed began to cry out.

"Larry, please open your eyes. It's Sara."

Don't open your eyes! exhorted the other inner voice.

Who could it be? Why aren't my uncle and younger brother not hearing the crying voice? Why can't they feel the heat on their bodies? I wondered.

Regardless of the answer, I refused to open my eyes to see who it was.

"Larry, you have something in your ear," it moaned, and I could feel something touching my left ear. Reflexively I reached up to touch my ear. I immediately regretted that instinctive act, knowing that whoever or whatever it was would know I was awake.

I could feel it leaning over me, its face next to mine. "Larry, this is Sara; please wake up."

The heat continued to grow within me and felt hotter than the sun, yet it was not burning my skin. I firmly believed that whatever was next to my bed was an evil spirit named Sara. *I don't want to open my eyes. I don't want to see the evil spirit,* I thought as I silently prayed.

The heat was getting so bad, and the crying voice begged me to open my eyes. With God's blessing, I did not open them.

I suddenly heard Grandpa's alarm clock waking him up to go to the milk barn. The presence moved quickly away, running upstairs. I no longer felt the burning heat and tumbled out of bed onto my feet. I ran to my Grandparent's bedroom and tried telling them what just happened. To my surprise, they didn't seem interested and didn't want to hear it.

"I've got to get up. I got to go milk those cows," stated Grandpa.

Grandma went to the kitchen to start making breakfast. I went to help Grandpa clean up the poop off the barn floor, but I felt sick. I wondered if I felt that way because of what had happened that night. I also felt an unshakeable urge to walk up to the graveyard behind the milk barn.

After breakfast, I went to the gravesite. The hoe was on the ground where my uncle had left it the day before. Something told me to pick up the white marble tombstone beside the hoe. The thought of picking up the tombstone scared me. *What am I going to see on the other side of the tombstone?* I thought.

Pushing aside my fear, I struggled to lift the tombstone upright. I could see the vague hint of a name and started rubbing the dirt away from the chiseled words. Slowly the name revealed itself: Sara Robinson.

The name filled me with fear. *Was Sara Robinson the presence telling me to open my eyes last night? No. It was the devil.* I was terrified and dropped the marble tombstone on the ground, returning to the old farmhouse. I thought, *that's why my uncle left the oil lamp burning all night. It happened to him. He heard the devil.* I never stayed all night at Grandpa's home again.

"So, the great dragon was cast out, that serpent of old, called the Devil and Satan, who deceives the whole world; he was cast to the earth, and his angels were case out with him."

(Revelation 12:9, King James Version)

Chapter 18

Heal Me, O Lord, and I Shall be Healed

I dropped out of High School in my senior year, just three months before graduation. There were moments when I found myself sitting down on a flat rock near the edge of a creek and wondered why I quit school when I was so close to graduating. I regretted my decision and asked myself if I had made a big mistake by not getting my high school diploma.

One hot August day, I was cutting tobacco for a farmer. The day grew hot and humid as several large black bees circled around my head. Thinking of them as harmless bees, I whipped out my bacco knife and swiped at them.

"Larry Ray. They're Bumble bees. They're not wood bees," Daddy warned me.

The bees began to sting me on the arms as I continued to swing my knife at them, but the more I fought with them, the more they continued to sting me.

"Boy! Stop fighting with the bees. You better walk away from them. I told you to stop swinging at them with your bacco knife."

"Ouch!" I yelped at the growing pain from the stings. "Why're the bees still stinging me, Daddy? I got to run. I got to get away from them."

I ran out of the bacco field as fast as a rabbit dog. Glancing over my shoulders, I saw the bees closing in on me. I continued to holler out in pain as the bees focused their stings on my back, butt, head, and legs. Running as fast as a wild buck deer chasing a doe, I finally reached Daddy and Momma's house with the bees in hot pursuit. Momma was startled as I darted through the back screen door.

"You scared me. What's wrong with you, Lawrence Raymond," she exclaimed.

"I got stung by black bumble bees. I thought they were wood bees," I replied, struggling to breathe.

My body started to itch, and I scratched at the growing irritation like a raccoon dog with fleas. Momma watched me with concern.

"Lawrence Raymond. You have red swelling welts on your skin. There are red patches on your arms, face, and legs."

"I can't stop scratching. I can't hardly breathe. You think I'm drying?"

"Get in the car now," insisted Momma. "You have to see the doc."

We got into the car, and Momma raced into town. It took no time to cover the ten miles to the doc's office.

"Momma. Are you okay? I never seen you drive so fast before. You didn't stop at the only stop sign on the street. Did you see the old man crossing the street?"

Momma ushered me into the doc's office, and soon I was seen by the doc.

"Your boy is allergic to bee stings. I need to give him a shot in the butt now," he informed us as he completed his examination.

"Pull your pants down to your ankles. Bend over and touch your toes," he instructed me. "This is not going to hurt you."

I did as he said, then glanced around to see what the old doc was about to do. He was holding a long needle that he suddenly jabbed into my right butt cheek. "Ouch!" I exclaimed. It felt like I had just been stung again. The doc talked to Momma while I was pulling my shorts up.

"Your boy's allergic to bee stings," he said, "Also, to penicillin. Without the shot, you would have lost him in a few more minutes."

"What's penicillin?" I asked Momma as we drove home.

"Heal me, O Lord, and I shall be healed; save me, and I shall be saved: for thou art my praise."

(Jeremiah 17:14, King James Version)

Chapter 19

Their Fear of Death

After arriving at the hospital, I asked the emergency room nurse if I could see my little brother. I entered the white, sterile room alone. Lying in the middle of the examination room, I saw my brother's face. It felt cold and devoid of life. Earlier that morning, Daddy found my brother lying on the garage floor. He had accidentally hung himself inside the garage.

A white linen sheet covered his lifeless body as it lay atop a silver metal table. I leaned over his face and whispered in his ear, "I'm sorry. I never told you I love you."

He looked so peaceful, so beautiful, lying on the table. I believe he heard me.

I talked to Momma in the emergency room, and she tearfully told me what she experienced as she rode with her baby boy in the ambulance.

"I kept looking at my little boy's face, praying to God to save him," said Momma. "God's voice whispered in my heart, saying HE gave HIS only son."

Several years later, Daddy and I were fishing on one of the farm's ponds. Daddy mentioned how our baby brother enjoyed fishing with him at this pond.

"After he died, I cried a lot," said Daddy. "I missed him so much. I kept questioning God: Where is he?"

"One day," he continued, "I was in the bedroom, alone, crying so much about how he accidentally took his own life. Suddenly, I heard Dad yelling at me from outside the window above the Water Maple trees, "Junior, why are you asking where your boy is?"

"I couldn't see Dad above the trees, but his voice was so clear coming from there. Dad said again, 'Junior, why are you asking HIM where he is?"

"I had this strong feeling that Dad was no longer above the trees, but that he was walking up the driveway towards the house."

"I tried to look for Dad but couldn't see him. Suddenly, I heard Dad's voice so loud and clear again as he came closer to the outside bedroom window, saying, he's over there with Ima (Grandma)."

"I looked behind Dad's voice to see if he and Mom were there. I could hear them laughing, but I wasn't able to see them. Dad told me, 'Stop asking. He's okay."

Then Daddy said, "I never again asked God, "Where is he?"

Momma and Daddy grieved for the rest of their lives for how he died. After several years, Momma and Daddy finally joined their baby boy in heaven.

"Since the children have flesh and blood, he too shared in their humanity so that by his death he might destroy him who holds the power of death--that is, the devil--and free those who all their lives were held in slavery by their fear of death."

(Hebrews 2:14-15, King James Version)

Chapter 20

Be Strong and Courageous

"Why does your mom have a gun in her hand? Why's she pointing a gun at me? What did I do?" I said to the girl in the passenger seat.

Earlier in the day, I was driving through the park with Bubba. We were drinking a few beers, and I noticed a young girl sitting alone at a picnic table. Her breasts were huge, like two cow hooters! She was a little heavy around the waist and not exactly beautiful, but I found myself enticed.

"Do you want to join us? We're just riding around drinking beer," I shouted over to where she was sitting.

"Sure!" She said, smiling.

Bubba opened the front passenger door and quietly climbed into the backseat.

"Come on. Get in," I said.

I turned to look at her as she took a seat in the car, and it looked as if she had been crying.

"Why are you sitting alone at the park?" I asked. "Did you walk to the park? Have you been crying?"

We hung out and drank a few beers, and the day continued.

"I'm going home," I told her. "Do you want a ride to your home?"

She accepted my offer to give her a ride home, and we started to drive down the road. She seemed nervous and uncomfortable, as if something was bothering her.

"I don't want to go home," she said at last. "I want to stay with you."

"No. I have to go home," I reluctantly replied.

"We don't have to take her home now," interjected Bubba.

I had already decided, though, and soon we pulled up in front of the girl's house. Her parents were standing in the driveway. The girl's mom was about 4 feet tall and skinny, and the girl's daddy looked like the fat giant from "Jack and the Beanstalk." I had never seen anyone that big before.

The skinny mom was pointing what looked like a handgun at me. Everything about the situation felt wrong, and I wanted to leave as fast as I could. The girl started to cry.

"I don't want to stay here," she pleaded. "I want to go with you. I'm scared of her."

"How about your dad? Why's he so big? Are you scared of him too?" I asked, hoping she would hurry up and get out of the car.

She just sat there, reluctant to leave the safety of the car. "Can you get out of the car now!" I politely insisted. "Your mom's going to shoot me. Your dad will stump me to the ground if she doesn't shoot me first."

"No. I want to stay with you," she continued to plead.

I tried to leave, but Skinny Mom leaped in front of the car, yelling,

"Stop! Get out of the car, Boy!" she demanded.

I wanted to throw the car into reverse, but her dad had stepped behind it, blocking me in. My heart was racing, and I was becoming desperate.

"Your mom is in front of the car screaming. Your dad is behind the car. I can't move forward or backward."

"Get out of the car," I begged her. "Your mom has a gun, and she's dangerous. Why is your dad so upset with me."

I turned to Bubba, hoping he could convince her to leave the car.

"Hey Bubba, tell the girl to get out of the car. Why're you afraid to say anything?"

Bubba just sat there like a deer in the headlights, not saying a word. I feared for my life, and I was growing angry. The girl wouldn't get out of the car, and Bubba wouldn't say a thing.

"What's going on with you? Why does your mom want to shoot me?" I demanded. "Did you run away from home? How old are you?"

"I'm 13," she admitted.

"You can't be 13," I croaked. She had seemed so much older when we had seen her in the park, and it had never occurred to me that she was that young. Did her parents think I had sex with her?

"Your skinny mom has a gun in her hand. She's going to shoot me in the head! Get out of the car," I demanded.

Skinny mom screamed louder as she waved the gun above her head.

"Boy, you get out of that car now. I will kill you if you don't get out of the car!"

"Your skinny mom's going to shoot me in the head!" I yelled.

The booming echo of a gunshot echoed in the air.

"Don't shoot me! I'm getting out of the car," I screamed. "Please don't shoot me!"

I slowly opened the car door and raised my hands as far as I could. Big Daddy swung around the back of the car and quickly walked towards me. He was several feet higher than me and must have weighed a ton. The guy looked like a deformed gorilla. Tossing the car keys on the ground, I hoped it would persuade him not to hit me with his massive fists.

"Boy! You get in the house now!" impatiently demanded Skinny Mom.

"Did you hear her, punk? Get in the house now.

Don't you run from me, Boy. I'll grab you by your long hair," echoed Big Daddy in his booming voice.

"I think he's really upset?" I told Bubba. Big Daddy started reaching for my long hair, and I ran like a wild dog that had been shot several times in the butt with a BB gun. Jumping over the doorsteps, landing on the front porch, and entering the front door, I slowly walked into the living room. Somehow Bubba had made it into the house before me, and he was sitting alone on a couch, not saying a word. I hadn't even seen him get out of the car, let alone enter the house. I was amazed at how quick he was, but he was still not as fast as Pepper.

"Sit down on the couch now before I shoot you in the back," demanded Skinny Mom.

I felt a terrible sense of dread, as though I had just walked into a death trap. The last thing I wanted to do was sit down on that coach. I wanted to flee, but Big Daddy stood at the front door, and Skinny Mom still had the gun pointed at my face. I wondered if I could make it out of the large living room window that I had noticed behind the coach. Reluctantly I sat down.

Satisfied that I was not going anywhere, Skinny Mom turned away from me and strode over to her daughter. Suddenly she drew back her arm and slammed the butt of the pistol into her daughter's head. Her daughter screamed out in pain as Skinny Mom repeatedly pistol-whipped her.

Every muscle in my body tensed as I contemplated running for it. If it looks like she will shoot me in the face, I will try jumping on Big Daddy's back. Maybe Bubba will jump on his back, too, I thought. We might have a chance to run out the front door. If not, we can jump out the living room window.

Skinny mom suddenly turned to look at me as though she could read my thoughts and pointed the gun at me.

"Boy! Did you rape her? She's only 13 years old," asked Skinny Mom accusingly.

"Rape who?" I asked. The question only served to infuriate them.

"My little girl? Don't you play dumb," screamed Big Daddy.

He had spit coming out of his mouth as he said the words, and the mother's eyes were red with anger. *These people are mad, I thought. But why me. Why do they believe I had done her in the car?*

"Boy, I know you did my little girl. You're one of those Boys from the hollers. I know you did her, Boy!"

"No, sir. I didn't touch her!" I insisted. "I didn't even kiss your beautiful, sweet daughter."

What had I done to make them think I had done anything so terrible. Big Daddy's huge fists clenched in anger as though he were ready to plummet me into another world. *This skinny mom's evil, I thought. She and Big Daddy are going to kill someone tonight, and it isn't going to be me.* I looked to Bubba, who sat cowered on the couch without saying anything. Why couldn't he just tell them that I didn't have sex with their daughter?

Bubba's knees were bent, his legs were tense, and his feet were planted firmly on the floor. It looked like he was getting ready to jump up from the couch like a bullfrog. *But how is he going to run around Big Daddy?* I wondered. *How's he going to dodge the bullets when the crazy evil mom starts shooting?*

"Boy, you're going to die tonight! I'm going to shoot you in your squirrel nuts for what you did to my little girl," screamed Skinny Mom.

"Lady, I swear to you. Your daughter didn't have sex with me. I wouldn't do her. She's too young," I pleaded.

Skinny Mom's handgun remained pointed at my face. It looked like a small .22 automatic, and I had learned as a Boy, hunting for rabbits and squirrels, that a small-caliber bullet can ricochet off anything. Even the red couch pillow sitting on top of my legs could potentially protect me. With that in mind, I slowly raised the couch pillow in front of my chest and prayed that it would save me if the crazy mom started shooting.

Skinny Mom decided she was not interested in Bubba and decided to focus on me.

"Get out of here, now," she told him.

In his haste to depart, he jumped up off the couch three feet into the air. He bounced off the couch as he landed and nearly tripped over himself as he ran out the front door. He fled like a scared chicken about to be shot without so much as a goodbye.

With Bubba out of the way, Skinny Mom focused on me and pronounced her judgment.

"Take this dumb-looking, nasty, filthy Boy by his long hair outside. I want you to beat the living poop out of him for raping our little girl," she demanded.

I was happy that she hadn't decided to shoot me.

"Yes, sir," I told Big Daddy. "I'm ready for you to beat the crap out of me. Come on. Let's go outside. Let's finish it."

I had no intention of taking a beating, though. This was a chance to run. Once I was outside, I could make a break for it and leave Big Daddy behind. I already knew Bubba wasn't going to be any help if I got into trouble. Heck! He was probably hiding behind a bush or running home.

I quickly leaped off the couch, running out the front door like a red tail fox squirrel jumping into a tree hole. I knew that Big Daddy could knock me to the ground at any moment, but I was certain I could outrun him. I darted out the door to my car and slid into the driver's seat.

Reaching into my pocket for the car keys, I suddenly realized that Big Daddy had taken the keys. The joy I had felt, having escaped a beating, came crashing down in the agony of defeat. I waited for Big Daddy to punch me in the head. He pulled back his arms and…threw my car keys on the driveway.

"Get out of here, Boy, before I stomp your head to the ground," he yelled.

I wasted no time and grabbed the keys off the driveway like grabbing nightcrawlers and jumped back into the car. I could hear Big Daddy screaming as I sped off.

"Boy, get the hell out of here. Don't you ever come back here. You hear, Boy? Leave my little daughter alone."

Sticking my hand out the window, I gave Big Daddy the nasty middle finger.

"I didn't do your fat ugly pimple-faced little girl. Take that and shove it where the sun doesn't shine," I yelled back.

I felt so proud of myself and wondered if he saw my middle finger waving at him. Did he hear what I said about his little girl? It was a dumb thing for me to say about his little girl, and he'd probably kill me if he ever saw me again.

Suddenly I heard something crawling in the back seat of my car, and I imagined the worst. It scared me to look over my shoulder at the back seat. *Please, it can't be that girl running away from her crazy mom and Big Daddy,* I thought. Praying not to find the girl, I glanced into the backseat. Bubba was lying on his belly like a snake, hiding on the floor.

"I know you didn't kiss her on the mouth. I was watching you. That girl's mom and dad are crazy," he sheepishly said.

I felt blessed to be alive as I drove home. Big Daddy almost stomped me to death, and Skinny Mom almost shot me in the nuts. My prayers were particularly heartfelt as I prepared to go to bed that night.

"Thank you, God, for saving me again."

"Have I not commanded you. Be strong and courageous! Do not be tremble or be dismayed, for the Lord your God is with wherever you go."

(Joshua 1:9, King James Version)

Chapter 21

A Time to Be Born, and A Time to Die

I suddenly felt something poking me in the back. Before I could turn around, a menacing voice whispered in my ear, "Don't move, or I will kill you, mother f----."

Several weeks earlier, I started a career pumping gasoline (gas), changing oil, repairing tires, and cleaning customer windshields. I wore a green uniform with a big red star on the front of my shirt. To this day, I remember the gas station's motto, "Trust the man who wears the red star."

The gas station could be a seedy place at times. It was not unusual for a customer to offer marijuana or sex in exchange for free gas. Many younger girls offered sex to me or co-workers in exchange for free gas. Some of the younger married girls even had small children inside the car. Some older married women just wanted sex at the gas station or the motel behind the station.

I asked Daddy how a guy could have sex with a married woman. This was something I had resolved that I would never do. Maybe it was my long hair and smile that attracted the women, or perhaps it was the free gas. Nurses going home after a long day at work would also stop by the station to fill their cars up with gas. A few single nurses would ask if I wanted to come to see them after work. Heck, I had gay men trying to pick me up for free gas. But I stayed away from them.

One day, one of my gas station co-workers drilled a hole the size of a penny in the ceiling of the women's bathroom. He liked watching women through the peephole as they sat on the toilet seat to clean their butt. I found his behavior to be sick and repulsive.

After a few days of pumping gasoline into cars, I started working alone on the night shift for the first time. Before the manager went home that night, he gave me some advice I would remember in the coming days.

"If someone tries to rob you tonight or any other night, don't go into the back office. If you do, the robber will kill you. Stay out in the open area where the gas pumps are so other customers can see you being robbed, especially if law enforcement is driving by the station. The robber won't shoot you out in the open."

One hot summer night, I was busy pumping gasoline for a lot of customers. In addition to pumping gas, I had to finish repairing a tire for a customer inside the garage. It was getting late, and I needed to repair the customer's flat tire before closing. I didn't have time to put the cash away in the office safe, so I rolled it up and put it in my pants pocket. Suddenly an inner voice told me to take the cash out of my pocket and hide it in my sock. I put the cash in my left sock without thinking more about it.

A few minutes later, a gray four-door Mercury with two young men pulled up next to the gas pump. I walked out toward the vehicle and watched as the driver and passenger got out of the car and looked around nervously. The driver walked past me and into the front office without saying a word. When he saw that no one was there, he walked into the garage and saw the customer standing next to the flat tire. From the expression on his face, I could see that the customer with the flat tire was as confused as I was. I was about to go over and see what he wanted when the passenger suddenly hit me in the face.

"What are you doing?" I snapped.

"Just shut up!" He commanded as he poked me hard in the chest and drew back his other hand to slap me hard across the face.

I wanted to hit him back as I reeled from the slap, but I knew now was not that time. He searched my pants pockets, moving his hands quickly down my legs. At last, he came to my socks and found the cash hidden inside my left sock. I was surprised he found it, and I wondered what gave him the idea to search my socks.

Pocketing the money, he slapped me again with an echoing whack! The driver walked out of the garage and strode up to me. Together they grabbed my waist and arms.

"Let's go," they demanded as they tried to force me to go with them inside the office.

I remembered what my boss had told me earlier, "... they'll kill you once you are in the back office."

"No! There are cops driving everywhere around here," I insisted. As if on cue, a squad car drove past the station.

"Look! There is a cop driving by the station now," I said, pointing to the vehicle. "Man! The cops and customers might see you guys robbing me."

The driver reluctantly let go of my arm and got back into the car. The passenger refused to let go and stared hatefully into my eyes.

"I'm going to shoot you, mother f-----."

Suddenly time seemed to slow, and it was as if I were in a dream. I could see myself being shot in the back, crawling on the ground, fighting for my life, saying, "I'm not going to die."

Finally, the passenger let go of my arm and shoved me aside. I saw a small black revolver in his hand and wondered if he would shoot me in the back. When he didn't do it right away, anger surged within me. Here's a chance to wallop this guy before he shoots me, I thought. Maybe I could get the gun. I tried to lash out on that impulse, but I couldn't move my arms. It felt as if some unseen hand had reached out to hold me back. The passenger pushed the revolver back into the front waist of his pants and hopped back into the car, slamming the door behind him.

I could have died that night, but I was alive. The passenger isn't going to shoot me in the back. I'm not going to die, I thought with relief. Why didn't he shoot me in the back? What stopped him?

The robbers sped off, leaving me there with my thoughts. Why was I still alive? What had stopped the passenger from putting a hole in my back? I watched as they faded into the distance, passing another gas station on the way.

"Hey! Are you okay?" shouted the customer from inside the gas garage.

"Yep, I'm okay. Thanks," I replied. I was very thankful to be alive, and the question echoed in my thoughts, *Why*?

I immediately ran into the office and called the police. I told them everything that had happened, as they listened with interest. Within minutes, two state troopers arrived at the gas station.

"Who is the man inside the garage?" asked one of the troopers.

"He's a customer with a flat tire," I replied.

One of the troopers stepped away and approached the customer to get his account of the incident. The other trooper asked me for a description of the robbers and their car.

I described the robbers and their vehicle in as much detail as I could remember. Then I explained how one of the robbers pointed a small black revolver at my back and threatened to kill me.

"I thought he was going to shoot me in the back," I said.

"These are the same robbers who raped a woman inside her car tonight at the shopping mall where she worked," he informed me. "Those guys stole the woman's car. They came over here to the gas station to rob you. She's lucky to be alive! So, are you!"

The customer's car backed out of the garage as I talked to the state trooper. He pulled out onto the street and left without bothering to pay for the repairs to his tire. I stared at the customer as he drove away. *You could have at least waved goodbye,* I thought.

"Did the customer give you a description of what happened?" I asked the trooper.

"Nope. The customer didn't see anything," he replied.

It wasn't long before the troopers left, and my boss arrived.

"I'm glad you didn't go inside the office with them," he said. "But Larry, why did you put the money in your sock, not the office safe?"

I asked myself that same question. Why did I hide the money in my sock? I have always put the cash inside the office safe.

Again, I was truly blessed; I could have been killed that night. *Whose voice assured me I was not going to die? Did God have a plan for me?* I could not explain to the boss why I did not put the money in the office safe, but I felt certain that decision had saved my life. He helped me to close the gas station.

I needed to listen and trust in the Lord.

"A time to be born, and a time to die."
(Ecclesiastes 3:2, King James Version)

Chapter 22

Flee Fornication

My co-workers frequently smoked weed after work, and it wasn't difficult for them to find willing sexual partners from among the nurses who came by the gas station. The sex didn't bother me, but I was confused about why some of my co-workers would smoke weed after work.

I eventually quit my job at the gas station and found work at the hospital as a surgical orderly. The hospital was full of beautiful women. I knew I had made the right choice in taking that job from the moment I walked in the door. It wasn't long before I discovered that sex was available from some of the women working there during and after work. I felt like a young French Charolais farm bull. It was crazy!

I enjoyed "hanging out" with many beautiful women throughout the day and drinking beers after work. A lot of the women did not have time to find the right man. Their careers in the medical community kept them busy, working long hours.

I had five nurses and nurses' aides to date at any one time. When I wanted a date, I would call one of them to find out who was available to go dancing or drink beer after work. Five was the most women that I could handle. After all that partying, it was impossible to save money, but I was smiling like a fox in a hen house. I didn't care if they were beautiful, ugly, fat, skinny, tall, or short. A great personality went a long way.

One of my favorite nurses had a little fat belly, but she also had a beautiful smile and laughed about everything I talked about. She loved drinking pitchers of beer and eating fried catfish. I couldn't help but wonder if the fat around her stomach was from drinking too much beer. After a few dates, I learned she was engaged to get married. But that never stopped her from calling me when her fiancée traveled out of town on business.

After a couple of years working in the hospital, I found a girl that was saving herself for marriage.

"I love playing the piano at the Southern Baptist church," she said on our first date. "My parents are very active members, and I want you to know I'm a virgin."

I was surprised. Working at the hospital, I had never met a woman who claimed to be a virgin.

A few days later, I was sitting on a brown sofa with her while her parents were in the kitchen drinking coffee. She slowly laid down on the couch and pulled up her dress above the hips. She was not wearing any panties.

"I love you. Let's get married," she whispered.

She jerked my pants zipper down as her parents, who were still in the kitchen, asked her about the job at the hospital. She replied to them casually as she pulled me closer. Primitive instincts raged inside of me. Without any thought of her parents in the kitchen, I jumped on her like a wild pig into a mammoth cave. We were making out on the couch as her parents continued to drink coffee in the kitchen. I was amazed; did her parents know what we were doing on the couch?

Later, as I thought about it, I was really upset. She had told me she wanted to wait for marriage to have sex, but it seemed she had done this many times. I was wrong to think she was a virgin, but I continued seeing her.

Daddy and Momma met her later. "She's not ready for marriage," they said. "Watch her with other men around. When you drop her off at her parents' house, go back and see what happens."

It saddened and disappointed me that they would say that about her. One hot summer night, my future wife wanted to go home early.

"I'm sick. I need to go home," she said.

We had sex at the ballpark behind a tree. Later we hung out in the back seat of my white Chevy. She had not seemed sick at all, and it seemed strange that she wanted to go home now. Nevertheless, I dropped her off at her parent's home.

I had driven about a mile when I started thinking about it. *She was acting a little strange tonight,* I thought. *She didn't look sick while having sex twice.* Then I thought about what Daddy had said, and suddenly I turned the car around. I turned off my headlights right before returning to her parent's house. It was already dark, and the front porch lights were on. There, fully visible under the revealing illumination of the lights, I saw my future bride hugging a guy on the front porch. I could see them both clearly. How stupid they were!

I was hot mad. To make matters worse, that guy went to the same church. *Where did he park his car?* I wondered. *He must have been waiting inside her parent's house when I dropped her off.* I felt like a fool. This was not the first time she cheated on me. Daddy and Momma were right, after all. She was no good.

I pulled into the driveway and slowly got out of my car. My hand was flat and stiff, and my arm was poised to deliver the hard slap this guy so richly deserved. My feet touched the first step, and she leaped off the porch like a deadly snake into my arms. I stared into her lying eyes as she bit me hard on my chest. I felt no pain from her poison bite. Pushing her away, I turned around and walked back to the car. What a fool I had been.

Without looking back at her devilish face, I got in the car and drove away. My emotions caught up with me as I drove home, and anger turned to sorrow. Tears fell from my eye's as I cried out loud. I had given up all my girlfriends at the hospital for her. I had thought she was special. I swore I would never let another woman make a fool out of me again.

A deep sense of sorrow filled me in the days that followed. I had been ready to settle down and have a family. One day I drove down to a property on Plum Creek Road that I had purchased from an old farmer. We had planned to build a home and raise at least two children. I sat in my car, crying all night until the next day. Right then, I gave up on ever finding someone to marry and have children. If only I had listened to my parents. I never saw her again, but I thanked God that I didn't marry the devil woman.

Early in the morning, Daddy came to the property in his Chevy pickup truck, searching for me.

"Daddy, you're right about her," I said as he got out of the truck. "I made a fool out of myself."

"Come on home when you're ready," he said.

What am I going to do now? I wondered.

"Flee fornication. Every sin that a man doeth is without the body; but he that committeth fornication sinneth against his own body."

(1 Corinthians 6:18, King James Version)

Chapter 23

I Am The Light of The World

Suddenly, the whispering stopped, and I wondered why? I felt someone near; the wind blew, yet no leaf waived in the trees. Nor did the tall grass sway gently to and fro as it should in the wind. Even the water in the creek was smooth and devoid of ripples. Why couldn't I understand the voice of the whispering wind in my ears?

It had only been a few weeks since I had seen my future wife in the arms of another man. She made a fool of me, and I decided never to see her again. I was deeply embarrassed by what had happened. I was ashamed to see anyone, especially at work. As a result of my shame and embarrassment, I spent a lot of time alone with my thoughts. One question weighed heavily on my mind.

What is life all about?

I found myself walking near the rocky creeks and cattail ponds. Sometimes I wandered into the dark backwoods and the hollers. Other times I found myself walking in the hay fields, watching the groundhogs pop up in the green alfalfa grass. Frequently I looked up into the sky and pondered the purpose of my life.

Late one summer night, I was lying down in the tall bluegrass next to the rocky creek. It was hot and humid, but I could feel a soft wind that blew cooly across my face. I stared up into the stars and at the moon that cast its soft illumination over the countryside. *What is my purpose in life?* I wondered. I needed to know.

As I stared up into the sky, I noticed the wind was not moving the leaves on top of the oak trees. Perhaps even stranger, the tall bluegrass stood motionless. The creek water was smooth as glass. Yet the wind continued whispering in my ears.

A few days later, I returned to walk barefooted in the woods. I listened to the noise of stillness and hoped to find the answers I sought in the whispering wind. They did not come, and I returned home that evening, no closer to any meaningful answer than when I had left.

The question continued to weigh on my mind as I lay in bed that night. What did I want to do with the rest of my life? I knew for sure that I wanted to travel and see the world. My little brother joined the Navy at seventeen and traveled a lot. If I joined the Navy, I could travel the world like my little brother.

Suddenly I found myself alone, walking up a rocky hill devoid of vegetation. It felt like daytime, yet I looked up and saw that the sky was dark. I had the terrible feeling that something horrible was in front of me. I saw a wooden pole with someone's feet nailed to it as I looked up. This can't be real, I thought, it must be a dream, a horrible dream. The feet had several deep wounds that left blood trickling down to the toes. It was terrifying to see someone dying such an agonizing death.

To the right of the pole, I saw what appeared to be three men dressed in strange clothes. One man seemed to be holding a spear. I looked to the left and saw a lady with a sad expression. A young man was standing next to the lady and seemed to share her sorrow. Neither of them shed a tear, but it was evident they were troubled. They had brown skin and looked at me with dark eyes that reflected their sorrow. Each wore dark robes, and the lady had a dark scarf over her head.

I turned back to face on the wooden pole and gently raised my hand toward the nailed feet. Suddenly the man with the spear drew back the weapon and thrust it forward. The sight sickened me, and I felt something terrible had just happened. I felt something splattering onto my face. Looking up at the pole, I saw what looked like blood running down the body.

"Help him," I cried.

I suddenly had the feeling that it was Jesus Christ that died on the pole. My eyes drifted upwards. I wanted to see the body on the pole and know if what I felt was true. I stared at the body's feet, then continued my upward gaze. Dark streaks of dried blood highlighted long cuts on the legs and chest. This was the body of a man, and I wanted to see his face.

A blinding white light filled my eyes as they looked upon the man's face. The warmth and intensity of the light brought me to my knees. I begged for someone to help this man as I knelt on the ground in the glow of the intense light. *How could that light be so bright, I thought. The man's face is brighter than the sun, so bright that I cannot look upon it.*

It is Jesus!

With tears streaming down my face, I knelt in shame and cried out for mercy. Eventually, I found the strength to rise slowly to my feet, but I could not look at his face. I felt so dirty, ashamed, unable to look into the holy white light from his face. I longed to see Jesus, to look upon him, but I could not. The light from his face was so intense it filled me with shame to look at him.

In my shame, I turned to walk away from the light. As much as I desired to do so, I was unable to look back at Jesus on the wooden pole. Though I could not bear to look upon him, I could feel the light of Jesus shining all around me. I felt so cowardly not helping him on the pole and turned to walk down the hill in my shame. Suddenly I was filled with the presence of Jesus, and I could hear his gentle voice.

"You will be my disciple."

Such was the sense of shame that I felt I could not bring myself to say the words I wanted to say, *yes, I will be your disciple.* I continued to walk away and did not look back at the wooden pole.

For several days, I asked myself; what is a disciple? Finally, I went to Plum Creek Baptist Church to tell the preacher about seeing Jesus Christ alive on the cross. The preacher had helped my family as we struggled with the death of our brother-in-law and little brother. I hoped he could help me with the thoughts that troubled me following what I had seen.

"I saw Jesus on the cross. His face was brighter than the sun. The light from Jesus' face shined on me, knocking me to the ground. A lady and a young man were standing near the cross," I told him.

The preacher looked at me with understanding and compassion. "You had a vision," he said.

Suddenly I realized; Jesus is alive, and HE is helping me not to walk the path of the devil but believe in HIM.

"Can you baptize me in the creek next to the bridge?" I asked.

On a Sunday afternoon, I was baptized. Several of the wonderful Christians of Plum Creek Baptist Church witnessed as the preacher immersed me in the water of Plum Creek. I later learned from reading the Bible that women were at the cross with Jesus. I believe the woman and the young man I saw next to the cross might have been Mary, the mother of Jesus, and John the Apostle.

"I am the light of the world: he that followeth me shall not walk in darkness, but shall have the light of life."
(John 8:12, King James Version)

Chapter 24

They Shall Be One Flesh

That night, I was hurting. The military doc said I needed a wisdom tooth jerked out of my mouth. He hadn't said anything about two wisdom teeth. I had no idea why he had to take out two. And why did he have to use so many stitches? I wouldn't be able to eat for a week. That problem was solved by eating eggs with taters (potatoes) for breakfast, lunch, and supper. My mouth hurt so bad. Heck! I couldn't talk to anyone.

A few days before, I had enlisted in the Navy. At boot camp, they checked us over from head to toe, and one of our first checkups was at the dental office.

"Open your mouth wide," ordered the Navy dentist.

He poked and prodded for a couple of minutes before coming to a conclusion.

"Well, I need to remove your wisdom teeth," he flatly stated. It wasn't long before he was doing just that. Once he started, I thought the doc would never stop pulling my teeth out.

After graduating from boot camp, I was assigned to the Navy Seabees. Although I was assigned to the Seabees, I had many different assignments in the Navy. One of the assignments that influenced me greatly was to assist the Chaplain and protect him in times of war.

After a couple of years, I was given temporary orders for an eight-month assignment to the Naval Base in Spain. While working in Spain, I met a woman with big dark eyes full of passion for living and faith in God. Her mom had already died before I ever had the opportunity to meet her. I wondered if her mom had the same eyes, full of passion for life, or had the hardship of facing death left them full of sadness.

We never kissed or held hands until about six months later. I was enchanted by her passion for life and realized I wanted to share my life with her.

"Hey, you want to get married?" I said one day as we talked on the phone.

"Yes," she answered with a laugh.

"What's so funny?" I asked.

I wondered if she even understood my Kentucky English.

While still on duty in Spain, I joined the Rodeo. I wanted to ride the bulls, but sometimes the bulls rode me. On one particularly bad ride, a bull stabbed me in the butt with its horn. My future wife was growing concerned, and I promised to stop pretending to be a Kentucky cowboy. Back home on Plum Creek Road, it was easier for me to ride hogs.

I was selected to attend training for seven weeks with the Marine Corps at Camp Lejeune. With the Marines, I felt like I was back home in the hollers, walking up and down the hills, crossing the creeks, camping all night, and carrying my shotgun. I quickly became an expert marine rifleman. After finishing the Marine Corps training, I returned to Spain to get married.

After returning to Spain, I had never met my future bride's father. Trying to calm my nerves as best I could, I introduced myself to him for the first time upon my return. In my best Kentucky English, I let him know that I wanted to marry his daughter. I did not go empty-handed, though; I had come with gifts. Among my offerings were an American smoked Hickory sugar ham, a case of American Budweiser beer, and a pack of boxer underwear.

After I gave him the gifts, I explained that I wanted to marry his daughter. I think he already understood that because of the gifts, but he seemed to be confused. Later that day, I found out he could not understand any English. I also learned that he gave the ham to his oldest daughter, did not drink beer and that the underwear was too big for him. I was disappointed with how our first meeting went. I also wondered who got the beer and underwear?

We got married in Spain a year later in a beautiful 18th-century church. I stood there waiting in front of the altar for my future bride as the priest was looking down at me. Suddenly, I felt a warm light touching my face and looked upward. A bright light was shining through a small window below the ceiling, and I heard a whispering wind calling me.

"You will not be a priest," it seemed to say.

When I walked out of the church with my Spanish bride, a young girl standing next to the large wooden door jabbed me with a needle several times in the butt. The girl's eyes glared at me as she jabbed at my butt. I wondered if she was expressing her dislike of Americans, but she smiled when I looked at her without stopping what she was doing.

"It hurts. Stop!" I said tersely.

Finally, she stopped sticking me in the butt, but I was confused about why she did it in the first place. Wouldn't it have been enough to pinch my butt? Later I learned that it was a Spanish tradition for a single girl to jab the bridegroom in the butt, hoping to find a husband soon. Did she really need to be so enthusiastic about it, though? Maybe she just enjoyed the sound of me yelling "Ouch!" in my Kentucky English.

After the wedding, my father-in-law walked up, staring me in the eyes, and smiled. He made circular motions along the side of his head with his finger and spoke words in Andalusian Spanish that I could not understand. It scared me a little bit, to be honest. His eyes seemed so dark, and I didn't understand what he was doing with his finger. *Maybe he was mad at me for marrying his daughter, I thought. Or perhaps he was upset about the oversize underwear.*

"What's your grandpa trying to say?" I asked my wife's nephew. He laughed as he responded with perfect "Yankee" English.

"My Grandpa asked you, "Why would you marry his crazy daughter?"

Then my wife's father moved very close, within inches of my face. His expression became very serious, and he looked straight into my blue eyes with a piercing stare that seemed to last for an uncomfortable eternity. He slowly moved his finger across his throat with a cutting motion, and there was no hint of a smile. He said something else to his nephew while looking directly at me.

The nephew turned to me, "If you ever hurt or mistreat his daughter, he will go to America. He will find you and cut your throat."

There was a pause as my new father-in-law said something else to my wife's nephew. I waited patiently to hear what he was saying.

"Now, he is asking for a box of Cuban cigars," my wife's nephew responded.

Not having any Cuban cigars, I decided to politely excuse myself.

I soon encountered my wife's aunts. They were trying to tell me how to treat their niece on our honeymoon night. My wife's nephew had come over once again and translated.

"Her aunts are telling you to be gentle, not to be a wolf with their niece on your wedding night. Don't hurt her."

"Okay," I said with a smile, and her aunts all smiled back. I wondered if I had married her entire family.

After a while, I quickly discovered that my wife could cook a pot of garbanzo beans (chickpeas) while dancing Flamenco. She maneuvered her skinning body, tapping both feet on the floor, waving her left hand over her head, and yelling "Ole! Ole!" as she cooked. She loved Flamenco music and could even flip a Tortilla in a frying pan while dancing without missing a step. Heck! She could even patch a hole the size of a silver half-dollar coin in my stock and underwear if needed, and I wondered what other amazing things she could do. I had discovered a soul mate, a woman I could trust. And she could trust me.

We tried to have children, but she did not get pregnant.

"Why can't you get pregnant?" I asked.

"Why can't you get me pregnant," she replied.

Later, Momma told me, "Lawrence Raymond, you might not be able to have children. You had the mumps as a child. The mumps could have affected your 'Marbles' (testicles). It makes your stuff lazy."

I had not known this, but maybe Momma was right about the mumps. Later I told a doctor I couldn't get my wife pregnant and explained what Momma said.

"What do you think, Doc?" I asked.

The doctor explained that mumps could affect the sperm, making it weak. The weak sperm could not travel up to the "home sweet home." The sperm would need some help to push it to the target to get my wife pregnant.

"You need to push it way up to get her pregnant," he explained.

I never told my wife what Momma said about the mumps or what the doctor said until years later.

My six-year contract with the Navy ended, and I was again left to ponder what I would do with my life. Both my wife and Momma strongly encouraged me to leave the military.

"Why don't you become a preacher?" said Momma.

"Why don't you become a Chaplain in the military," replied my wife.

I agreed to end my career in the Navy. But I expected to return someday as a Naval Officer in the Chaplain Corps.

Wow! Did God have other plans for my life?

"Therefore shall a man leave his father and his mother, and shall cleave unto his wife: and they shall be one flesh."

(Geneses 2:24, King James Version)

Chapter 25

Not to Please Ourselves

The FBI agent sat in front of me and began asking me a series of very personal questions.

"When was the last time you cried?"

"Did you ever abuse animals?"

"Do you like girls?"

"Did you ever lie?"

"Did you ever steal?"

A few weeks before leaving the military, I wondered if I was qualified to be an FBI agent. I visited a Federal Bureau of Investigations (FBI) office in Yuma, Arizona, to inquire about their qualification process. When I arrived at the office, I was met by a Hispanic agent. He wore black slacks, a red tie, and brown leather slip-on shoes.

"Welcome to the office. I'm the only agent here," he said cordially. I responded that I was interested in becoming an FBI agent.

"Do you have a college degree?" he asked.

"Yes, sir. I also have two master's degrees," I proudly replied.

"Okay. You passed the agent's interview. Next week return to the office for a pre-mental exam interview."

"Sir. Why do I need to take a mental exam?" I inquired.

He laughed at the naivety of the question, "Because you want to be an agent," he replied with a grin.

The following week, I met the agent at the FBI Yuma office. He politely smiled and said, "Are you ready for the pre-mental exam questions?"

"Yes, sir."

The questions that he proceeded to ask me made me angry. What's going on here? I wondered. A mental exam. For what? Did he think I might be crazy because of my military service in the Navy? Perhaps he believed that the rigors of Navy life, living with a bunch of guys with very few women around, had made me crazy. I kept a lid on my anger and answered the questions as best I could.

"I cried when my little brother died at age 11."

"I killed several chickens and hogs on the farm."

"I hit my brothers and sisters growing up."

"Heck! I never did stop liking my sister's girlfriends."

I answered all the questions honestly, but I was becoming more frustrated with each one.

"Did you ever lie or steal?" he asked.

"How about you? Have you ever lied and stolen?"

"I'm asking you," the agent coldly replied. I calmed myself and continued to answer his intrusive questions.

"Heck! The first time I lied was when a pickup truck hit me in the right leg. I told Daddy I fell at school. At age 7, I took a "Musketeer" candy bar at a country store without paying for it. I hid it in my pocket. Later I ate it. It was good." I replied to the agent.

I wondered. Why was he asking so many weird questions? Could you really fail the mental exam for not liking girls?

"Sir. Are you serious about the question of not liking girls? I'm married to a woman." The agent did not say a word, but I was sure I could smell alcohol on the agent's rotten breath.

The interview was after lunch. I thought maybe he had a beer or two while eating. Or perhaps he was a closet gay guy. The thought made me burst out in laughter.

"What's so funny?" he asked. I politely dismissed the laughter. "Well, you passed the pre-mental exam," he continued. "Congratulations! The FBI main office in Washington D.C. will call you for a physical examination soon."

Between the crazy questions and the smell of alcohol on his breath, I wondered if this guy was really an FBI agent? Later, I was speaking to a local town police officer.

"Hey Larry, the FBI agent interviewing you is a little crazy. He's an alcoholic," the officer informed me.

“We then that are strong: ought to bear the infirmities of the weak, and not to please ourselves.”
(Romans 15:1, King James Version)

Chapter 26

I Am with Thee: Be Not Dismayed

"I have an interview with the FBI. They think I'm a minority, a Kentucky Cherokee Indian," I shouted out excitedly.

One of the federal agencies I considered applying for after leaving the military was the Secret Service. I called their office in San Diego to see if they were hiring. They called me to meet with an agent at his San Diego Federal Building office. I told the agent about my education, military service, and my marriage to a Spanish woman.

"Is your wife looking for a job in the Federal Government?" he asked.

"Why, my wife?" I replied.

"Congress wants Secret Service and other federal agencies to hire minorities. You need to change your last name to your wife's Spanish name. Without a doubt, your education and military experience make you qualified for the Secret Service job. But all law enforcement agencies are searching for minority applicants."

The statement puzzled me. "Are you saying I must change my last name to Spanish to get a job with the Secret Service and in the Federal Government? She's not an American by birth. But I am."

I felt disappointed when I left the Secret Service office. It seemed unfair that the U.S. Congress was putting pressure on federal law enforcement agencies to restrict their hiring to minority candidates at the exclusion of other qualified candidates.

As I left the Federal Building, I walked past the Federal Bureau of Investigation (FBI) office. There was a notice on the front door announcing the FBI was hiring. My disappointment with the Secret Service was still fresh in my mind, but I recalled something Momma had said. She told us stories about her great-great-great grandfather, who was a full-blooded Cherokee from Kentucky. My great-great-great grandfather was a Native American. I thought about it and decided that made me a minority.

I walked into the FBI office feeling confident about my family heritage as a Cherokee Indian. There was a receptionist at the front desk, and I politely asked her for a job application. As expected, the application wanted to know my race and color. I marked the box that said white and found a line on the application where I could acknowledge my Cherokee heritage. Within two weeks, I received a letter from the FBI to report for a job interview.

Several days later, I returned to the FBI office at the appointed time. I proudly sported a $5 grey jacket with dark paints that I had purchased from the Salvation Army.

"Can I help you?" asked the receptionist.

"I'm here for a job interview. Here's the letter," I said with pride.

"Go to the waiting room. Wait for instructions."

I felt out of place as I entered the waiting room. The other candidates came from minority backgrounds, and I wondered if having a Cherokee great-great-great grandfather would be enough for me to be considered.

Two men arrived in dark suits.

"Those guys are FBI agents," said the girl sitting beside me.

One of the agents approached me, "What is your name?"

"Larry Ray Hardin."

"You marked Native American on the application. What tribal affiliation are you?"

"Cherokee," I replied confidently. I was happy that my Cherokee heritage had gotten me an interview with the FBI.

"Do you have Indian tribal papers with you?"

"What are tribal papers?" I asked.

"Can you speak Spanish?"

I wondered what speaking Spanish had to do with being Cherokee. My wife was from Spain, but she was not a Native American. Fortunately, I learned some Spanish during my time in Spain.

"Yes, sir, I can speak Spanish."

"You can follow me. You are going to take a Spanish exam."

Another exam, I thought, as we walked to the exam room. I hoped I would not have to take another one of those crazy mental exams like when I had applied with the FBI. The exam room was tiny, with plain white walls and no windows. A single door and small metal tables lined up across the room. When I arrived, a young Hispanic man was already sitting alone at one table.

"You need to listen to the tape recorder on the table. After you listen to the tape, write down the answers in Spanish on the papers I am giving you. You have one hour for the exam," said the agent before he left the room.

I started listening to the Spanish recording on the tape and couldn't hardly understand any of it. The man next to me saw that I was having trouble with the exam, as I quietly whispered my frustration.

"Man, this is difficult," he said. "I can't understand some of these words on the tape recorder either."

"Where are you from?" I asked.

"From TJ."

"Tijuana, Mexico?" I replied.

After about an hour, the door opened, and the agent entered the room.

"The Spanish exam is finished. Within two weeks, you will hear back from the FBI with the results of your Spanish exam." Within two weeks, I received a letter from the FBI. The letter said I did not pass the FBI Spanish exam. *What a surprise!*

"Fear thou not; for I am with thee: be not dismayed; for I am they God: I will strengthen thee; yea, I will help thee; I will uphold thee with the right hand of my righteousness."

(Isaiah 41:10, King James Version)

Chapter 27

Thy Nakedness Shall be Uncovered

"So, you want to be a DEA agent?" said the DEA recruiter. "Well, I was shot in the neck and hip, wounded, and almost killed during an undercover narcotics case."

Several days after losing interest in becoming an FBI agent, I decided to find out what the Drug Enforcement Administration (DEA) was all about. Until recently, I had never heard about DEA, and I didn't have any idea what they did. That didn't stop me from calling the DEA office to look for a job.

"Okay. I'll transfer you to the recruiter's office," the receptionist politely responded to my call. I waited patiently as she transferred my call.

"Hello. Can I help you?" asked another voice.

"I would like to be a DEA agent."

I considered what the recruiter said about being wounded and almost killed. If he was trying to dissuade me, it didn't work. Despite my young age, I had already been through a lot, and his stories did not scare me.

"Do you think I can be a DEA agent?"

"Do you have a college education?" he asked.

"I have two master's degrees and just got out of the military."

We set up a time to meet, and a few days later, I met the recruiter at his office. The recruiter was an older Hispanic man dressed in tight blue Levi jeans. The stiff formality of the FBI and Secret Service Recruiters was utterly lacking. He wore a big gold-colored belt buckle with a long silver horn and a bull's face, brown leather pointed-toe boots, a large beige hat, and a long sleeve western shirt with ivory buttons. He looked like a cowboy from the old Western TV series Gun Smoke. His pants seemed tight, though, and I wondered how he could bend over to put his leather boots on without hurting his "family jewels?" My first impression was positive, and I felt at home there.

This was an authentic Mexican cowboy working as a DEA agent. Other agents walking around the office looked like they were at home on the streets with worn-out clothes and shoes. The kind of streetwise guys that could blend in with a crowd of homeless people.

The appearance of the agents made me think I could be one of them. I felt the excitement in my stomach I had known as a kid while eating a bag of salted peanuts or drinking a Big Red soda. I could work on the streets as a DEA cowboy, a homeless man, or a Kentucky farm boy. This was my kind of job. It was an incredible sight, with agents carrying different types of guns on their shoulders, waists, and ankles. It only takes one gun to shoot someone, I thought. Back home, I only used a single-barrel Shotgun to kill a rabbit and a squirrel. Still, it felt like my kind of job.

"Let me show you the office. I want you to meet some of the agents working on a case where an agent was kidnapped and tortured to death by a Mexican Cartel," said the agent.

"What happened to the agent?" I asked.

"The agent and his informant were kidnapped in Mexico. The informant was killed immediately. A cartel doctor gave the agent drugs to keep him alive so the kidnappers could torture him even longer. Eventually, the agent was skinned alive." I was saddened and angered to hear how the agent died.

After meeting the agents at the office, I was highly impressed with how casual yet functional they dressed, how they carried their guns, and how they acted. I wanted to be an agent. I thought, if you're going to do enforcement work on the streets, this is what it's all about. I suddenly felt an inner voice telling me this was what I would do.

"I want you to review some recruitment paperwork to understand the DEA's mission," said the recruiter.

He called me back into the DEA office a week later. There wasn't any pre-mental exam like the FBI. The recruiter never asked if I lied, liked girls, stole, or if I ever abused animals. Nevertheless, he did give me a written exam.

The DEA written exam was a two-page essay about my life and experience. I wrote about my family back home, my wife, and my experience in the military. It was easy to write about everybody back home. Heck! I could write a book about them.

Later, he had me take a pre-qualification physical fitness exam. The exam tested how many push-ups and chin-ups I could do without pulling a muscle and how fast I could run a mile without fainting. It also tested practical skills, like how many times I could squeeze the trigger on a .38 caliber revolver. Of course, they didn't give me any live rounds to fire.

I felt like I was back in the hollers as I squeezed the revolver's trigger. It wasn't like squeezing the trigger on my 20-gauge single-barrel shotgun back home, but it reminded me of home. The revolver shot six bullets. Heck! With a revolver in the woods, I would have had six bullets to shoot snakes.

Several weeks passed, and I didn't hear back from the DEA. I decided to call the recruiter to find out about the status of my application. The recruiter sounded concerned about my application as he took my call but didn't want to say much on the phone.

"Can you meet tomorrow at my office? I need to discuss if you or anyone else in your family has ever been arrested."

The next day I was in his office for the requested interview.

"Have you or anyone in your family ever been arrested?" he asked.

"Yes, sir. I was arrested once. But I only stayed in the jail for just a few hours."

"What happened?"

"I was at the softball game with my girlfriend, watching my sisters play softball. I decided to run naked across the ball field. My girlfriend didn't want to get naked with me because her father was a

Taylorsville town cop. She said no. Her daddy would have killed her. I really wanted to see her run naked.

The recruiter chuckled, and I continued with the rest of the story. I had seen a tall skinny guy with a mustache drooping down over the corners of his lips and blond hair down to his shoulders standing next to me.

"What are you looking at, buddy?" I asked him.

"I'm watching your sister playing softball."

I didn't really want to run naked across the ballpark by myself, and it occurred to me that this guy might be up for that kind of stunt.

"Hey, do you want to get naked and run across the ballpark with me?"

He laughed and said, "Yea! Let's do it."

Two days later, there was a knock at the door. It was my girlfriend's dad and another cop. They politely addressed Momma, who had answered the door.

"Your son needs to come with us. Your boy is being arrested for running naked at a girl's church softball game. The judge is charging him with indecent behavior."

"Are you sure it's not my other son?" asked Momma, surprised.

"No," the cops said. "We're sure."

Wow, I couldn't believe I was being arrested. My first arrest was for running naked at a girls' softball game. It had just seemed like a harmless prank at the time.

Later that day, Daddy talked to the town judge about my arrest.

"Junior," he said to Daddy. "I didn't know he was your son. Go get your boy out of jail."

A few days later, I had to appear at the county courthouse and face the judge.

"Hardin, why did you run naked at the girl's church softball game?" he asked.

"I'm sorry, judge. I didn't know it was a "church" softball game. I just wanted to see my girlfriend naked, and I thought she might do it if I did it."

The judge shook his head while forcing himself not to laugh. He dropped the charge for indecent behavior and fined me $60. I paid in cash.

The guy who ran naked with me later married my sister. Sadly, he died a few years later at age 23 from an accident at work. Daddy was with him at work when the accident happened. My sister was left to raise their two girls alone.

The recruiter listened thoughtfully to what I had told him and paused to consider his reply.

"I'm going to call your mom about what happened at the church softball game. Don't say anything to her while I'm talking on the phone." He dialed the number as I waited quietly. "Hello," I heard him say as Momma answered the phone.

The recruiter politely introduced himself and explained that he was calling about my past incident with the law.

"Larry Ray's a good son," Momma told him. "His daddy and I never had any problems with him. We're proud of Larry Ray. My other son is the one having problems with the town cops. He was arrested for growing marijuana and went to jail for a few days."

The recruiter thanked Momma for her time and hung up the phone.

"Anything else?" he asked.

"Yes, sir! I had a couple of traffic tickets. The cops said I was driving too fast through town. I paid the ticket in cash and didn't do any jail time." I replied. "Once, a town cop did stop me and searched my car. He found a quart of homemade whiskey under my car seat. He took it without charging me."

"Anyone arrested in your mom's family?" he asked. I found it interesting that he was asking specifically about Momma's family.

"My Momma said revenue officers arrested her dad. He was making homemade whiskey inside a cave somewhere in Kentucky. He needed to make some money to buy food and clothes for Momma's brothers and sisters. Momma said her dad went to prison for five years for making whiskey."

"Momma said her brother went to prison for holding a gun when he robbed someone. She said her younger brother had never robbed a bank. His buddies robbed the bank. He was only driving the car. He served five years in prison for the bank robbery she said he never did," I truthfully acknowledged.

"Is there anybody else who was arrested and went to jail on your mom's side of the family?"

"No. I don't think so."

"Okay," he continued. "How about your dad's family. Has your dad ever been in jail?"

"My daddy went to jail several times when he was a young boy for fighting on public streets and driving while drinking alcohol."

"How about your dad's brothers and sisters?"

"No. If my uncles and aunts did something wrong, they never got caught by the cops."

"We are done with this interview," he said.

Later that evening, I called Momma to talk to her about the phone call she had received from the DEA recruiter.

"I was so nervous," she said. "I wondered why he wanted to talk to me about you, not your brother."

"Momma, you did okay, but why did you mention my brother?"

"It's the truth, Lawrence Raymond," she stated unapologetically.

I told my wife about the interview with the recruiter. "You'll never get a job with DEA because of you and your family's criminal past," she said.

"I'm not ashamed of it," I replied.

I met with the DEA recruiter over the next several months, and we became good friends.

"Thy nakedness shall be uncovered, yea, thy shame shall be seen: I will take vengeance, and I will not meet thee as a man."
(Isaiah 47:3, King James Version)

Chapter 28

Ye Shall not Enter into the Kingdom of Heaven

What really happens to women and children before crossing into the United States from Mexico? What happens to most children when they are left scattered, alone, and afraid throughout the United States? Without a doubt, the children would be sexually exploited and preyed upon by pedophiles.

DEA's hiring process was extensive and took quite a long time. While waiting for DEA to hire me, I was blessed to find a job with the Federal Bureau of Prisons in California as a Correctional Officer (Prison Guard).

At the Federal prison, I frequently overheard other correctional officers saying most prisoners illegally entered the United States from the Southwest Mexican Border. They said many prisoners were smuggling drugs (heroin, cocaine, methamphetamine), women, and children into the U.S.

It upset me to know that Drug Smugglers were exploiting women and children. I wondered, *Why they were bringing women and children into the United States. Was it for money and sex?*

One day I decided to ask the guard supervisor. "Why're these drug smugglers bringing children without their parents into the U.S.? Do you think the women and kids are sexually abused by the smugglers in Mexico and the U.S.?"

"Yes," he responded. "Drugs, money, and sex."

I was shocked that these children were traveling alone. I wondered if the smugglers found the trafficking of women and children to be as profitable as smuggling drugs.

"Verily I say unto you. Except ye be converted, and become as little children, ye shall not enter int the kingdom of heaven."

(Matthew 18:3, King James Version)

Chapter 29

Be not Deceived; God is not Mocked

Once inside the prison, illegal immigrants ate three healthy meals daily, were given clean military surplus clothes, and received medical and dental checkups. The prison also allowed them to learn English if they wanted to. They seemed to be cheerful and fortunate to be in the United States of America, even if they were in prison.

While I worked at the Federal prison as a correctional officer, I saw many illegal immigrants in ill health. They were primarily young men and women from poverty-stricken Mexico, Central America, and South America. Their hygiene was poor, and many of them had dental problems. I noticed some prisoners were unwell and had many forms of illness.

The illegal immigrants inside the federal prison were given a complete medical examination as part of their in-processing. They were seen by doctors, dentists, and nurses to assess if they had any physical injuries, infections, or diseases. Many had coughs, sores on their faces, or missing teeth.

After the physical evaluation, the illegal immigrants were moved to their temporary holding cells. The cells allowed them to relax after a long and dangerous journey. They were safe and, at least temporarily, free of the smugglers. The prison was not the ideal living situation, but it did provide them with medical care, a hot shower, food in their stomachs, and clean beds to sleep in. It was a sad life for them. I wondered how many illegal immigrants ever had three meals a day while living in their home countries.

The illegal immigrants would eventually be given a hearing before a federal immigration judge. They were provided legal advice from public defenders with Spanish interrupters, courtesy of United States taxpayers. Most public defenders instructed the prisoners on how to deny any federal criminal charges brought against them.

If the immigrant prisoner wanted to work while waiting for their "due process-of-law," they received "award points." These were given for tasks such as making up their beds, cleaning the bathrooms, removing trash, taking their showers, etc. They could use the points to buy food or snacks at the prison store.

The plight of the immigrants was a tragic one. Still, it was heartbreaking to see how American taxpayers bore the economic burden of illegal immigrants and drug traffickers in prison. While in prison, the immigrants learned how to take advantage of "due process" in our legal justice system from public defenders and many churches that visited the prison. They used what they learned to become legal residents and United States citizens, and I felt they were being rewarded for entering the United States illegally. It was discouraging to see how our federal and state court systems were being used by corrupt lawyers abusing the "Scale of Justice."

Many "coyotes" and smugglers continued their human trafficking and drug smuggling activities along the Southwest border with Mexico. Eventually, most of the immigrant prisoners were released into United States communities pending a deportation hearing. The other prisoners were given a temporary reprieve from their sad lives. For the moment, at least, they were safe in the United States, away from the terror of the Mexican cartels, human traffickers, gangs, and corrupt cops and politicians.

After a few weeks, I left the job at the federal prison to take another federal job at the Immigration and Naturalization Service (INS). I worked as an adjudicator, and it was my job to adjudicate an immigrant's legal status to live in the United States.

During my time with the INS, I interviewed many illegal immigrants. Most of them were from Central and South America and wanted to live in the United States. Most of them came from poor conditions and without adequate health care. They wanted a better life than the one that awaited them in their home countries. Since childhood, they had known nothing except for hardship, and now they were living the American dream, having a home, car, free health care, welfare assistance, free education, and other benefits. I wondered who was paying for all these free benefits, particularly how that burden affected middle-class taxpayers.

"Be not deceived; God is not mocked: for whatsoever a man soweth, that shall he also reap."
(Galatians 6-7, King James Version)

Chapter 30

But Whoso Shall Offend one of These Little Ones

"The surveilling DEA agents killed two of the Asian gang members. A third man was shot several times by agents," said the instructor. He paused to let the implications of that statement sink in.

"Do you realize how dangerous this job is?" he asked.

I was finally hired to work for DEA and was in my fifth week of training at the DEA Academy. The instructor seemed oddly upset as he walked into the classroom.

"Today, two agents were assassinated in Los Angeles. One agent was severely injured. The agents were negotiating to purchase white heroin from Asian gang members. It was an ambush, to rip off the "buy money" and kill the agents."

It angered me to hear how callously the agents had been killed. Evil men don't understand God's justice, I thought. They will kill again if justice isn't quick. After 13 weeks, I completed training at the DEA Academy in Quantico, Virginia. I was officially a DEA agent, ready to hand out justice and "Win the War on Drugs."

I returned to California as a DEA Special Agent. Within two days of reporting for my assignment, I was "working the streets." It was exciting, and I was ready to hit the streets running, develop my first Informant, and buy cocaine, heroin, and meth. I was prepared to fight "the war on drugs."

Before running out the door to find "dopers," the supervisor called me into his office.

"Shut the door," he said as I stepped inside. "What you learned at the academy was a perfect world where no one gets hurt. Well, Hardin, you're in the real world now. Bad guys don't follow the rules on the streets when they're trying to kill you. Watch and learn from the guys that have been on the job for several years. There are some bad agents, but there are also a lot of good agents with integrity who get the job done right."

"Now listen carefully," he continued. "Don't get caught drinking or having sex with women in your government car, especially informants."

It disappointed me that the supervisor talked so much about women and drinking. The DEA academy didn't feel the need to talk about that. I wanted to focus on the job.

After the first week on the job, the supervisor asked me to take his new, government-issued Chevrolet for its weekly car wash.

"Hey, Hardin, here are the keys," he said. "My car needs gas. Make sure the tires are okay." Then he threw the car keys on top of my old metal desk.

The request left me feeling deflated, and I slumped down into my broken chair. I'm a DEA agent, I fumed silently, But I can't fight the war on drugs because I must wash my boss's car. Heck! Why am I his personal errand boy when there are other agents in the office? Is it because I'm a new agent? It was shameful, I thought. Did the taxpayers know how much money they were paying me to wash my boss's car?

Eventually, I found myself being given more responsibility. I was helping other agents, and cops, with routine enforcement work like handcuffing criminals who were smuggling dope and large amounts of cash across the Mexican border.

After working on the streets for several weeks, I realized that the DEA had entrusted me with a lot of power. My work primarily targeted narcotics traffickers, but I could detain and arrest anyone for just about anything – drugs, bank robbery, spitting on a public sidewalk. I understood that the broad powers and authority I had been given also came with great responsibility, which was an intimidating thought. *Wow! I was finally working on the streets as a federal narcotics agent.*

Every day I worked the streets was an education, and I became increasingly street-smart every day. I was learning from the agents, narcotic cops, sources, informants, and even the dope smugglers. The dope smugglers were incredibly resourceful and used cars, trucks, boats, planes, and anything else to move drugs (marijuana, cocaine, heroin, and methamphetamine) into the United States from the Southwest border with Mexico. Their activities generated a lot of dirty cash, which they had to launder and smuggle back into Mexico and South America.

In addition to smuggling drugs, the dopers were also smuggling women and children whom they used as "mules" to bring drugs across the border. First, they hid small amounts of drugs in party balloons or clear plastic baggies. The pre-packed drugs were then ingested or inserted into the body cavities of women, children, or other smugglers.

It shocked me that women and children were shoving the dope and pills into bodily crevices such as their vaginas or anus. I learned that the drug cartels knew the American cops do not like searching the body cavities of women and children for fear of being accused in a sexual harassment lawsuit. The dopers also knew that cops must get a federal or a state search warrant for a doctor or nurse to take a peep inside of a woman or child's "private parts." With a male dope smuggler, an agent can simply tell him to bend over and spread his "cheeks" to see if anything was bulging out from the anus.

I remember the arrest of a Hispanic female at the Mexico border. A doctor removed one pound of Mexican black tar heroin from her vagina. The heroin was rolled up in roughly the same size and shape as a penis. That pound of heroin was worth over $70,000 on the streets.

In addition to drugs such as cocaine, heroin, methamphetamines, and marijuana, the traffickers also transported narcotic pain pills. As a new agent working far and wide, night and day, to apprehend traffickers, I wondered if the traffickers were bringing the pills across for personal use. Were they sick, I wondered. Had snorting cocaine and injecting heroin into their bodies taken a painful toll?

I was amazed by the sheer quantity of drugs, pills, and pre-cursor chemicals I was seizing from bad guys. The pre-cursor chemicals were for use in the manufacture of methamphetamines. They could be found anywhere, homes, cars, boats, businesses, and even within the medical community. The DEA academy in Quantico never taught me why these drugs were being abused.

We thoroughly searched traffickers and their property for additional dope to be used as evidence. I would find clear plastic baggies and plastic medicine bottles inside the trafficker's clothes, cars, homes, storage units, boats, airplanes, and on or in their person. Sometimes I would find packages containing hundreds of narcotic tablets (pills) and capsules. The drug traffickers would frequently tell me that the pills were vitamins. Sometimes they would say that a doctor prescribed them for pain.

"Where's your prescription from the doctor? What's the name of your doctor?" I asked.

I doubted they had so many narcotics pain pills without a written prescription from a doctor. Depending on the quantity of pills and the situation, I might give the pain pills back, dispose of them, or confiscate them. I wondered if doctors were aware that some of their patients might be traffickers or if they knew how many pills had found their way into someone's hands. I learned from the DEA Laboratory that dopers were trafficking in Ecstasy, Percocet, Oxycodone, Vicodin, and many other kinds of narcotic tablets and capsules; so-called "feel good" drugs.

It seemed that some doctors were pushing "pain medication" on their patients without a physical examination. I found that to be very disappointing. How were the dopers getting the narcotic pills without a doctor's prescription?

"But whoso shall offend one of these little ones which believe in me, it was better for him that a millstone were hanged about his neck, and that he were drowned in the depth of the sea."

(Matthew 18:6, King James Version)

Chapter 31

Be Strong and of a Courage; be not Afraid, Neither be thou Dismayed

Looking over the woman's shoulder, I could see the glassware "cooking" vessels. The information the informant had given me about meth being cooked in the RV was true. I quickly grabbed the 9 mm Sig from my waist and pointed it at the woman's face.

"I'm a cop. A DEA agent. Don't move. Don't scream. I'll shoot you right here between the eyes."

I had finally gotten my first opportunity to work with an informant. The informant told me a nurse and her boyfriend were "cooking" methamphetamine in her dad's motorhome.

I questioned the informant carefully, not only to find out what they knew but what their intentions and motivations might be.

"Why are you telling me about this nurse and the boyfriend?"

"What's the location of the RV?"

"How do you know they are cooking meth?"

"Are you using meth?"

I noticed the informant's cracked, dirty hands, a tell-tale sign.

"When's the last time you "cooked" meth yourself?"

The question caught the informant off-guard, and he started to fidget nervously.

"I don't take that sh--- anymore. Stop cooking that sh—," he stammered.

I wondered when the last time this drug addict informant had taken a bath or brushed his teeth. His body smelled like a dead animal carcass. When he opened his mouth, I could smell rotten eggs. His face was covered in sores. He looked like a dead man who had walked across broken meth pipes with worn-out shoes. What happened to this human that God had made? Satan was destroying this man's body and soul.

"You're not cooking meth right now," I reiterated, staring directly into his red bloodshot eyes.

"Not right now," he said, lowering his head.

"Who's the nurse? How do you know she's a nurse?"

"She's a nurse working at a hospital. I used to work with her," he admitted. Looking back on who he had once been, I got the sense that the man was ashamed of what he had become.

"Give me the location of the RV."

After talking to the informant, two other agents and I went to where the RV was parked. It was right where the informant said it would be. I knocked on the RV's door.

"Who is it?" shouted a woman from inside the RV.

"The RV is burning outside," I lied. "There's smoke near the engine." I needed the woman to answer the door, and telling her who we really were at that point would have allowed her to flee or to arm herself with a weapon.

Slowly the RV's door opened, and a woman's face poked out and looked at me. I glanced through the crack in the open door and saw several pieces of laboratory glassware used to make meth near the stove and sink.

I immediately drew my weapon and forced my way inside the RV.

"Where's your boyfriend?" I asked as I put handcuffs on her.

"Sir, he's in the bedroom sleeping," she said nervously, yet politely responded.

I quickly tiptoed to the bedroom, not saying a word. I slowly opened the door and hoped that our entry had not alerted him. A man was lying on his back in a small bed. Without hesitating, I jerked him out of bed by his legs and threw him to the floor. The first thing he saw as he opened his eyes was the barrel of my handgun pointing at his head.

"Don't you move your hands! Don't even move your feet. If you so much as spit, I will blow your corrupt brains out of your ears. Now slowly give me one hand at a time."

The man complied, and I quickly handcuffed him. With the woman and her boyfriend safely in cuffs, we investigated the crime scene and questioned the suspects.

"Who's cooking the meth?" I asked.

"Are you really a cop. Did someone tell you we're here?" asked the woman.

"I'm a DEA Federal agent? Have you ever heard of DEA?"

"Yes, sir. My uncle's a DEA agent," she proudly replied.

"Are you a nurse?" I asked.

"Who told you I'm a nurse?" she yelled. The question and what it said about how much we knew clearly upset her.

"Where do you live? What hospital are you working at? Who owns the RV?" I asked the nurse.

"I live with my parents. The RV is my dad's. Who told you I'm a nurse?" she demanded.

It disappointed me that a "meth user" nurse was giving patients their narcotic medications, drawing their blood, and giving injections. *How many patients had overdosed on their own medicine or died while she was stoned out of her mind?* I wondered. *And did she say her uncle was a DEA agent?*

"So, this isn't your glassware to make meth? Can you tell me who's cooking meth? Don't you think it's strange that you both live at the RV but cannot tell me why the lab glassware is here?" I asked.

I stared directly into the nurse's bloodshot eyes, "Where're the chemicals?" I asked.

"What chemicals? Do you see any chemicals here?" she replied, grinning defiantly. "We don't have to tell you nothing."

They decided not to tell me about cooking meth or where the chemicals were hidden. It upset me that the nurse and her boyfriend continued to deny that the lab glassware inside the RV was theirs.

We formerly arrested the nurse and her boyfriend. After taking them to jail, I returned to the office and reported to my supervisor. I carefully explained the events associated with the arrest, described the glassware we had found for cooking meth, and told him that the nurse's uncle was a DEA agent.

When I told him the nurse's uncle was a DEA agent, the supervisor seemed very concerned. "Larry, you need to find out who the uncle is. Do it now!"

Another agent and I went to the nurse's parent's home to speak with the parents. We mainly wanted to know if what she had told us about her uncle was true.

When we arrived at the home, we were politely greeted by two older people who acknowledged that they were the nurse's parents. I identified myself as a DEA Federal agent.

"Your daughter was arrested today with her boyfriend inside your RV," I informed them. "I found lab glassware to make methamphetamine (meth) but no chemicals. I need to find out where your daughter has hidden the chemicals before a kid finds them and gets hurt."

The mother was starting to cry. "My daughter called telling us she's in jail. She said it was not her glassware. It's not her chemicals. The chemicals are her boyfriend The "stuff" is outside."

I glanced at the nurse's father. "Do you own the RV? Do you have a relative working for DEA?" I asked.

"Yes. That is my RV. I have a brother that works for DEA in Washington D.C." He cooperated and provided us with his brother's name and telephone number.

We ended the interview by thanking them for their cooperation and letting them know we had no further questions. As we walked away from the home, I wondered if they or anyone else had known that the daughter was using meth while working with patients at a hospital? The thought upset me, did her co-workers suspect she might have been high on the nasty meth? Or worse, did the uncle know she was a meth user and cook?"

The next morning, I called DEA Headquarters in Washington, D.C., and asked for the nurse's uncle. He answered the phone and wanted to know what I was calling about. I explained that his niece had been arrested for manufacturing meth.

"I have nothing to do with my niece. My brother has already told me what happened to her," he said in a hushed tone. The incident was obviously embarrassing for him, and he didn't want it to affect his career as an agent.

"Sir, I need to find the chemicals," I continued. "You know the chemicals are extremely dangerous, and I need to find them before someone gets hurt, maybe a kid. Can you ask your brother to help me to find the chemicals?"

"I'll ask him about the chemicals."

"Thank you, sir, for your help."

I hoped the nurse's father could convince her to tell me where the chemicals were. He called later.

"My daughter was released from jail. She will show you where the chemicals are hidden."

A day later, the nurse called, agreeing to show me where her boyfriend hid the chemicals used to "cook" the meth. I told her to meet me near the RV site.

The next day I drove to the RV location at the appointed time. Another agent was supposed to meet me on site, and I patiently waited in my government car. I got a call from him on the car radio.

"It's raining. The traffic's a mess. I'll be there soon."

We were already late, and I was frustrated by the delay. "You know I can't be alone with a female, especially a defendant female. Hurry up!" I urged him.

The nurse pulled up in her car, stepped out into the rain, and walked up to my car.

"I'm waiting for the other agent," I informed her.

"Sir. I don't want to get wet from the rain. Can I jump in the passenger seat?" she asked.

"Sure, jump in," I reluctantly replied.

As she jumped into the passenger seat, I noticed she wore an extremely short skirt that left little to the imagination. In like manner, the upper buttons of her blouse were unbuttoned, exposing ample cleavage. It became painfully obvious that I had put myself into a bad situation by allowing her to sit beside me without another agent being present.

The lessons I had received at the DEA academy came rushing back like a flashing light warning of danger ahead. I recalled the lectures we had received from lawyers and instructors.

"Don't ever be alone with a woman, any woman that has been arrested or an informant. She will tell her attorney you put your hands on her while saying something nasty."

My palms began to sweat as I looked around nervously. *Where was the other DEA agent?* I was becoming increasingly fearful that I was being set up.

As though to confirm my worst fears, the nurse flashed me a seductive smile. She fidgeted with her skirt, and it grew slowly shorter. I tried to rationalize my growing fears and convince myself they were unfounded. I suddenly saw the flash of headlights in the rearview mirror and looked to see another car pulling in behind me. Thank God! The other agent had finally arrived.

She suddenly straightened up, adjusting the skirt to its full length, and quickly moved to open the passenger door. Before opening it, she paused like an actress getting into character for a scene. She suddenly appeared to cry as she stepped out the door and back into the rain. The other agent approached her.

"I don't feel okay. I'm going home," she told him.

I jumped out of the car, confused by what was happening.

"What's wrong," I shouted over to the nurse as she walked away. "Why are you crying? Will you show me where your boyfriend hid the meth chemicals?"

The nurse said nothing else to the agent or me as he arrived. She got into her car and drove off without saying a word. I wondered if she ever intended to show us where the chemicals were hidden. I felt like I had been lied to, and I was angry.

"Why're you so late?" I snapped at the other agent.

"Wow! Why is the nurse wearing that dress if she's searching for meth chemicals?" asked the other agent, ignoring my barb. "She can't search for chemicals with that dress on her. If she bends over, she's going to show her butt to us. Why's she leaving in such a hurry? What happened? Was she crying? You know you're not supposed to be in the car alone with her?"

"What are you saying?" I protested, with no attempt to hide my anger or frustration. "Nothing happened. It's raining. Anyway, her uncle is a DEA supervisor in Washington, and she's a nurse at the hospital." I naively tried to convince myself that those facts meant that I had not walked into the trap that I feared I had.

"Hey! It stopped raining. Let's get something to eat and a beer," I said.

The incident was far from over, as I would find out when I went into the office the next day. The supervisor was waiting for me. Hearing me come in, he peered out of his office door with an angry glare.

"Hardin get in my office now," he demanded.

I wondered why he was so upset, and I dismissed the idea that it had anything to do with what had happened the day before. Maybe I scratched the boss's car while washing it a few days ago.

"Shut the door," the boss demanded as I entered his office. "That nurse is complaining you tried to rape her in your government car. She told her public defender lawyer that your hands were all over her legs. The nurse's lawyer has a reputation in court. She doesn't like men, especially cops. Why did you let her sit in your car without another agent?"

I was shocked but not surprised by the allegation. I wondered if the other agent had talked to the supervisor and, if so, what he had told him. *Had he told the supervisor that the nurse was oddly dressed, given the purpose of the meeting? Had he assured him that he never saw me act inappropriately toward her when he was there? Or had he said she jumped out of my car, pulling her dress down and crying? Son-of-a-gun, I was in trouble again.*

I started to speak so that I could tell him my side of the story, but he stopped me abruptly and continued. "I told you that you are not to be alone with any woman who's an informant or a defendant. You were set up by the meth nurse. It's your word against her word. She's a woman. You are an agent. You're in California with liberal jurors that don't trust male cops."

I tried to speak again, but he cut me off again loudly. "Hardin, don't you dare say anything to me. The nurse is going "to walk." No one is going to press charges against her. Why? She's claiming you tried to rape her. You will be lucky if her lawyer doesn't come after you. Her meth boyfriend is the only one charged for making meth."

The supervisor stood up and leaned over his desk, looking me in the eyes. "You're a new agent, and you just made one hell of a mistake being alone with that nurse, even for a few minutes. Nobody at the U.S. Attorney's Office believes what the nurse says about you trying to have sex with her. But Hardin, you played right into the nurse's attorney's hands. Get out of my office now, Hardin! Don't you ever make that mistake again."

A few days later, I spoke to the homeless informant that had provided me with the information about the nurse.

"The nurse is still working at the hospital treating patients," he said. "She's probably stoned out of her mind using meth and stealing narcotics from her patients. She and her lawyer are laughing at you."

It bothered me that the nurse was still working at the hospital, endangering her patients. I spoke with one of the DEA Diversion investigators tasked with investigating the illegal diversion of pharmaceutical drugs.

"You know the meth nurse is a danger to the patients at the hospital," I said. "Why can't you tell the hospital that the nurse was at a meth lab with her boyfriend? DEA arrested the nurse and her boyfriend for cooking meth. Tell the hospital the nurse's boyfriend plead guilty to manufacturing meth. He will probably go to prison for five to ten years."

"Larry, DEA Diversion can't contact the nurse's place of employment. The nurse wasn't charged with a felony," replied the Investigator.

It bothered me that the nurse was never charged, partly due to my rookie carelessness. It wasn't long before my homeless informant gave me the name of another nurse manufacturing and using meth. She was addicted to the nasty stuff. Within a year on the job, I arrested three nurses and their boyfriends for manufacturing meth in their homes.

When I became an agent, I never expected to investigate corrupt doctors and nurses wearing white lab coats and Stethoscopes. I had always viewed them as above reproach and never expected them to push pills illegally or make meth. Whatever happened to the Hippocratic Oath and the noble ideal of "Do no harm?" I was trained to focus on looking for illegal drugs like marijuana, meth, cocaine, and heroin, not prescription pain pills. I wondered who else in the hospital system was using meth, narcotic pain pills, and other dangerous drugs?

"Have not I commanded thee? Be strong and of a courage; be not afraid, neither be thou dismayed: for the LORD thy God is with thee whithersoever thou goest."

(Joshua 1:9, King James Version)

Chapter 32

For He Shall Have Judgment Without Mercy

I was surprised by how ragged and worn the girl looked. She was probably only 13 or 14 years old, but it seemed she had been through a lot. She was very thin and underdeveloped, and sores covered her young face. Worse yet, was the string of what appeared to be needle marks down her bruised arms.

I had observed the young girl standing next to a bus stop but going nowhere. She stood there, looking around nervously, and I could tell something wasn't right. I walked up to her, pulled out my badge, and identified myself as a DEA agent.

"Why are you standing on the corner? Are you waiting for a bus? You're not selling sex, dope, or pills?" I asked.

The girl giggled as though it were a joke. "Are you going to arrest me for standing on the corner?" she asked.

"Why? Should I arrest you? Are you selling sex or dope? How old are you?"

"I'm eighteen."

"Do you have any ID?"

"No!" She responded with a slightly defiant tone.

"Show me your arms," I insisted. "Are you on dope or pills?"

"Not really," she replied unconvincingly.

"Give me the pills."

She reached into her back pocket, pulling out two green pills.

"Okay. What kind of pills are they?"

"I think the pills are meth. But I'm not sure. Please don't arrest me." Her subtle defiance was turning to concern.

"Where did you get the meth?"

She started to cry as it dawned on her that she might be in trouble. "Are you going to put me in jail? I got the pills at that old grey stucco house." She said, pointing to a house across the street.

"I'm not going to arrest you," I assured her. "This is my personal phone number in case you need to talk." I felt bad for her; she was too young to be on the street. I pulled five dollars from my pocket. "Take it," I said. "Go buy something to eat."

I turned to the other narcotics officers I was with and pointed to the grey stucco house where she had supposedly gotten the meth. We crossed the street and walked up to the door, where I knocked.

"What do you want?" yelled someone from inside.

"I need something to make me feel good," I replied.

Within a few minutes, an old bald man opened the door. His eyes were droopy and red, sores covered the old man's face, and most of his teeth were missing. It seemed clear that he wasn't just selling meth but also using it.

"Hey, dude, I want to buy some of your pills," I said as he stood looking at us suspiciously.

"What? I don't know you. Who're the other guys with you? Why're you asking me for pills?"

The old man wasn't convinced that we were there to buy drugs. He turned to close the door, but I whipped out my badge and held it inches from his sore-ridden face.

"I'm a narcotics agent."

He stared at the badge and stuttered. "What? You're a dope cop?"

He fidgeted nervously and tensed as though he were getting to run. Using my right hand, I yanked my gun from the front waistband under my shirt and pointed it between the old man's eyes.

"Don't run! Don't you move your hands. Don't you spit on me," I said politely. "I'll shoot you right between the eyes."

Before I could finish the sentence, the old man swung around with a speed that defied his years and bolted back into the house.

"Don't shoot me in the back," he yelled, running down the hallway like a two-legged sick dog. Disappearing into the darkness at the end of the hall, he screamed like he had seen the devil.

"Go get 'em blue," one of the officers said in a hushed tone as I darted into the house.

Where in the house the old man had gone was anyone's guess. For all we knew, he might be getting a gun or dumping pills in the toilet. We carefully entered the house with our guns drawn, searching ahead and to the side as we moved cautiously forward.

We approached a side door partway down the hall. The other officers watched the hall as I threw open the door and assessed that it was safe to enter. I was stunned to see a young girl lying on a ratty old mattress in the middle of the room, naked as a "jaybird."

She lay there unmoving, oblivious to everything that was happening around her. There was not so much as a blanket to cover her nakedness, and for a moment, I wondered if she was dead.

She suddenly stirred and saw me standing in the dim light with my weapon drawn. Screaming, she kicked out with her legs and flailed her arms wildly about as she tried to get up from the bed. I can only imagine what fears entered her young mind as she awoke to find a strange man with a gun in her room. Her ear-piercing screams of terror echoed in the room. The old man could be anywhere, and who else might be in the house? Why did she have to scream so loudly?

I quickly restrained her, cupping one hand over her mouth and pointing the handgun at her head with the other hand.

"Listen to me. I'm a narcotics agent. Stop screaming. Stop kicking me. Where's the old man hiding? Where are the pills? Do you have a gun in bed with you? Where's the gun?"

Her hands moved to her crotch, and I feared she was reaching for a gun. I grabbed her quickly by the wrist and touched the cold metal barrel of my gun to her forehead.

"Don't move your hands, or I'll kill you. Do you have a gun and pills down there?"

"It's under my ass," she cried out.

I let go of her wrist and swept my free hand underneath her, recovering a clear plastic bottle of white pills. The smell of her was nauseating. After three days, she stank worse than dead "roadkill" lying on the highway. I wondered why she kept the pills under her butt and if they were there so that she could easily hide them inside herself. I felt rage boil up inside me and the urge to lash out. Her fearful brown eyes opened wide, and her lips quivered in fright. She could see the anger on my face. Taking a deep breath, I brought my emotions under control.

The other officers searched other rooms in the house while I restrained the girl and confiscated the pills.

"I found the old man hiding in the hallway closet," I heard one of them yell.

I turned to the girl, "Put on your clothes," I ordered. "How old are you?"

"I'm over 18," she said, but I was sure she was lying.

"Where's your ID (identification)?" I asked.

"I don't have an ID," she replied.

Nothing about the girl looked like she was 18. 12, maybe 14 years at most, I thought. I was sure she was underage. The other officers agreed, but I didn't have time to prove she was a minor.

"Are you having sex with the old man?" I asked though I was already sure of the answer. "How much did he pay you?"

"He gave me pills," she admitted.

"Did you run away from home? Tell me the truth. I won't arrest you. Where's the old man getting his meth pills?" I asked.

"I swear to God, I don't know. I can't help you. Please don't arrest me."

"I'll let you go home if you promise not to do dope and have sex with anybody else," I promised. It was the drug-dealing pedophile I wanted to put away.

She started to sob. "I won't do it again. I promise. I swear to God."

I gently took her by her quivering hands and stared deep into her tearful eyes.

"If you start doing drugs and selling your body for sex, I'm going to put you in jail for a long time," I said very seriously. Do you understand me?" I hoped the words would scare her away from the dark path she had begun to traverse.

After work, I went to have a beer with the other narcotics officers. They laughed about how I had rushed into the house to chase after the crippled old man and restrained the screaming girl. "Blue," they nicknamed me.

"For he shall have judgment without mercy, that hath shewed no mercy; and mercy rejoiceth against judgment."

(James 2:13, King James Version)

Chapter 33

God Shall Judge the Righteous and the Wicked

I grabbed the .38 Special I had nicknamed Sweet-Pea, from the ankle holster and jumped out of the van.

"Stop! Don't move! Hands up now. If you move your hands down to your waist, I'll shoot both of you with one shot between your crazy eyes. Hands on the ground, not your knees. I want you on your bellies. Stretch your hands out like you're trying to swim in a bathtub. If you don't get down now, I'm going to shoot. Kiss the ground now!" I demanded.

A narcotics officer had asked me to assist him with a case.

"Hey, Blue," he said, referring to my new nickname. "Go with me to meet an informant. She's got some information on someone selling narcotics and heroin. After we see her, we can grab something to eat."

I grabbed my things, and we jumped in his old, white, undercover van. We drove to an alley where the meet was scheduled and parked the van. While waiting for the informant, the narcotics officer listened to his police scanner. Two people had just robbed a bank near where we were parked. We listened with interest as they described two suspects, a female, and a male, who were seen leaving the bank.

"Hey, the bank's right in front of us," said the officer. We looked up and saw the two suspects departing the bank. "Wow! Look Blue! Here come the two robbers walking from the bank. Get them Blue."

That's when I reached down and jerked my 5-shot .38 revolver, "Sweet-Pea," from my right ankle holster and jumped into action. The two crooks were not expecting me and practically tripped over themselves to comply with my commands.

After arresting the young girl and the boy, I searched for weapons. I didn't find any weapons or money, but I did find a bottle of pills.

"Where's the money from the bank?" I asked.

"What money?" they said in unison. "The bank lady wouldn't give us the money. She kept it."

"What are these pills I found in your pockets?" I asked.

"Vitamins," they insisted.

I later learned from the narcotics officer that the two bank robbers never actually stole any money. They had entered the bank and demanded the cash, but the teller had adamantly refused to hand it over.

It was a thrilling adventure. A DEA agent and his trusty revolver, "Sweet-Pea," foiling a bank robbery.

"I said in my heart, God shall judge the righteous and the wicked: for there is a time there for every purpose and for every work."
(Ecclesiastes 3:17, King James Version)

Chapter 34

For if Ye Live After the Flesh, Ye Shall Die

I was working in the office when the phone rang.

"I have some information about a nurse buying glassware for her boyfriend," said a woman's voice.

"What kind of glassware? Are they making meth?" I asked. I could hardly believe I was getting another tip about a nurse cooking meth.

"Can I meet you somewhere? She inquired. "I don't like talking on the telephone."

I told her that would be okay. She suggested a bar where we could meet around lunch the following day and briefly described what she looked like; long reddish hair, thin, with light skin.

I nearly declined the meeting. This seemed far too like the situation with the nurse whose uncle was a DEA agent. One thing was for sure: I would not make the same mistake being alone with a female suspect or informant. My boss would surely kill me if I ever made that mistake again. I would probably lose my job. Then my wife would kill me too.

The next day my partner and I drove to the meet. It was at a local bar where many of the patrons were off-duty cops. I saw an attractive woman that matched the description I had been given by the informant waiting outside. Her long red hair shined in the sunlight and reminded me of a red-tailed fox that was killing and eating Grandma's chickens.

I introduced myself and made sure this was the woman I was here to meet. "I'm the guy you called about a nurse cooking meth," I said once I felt confident this was the woman.

"Who's this guy with you?" she asked warily.

"It's my partner. I can't be alone meeting with a woman," I explained. "Let's sit outside and have a beer."

Explaining myself reminded me again of my stupid mistake in allowing myself to sit alone with the meth nurse. I learned my lesson and wouldn't make that mistake again. My partner and I would sit close together like a pair of lonesome doves while we talked to the attractive redhead about the nurse.

"So why do you think the nurse buys glassware to cook meth? Is she a friend of yours?" I asked.

"She used to be a friend of mine," explained the redhead with a hint of sadness.

"Why do you think your former friend is making meth?"

"She's buying the glassware for her two boyfriends to make meth," she corrected me.

"How do you know they're making meth with the glassware? You said the woman's a nurse. How do you know she's a nurse?"

"She's addicted to meth. She once told me that she didn't like working at the hospital."

"Do you know where she lives?" I asked.

"Yes. I have her address. I believe she might be living with the two boyfriends," the redhead explained.

The tip seemed promising, but I needed to verify what I had been told. A few days later, I drove to the address the redheaded informant had given me. When I arrived, I found an old single-story wooden house surrounded by wrecked cars and old leafless trees. It was in an area away from the city where the suspects could avoid prying eyes while cooking meth. I was becoming increasingly confident that the information I had received was good, but I needed more information.

I found an informant who had been a former meth user. He agreed to go to the old wooden house to see if it was a meth house.

"I want you to buy a gram of meth," I instructed him. If he could purchase the meth, I would have the confirmation I needed.

The next day, the informant called. "Hey Larry, I went to the house. At the house, a middle-aged woman told me to come back later. She said her boyfriend has some meth he can sell me."

"Did you see glassware and chemicals?"

"Yes!" He responded confidently.

"Okay. Great job. I'll call you back in a few days."

Based on the information I gathered, I got a federal warrant to search the old house for meth and laboratory glassware. I called the informant back and asked for assistance on the next phase of the operation.

"I want you to go back to the house," I said. "Ask them if they got any meth."

I didn't have to wait long. The informant called me back later that afternoon.

"I went inside the house and asked one of the guys for some meth," he explained. "I saw another guy sawing off the barrel of a double-gauge pump shotgun. The man also was carrying a black automatic handgun in his waist."

"Did you see anything else?" I asked.

"I heard a woman yelling in the bedroom for one of the guys to see her. Then I saw a filthy, starving, hairless dog lying beside some chemicals."

"You did see the chemicals?" I asked him to confirm. "Do you think they are making meth?"

The informant confirmed my suspicions, but I was concerned that two guys were in the house with weapons. I requested SWAT officers (Special Weapons and Tactics) to enter the house first and arrest the people inside. I reasoned that bringing in the SWAT team would help avoid a shootout between the suspects with DEA agents and narcotic officers. I also wanted to avoid hurting or killing the dog.

The operation went like clockwork. Four SWAT team members threw a flash grenade into the house to stun the nurse and the two men. The rest of the SWAT team quickly entered the house, capitalizing on the element of surprise they had gained from the flash grenade. I followed the SWAT team as soon as it was clear to do so.

I cautiously entered the house and found the nurse and two men lying with their bellies on the floor and their hands cuffed behind their backs. The two men were dirty looking and shirtless, and the nurse had the gaunt appearance of a meth addict. Her torn black dress had ridden up her back, she was not wearing any panties, and her nakedness was exposed. The SWAT team had not wasted any time restraining the suspects. I gestured for a female cop to come over and assist.

"Can you pull her dress down over her waist and cover her up," I asked.

The female officer happily complied, and I knelt and turned to look at the nurse once she was covered up.

"I heard you're a nurse," I said.

"Who said that?" She demanded.

"So, you are a nurse. Do you work in a hospital?"

"I'm not working in the hospital. But I was a nurse," she admitted.

"Lady, who are your boyfriends?" I asked, pointing to the two males.

"Both of them live here with me," she replied with a hint of venom in her voice. She looked over at the two filthy toothless guys lying on the floor. I got up and stepped back to address all three suspects.

"I found some meth, chemicals, laboratory glassware, and guns in the house," I said, pausing to let the ramifications of that statement sink in. "Okay, who wants to talk first?"

The woman glared at me from her sore-covered face and practically snarled at me with her yellow-stained teeth. No, she wasn't going to talk, I thought to myself.

She smelled bad, like a dead skunk, and I wasn't sure which one smelled worse between her and the dog. The meth had driven her insane, causing her to abandon personal hygiene and modesty to the wind. She did not seem to have any problem walking around the house with no panties on, although it was occupied by two men. That nasty woman would probably kill them all in a fit of rage. The most likely person in this group to talk to would be the toothless dog, and that wasn't going to happen.

I waited for someone to break and squeal like a dirty sewer rat. Whoever squealed first would get the best deal and spend the least time in jail. All three suspects remained defiantly silent. Why wasn't the nurse talking, I wondered. I explained to the nasty nurse and the two homeless-looking men they were going to jail.

I had been in the DEA job for two years. During that time

I had arrested two nurses for manufacturing meth. Why were they cooking meth? Why were they using the nasty stuff? The nurses were working with patients at hospitals. Why couldn't they drink beer or wine after work to unwind or get whatever "high" they wanted?

About a week after the arrest, I received a call from an Assistant United States Attorney (AUSA).

"Larry, you have a problem with the nurse you arrested for manufacturing meth. Her lawyer is claiming that someone from the SWAT team bruised her breast. Then someone gripped her vagina and squeezed it."

It frustrated me to hear that this woman was saying a SWAT team member had copped a feel. The way she looked and smelled, I couldn't even imagine who would want to touch her. I wasn't the one who had searched her for dope and weapons, so I was 100% sure it wasn't me.

"Not again. Are you joking?" I asked. "That nurse is a danger to law enforcement and the public. She will eventfully kill someone. The SWAT team guys did their job searching the nurse's body for any weapons and dope. How do we know she's telling the truth?"

"We will find out next week with the judge. The judge wants to know what happened when the search warrant was executed at the nurse's house. The judge wants to learn how the woman's body was searched. Who grabbed her vagina then bruised her breast?" said the AUSA.

I couldn't believe this was happening again. Did she have the same female public defender as the meth nurse that accused me of trying to rape her in my car?

Several days later, we appeared before the judge in federal court.

"Special Agent Hardin did you search the defendant's body for illegal drugs and weapons?" asked the female judge.

"No, your honor. But, your honor, I would search below the waist if I had to search a dangerous suspect, woman, or man."

"Would you have gripped a women's breast? Would you then squeeze her virginal?" the judge asked curtly.

I noticed the public defender sitting at a wooden table beside a woman who looked like the nasty meth nurse. It was hard to believe that the same woman smelled like a dead skunk at the meth house. She looked different after cleaning herself up. Her face was clean and free of dirt, she had dressed up very nicely, and her teeth appeared much whiter. I could hardly believe that it was the same person.

"Special Agent Hardin," said the judge, interrupting my musings. "The defendant here in court cannot identify the SWAT member who bruised her breast and squeezed her vagina because of the mask and the eye protector."

"Your honor, the SWAT team wear masks and protective eye equipment to hide their faces and eyes from dangerous objects thrown at them by the bad guys," I explained. "I'm sorry, your honor. I cannot identify the person from the SWAT team that searched the nurse."

I would not insult the professional and hardworking members of the SWAT team. There was no way I would ask the SWAT team who had searched the nasty nurse for weapons. These guys were doing their job, and that's all there was to it. They had done what they had to do to protect themselves and ensure the suspects were not armed.

The AUSA called me after the hearing. He sounded disappointed, and I got the feeling he wasn't calling with good news.

"I must drop the drug charges on the nurse for manufacturing meth and possessing weapons. The nurse's attorney will accept probation for five years for meth possession. The nurse's two boyfriends will plea to manufacturing meth and possessing weapons."

"So, the nurse isn't charged with manufacturing meth because of the sexual remarks she made against the SWAT team? It's the nurse's home. There's chemicals, glassware, meth, and weapons inside the house," I said.

"That's correct, Larry. We will not find a jury to convict the nurse after they hear that a police officer molested her, twisting her breast and squeezing her vagina. The case is closed."

It frustrated me that, yet another criminal had avoided being charged by making baseless allegations. It wouldn't always be women, either. Of this, I was sure.

One day a dangerous man would employ the same tactics, saying a cop had squeezed his penis and testicles, claiming it was sexual assault. When that happened, who knows what crimes he would go on to commit or whom he might hurt or kill while walking free.

"For if ye live after the flesh, ye shall die but if ye through the Spirit do mortify the deeds of the body, ye shall live."

(Romans 8:13, King James Version)

Chapter 35

Blessed are They Which do Hunger

A Sig Sauer 9 mm automatic was hidden inside my pants on the right side of my waistband. I learned this trick by watching members of street gangs stick their guns inside their waistbands.

While working on the streets, I decided to try it for myself. I slowly pushed the Sig Sauer into the right inside of my waistband. Keeping the 9 mm close to my right hand and under my belt felt great. Since I wasn't wearing any underwear, I could feel the Sig Sauer lying against my bare skin.

Another day a narcotics officer and I were waiting for an informant to give us information about heroin and pill traffickers. I decided to put the Sig Sauer 9 mm behind my back while I sat patiently waiting in the driver's seat. Suddenly we heard someone yelling loudly from the parking lot.

"Hey, stop! Stop! Help me," the voice yelled.

I saw a fat little white man with dark pants, a short white-sleeved shirt, and a small black tie hanging just above his bulging belly. He saw us sitting in the car and ran towards us, huffing and puffing from the exertion of the short run.

"Stop him," he pleaded.

I had no idea who he was talking about. "Stop who?" I asked. Between the parked cars, I saw a short, thin-looking Hispanic man jump out directly in front of our car.

"She's here," said my partner.

"Who's here?" I asked, trying to make sense of the confusion.

"The informant."

Meanwhile, the fat little man continued yelling. "Help. Help."

The little Hispanic guy was running past the undercover car. I looked from my partner to the fat little man yelling outside our window and the other guy running away from our car.

"Get him Blue," shouted my partner.

I grabbed the door handle and hesitated. The informant was approaching the car, and I didn't want to leave the officer alone with her. I could also see that the man who was fleeing was quickly gaining distance.

On instinct, I leaped out of the undercover car like a bird on its wings and flew after the suspect. I could see he was holding something tightly in his right hand as I chased him. The guy was running like a Bluetick Coonhound dog, scared to death of getting a whipping from an angry old farmer. I ran as fast as possible and closed in on him, trying to grab him by the back of the hair.

I was concerned about what he might be holding in his hand. It could easily be a small gun or maybe a knife. I wondered what he had done. *Did he hurt someone in the parking lot? Did he rape a woman?* Regardless, if he didn't stop, I would run him down like Grandpa's coonhound dog, old Blue.

"Stop! Stop! I'll shoot you in the back. I'll shoot you in your head if you don't stop running. I will kill you for sure," I threatened the fleeing man.

I followed the suspect out of the parking lot and into a wood-lined park like a jackrabbit on two feet. He was almost close enough to grab him by the back of his hair for a second time. I reached down to jerk the beautiful Sig Sauer from my back waistband. It wasn't there, and I felt a sense of panic as I realized that I was pursuing a potentially armed suspect without my weapon. I slowed down as my mind raced in a thousand directions but did not break the pursuit. *Had I left the gun on the car seat? Did I drop it when I jumped out of the driver's seat? Was it lying on the ground? Hopefully, the officer would find it before the informant if that happened. He will take care of it,* I hoped. *But how could I stop this guy if he had a gun?*

Suddenly I saw the narcotics officer running between the trees with his gun in his right hand. He darted out from the trees on one side of the fleeing suspect and toppled the little man to the ground. Within seconds he was on the guy's back, forcing him into the dirt. The suspect flailed about wildly, attempting to throw the officer off his back.

"Don't move," commanded the officer. "I will hurt you if you don't stop fighting."

Exhausted from running, I dropped down on top of the struggling suspect alongside the other officer. He continued to resist. I hit the guy on the head with my fists to subdue him.

"Blue," cried the other officer. "You're hitting me on the head. Stop hitting me. Blue, you are hurting me."

Finally, the narcotics officer handcuffed the little brown guy. He handed me the Sig Sauer I left behind on the car seat as we caught our breath. I picked up a little brown bag from the guy's hand that had fallen into the dirt. I wondered if it contained money he had taken from the fat man in the parking lot.

We walked the suspect back to the undercover car in handcuffs.

"Tengo hombre," he shouted in Spanish.

"What's he saying?" I asked the narcotic officer.

"I don't know, Blue; I don't speak Spanish."

The fat little man waited for us in the undercover car when we returned. I didn't see the informant and wondered what had happened to her.

"What did this Mexican guy do?" I asked. "Here's the brown bag the guy had in his hand."

"That Mexican stole a bag of shrimp from the grocery store," replied the fat little man indignantly.

"What!" I exclaimed in disbelief. "Are you telling me that skinny little guy almost got shot for stealing a bag of shrimp?"

I looked at the other officer, disgusted by what had just happened. "This poor guy has blood on his head. We just beat the 'snot' out of this little guy over a bag of shrimp," I said, pointing to the hungry Hispanic man in handcuffs.

"Why did he steal the shrimp from you? Do you understand Spanish?" I asked, still in disbelief.

"Yes, a little. The Mexican guy said he was hungry. He has no money to pay for it." Disbelief turned to anger at that admission.

"What! I'm not arresting that guy over a bag of shrimp," I yelled. "I'm letting the little guy go." I looked the fat man in his eyes, glaring angrily. "Here, take your bag of shrimp," I said, tossing it roughly back at him.

When I arrived home, my wife noticed blood on my pants legs. "What happened to you? You have some blood on your pant legs. Did you get hurt?" She asked with concern.

"What blood?" I replied, looking down to where she was pointing at my pant leg.

I couldn't bring myself to tell her what really happened. "Hey, Honey. I got into a fight today with a tattooed gang killer from Mexico. The narcotics officer I was with almost shot the killer in the head. We beat him up bad for resisting arrest. The killer kept yelling, "I'm going to kill you, punks. He's lucky to be alive," I lied.

A little white lie is not going to hurt anyone, I thought. I couldn't tell her a little Hispanic guy almost got shot because he was hungry and had stolen a bag of shrimp. I felt ashamed, and I knew she would ask me why I didn't buy the little guy something to eat. I would think of it if I knew that he was hungry.

"Blessed are they which do hunger and thirst after righteousness: for they shall be filled."

(Matthew5:6, King James Version)

Chapter 36

But Every Man is Tempted When He is Drawn Away of His own Lust

I received a phone call from a Border Patrol agent who sounded very agitated. We had worked with the agent on a checkpoint case a few days earlier.

"We arrested that Mexican drug trafficker with meth," he said, recapping the events from the arrest. "We seized a lot of cash hidden inside the Mexican's car. I counted $75,000 in front of the narcotic officer with you. You took the doper into custody, and your partner took the money. I read his report, and according to his report, he only took custody of half of that amount from me. That's not true. My report shows how much money we seized." The border patrol agent made a serious claim against the narcotics officer for doing something wrong.

"Wait. Stop now," I said. "You need to talk to the narcotic officer about the money. It's probably a mistake. But listen to me. It's not my problem. This is between you and the officer. You and the officer counted the money. Do you understand? I took the bad guy to jail." I knew that I had done my job honestly. There was no way for me to know with certainty what happened after I left with the suspect, and I did not want to become involved in making unfounded accusations against the officer.

Later that year, on Thanksgiving Day, the same narcotic officer involved in the Border Patrol incident called me to assist him on another case.

"Blue, I need your help. A DEA fugitive wanted for narcotics trafficking violations is picking up some money at a "stash" house. I have an informant watching where the fugitive is."

The officer wanted me to come with him to arrest the DEA fugitive. I went with the officer to where the fugitive was supposed to pick up the "dope" money. We spotted the fugitive in his car, where the informant said he would be. The officer contacted the local police department to help stop the fugitive's car for a traffic violation.

Within minutes a marked police unit from the police department arrived and stopped the fugitive's car. The fugitive got out of his car per the police officer's instructions. When I approached him with my handgun pointed at his chest, the fugitive seemed shocked.

"Don't move. If you try to run, I will shoot you in the back. You are under arrest," I shouted.

The fugitive complied unquestioningly, and we quickly moved to put him in handcuffs.

"Do you have any guns or money inside the car?" I asked.

"I don't have any guns, but I have money in the trunk," he stated.

The narcotics officer searched inside the car for weapons, drugs, and cash. He rapidly went through the interior of the car and popped the trunk.

"Wow!" he exclaimed as he threw it open. "Blue, look at all that money."

I was surprised to see how much money the fugitive had in the trunk.

"Why do you have such a big pile of money dumped in your trunk?" I asked. "How much money do you have in there."

"About $245,000," he replied.

"You take the fugitive back to the police department. I'll take the fugitive's car back and count the money," the narcotics officer hastened to say.

The next day I picked up the local newspaper and quickly scanned it to see if there was anything about the arrest and seizure. I quickly found the article I was looking for and started to read. Suddenly I stopped reading as I came to a line that shocked and angered me.

"The fugitive's car was seized with $37,000 in it," said the article.

That isn't the amount the fugitive said he had in his trunk, I thought. I remembered the earlier incident when the Border Patrol agent had made similar accusations against that same narcotics officer. This did not seem like a coincidence.

I wrestled with telling my supervisor or someone else in the chain of command what had happened. While working with narcotics officers, I learned quickly never to question another officer's integrity. Saying anything to your supervisor about another officer's integrity could backfire very soon.

It certainly wasn't the norm for narcotics officers to handle money without counting it in front of other witnesses (usually other officers or DEA agents). Most of them were very careful and ethical when handling money. Unfortunately, there were exceptions, and not all of them could be trusted.

It was hard to ignore that some narcotics officers might be stealing from the dopers. It shook my fundamental belief that those who worked in law enforcement were good when I discovered that some might be the bad guys.

I heard other agents and informants about corrupt cops from time to time. There were always stories about drugs and money that were confiscated and had gone missing or never been reported. I never got involved with the hearsay about corrupt cops. If I thought another agent or narcotics officer was corrupt, I avoided them. I refused to work with them.

"But every man is tempted, when he is drawn away of his own lust, and enticed. Then when lust hath conceived, it bringeth forth sin and sin, when it is finished, bringeth forth death."

(James 1:14-15, King James Version).

Chapter 37

For He that Soweth to His Flesh Shall of the Flesh Reap Corruption

I sat in the driver's seat, talking with one of the women. The officer was in the backseat with another woman, trying to convince her to have sex with him. As much as I wanted to tune it out, I couldn't avoid hearing what was happening back there.

The narcotics officer rode with me to the county courthouse earlier that day. While there, he started flirting with two young married law clerks. Without consulting me, he invited them to join us for lunch. There wasn't any work-related reason for him to do that, and I was frustrated that he was asking these married women to have lunch with us?

As we drove back to drop them off at the courthouse after lunch, I kept quiet despite my growing anger and said nothing.

"How can you crawl like a venomous snake in the backseat with a married woman, trying to have sex?" I snapped at last once we were alone.

"Blue," he said, laughing as though my anger were a joke. "Why didn't you try to get some from her?"

"I'm married. The woman's married. I know your family. You have a beautiful wife and two little boys," I said.

He shrugged it off with a laugh, and we got back into the car. I was disappointed with the officer's behavior. A few narcotics officers take advantage of their position to hook up with women. I refused to participate in any sexual misadventures. The women on the streets, in the courthouses, female sources, female informants, female defendants, or the women lawyers I worked with were all off-limits as far as I was concerned.

A few agents and officers got drunk after work to blow off steam. I did too. One night I stopped by the cop bar after a long day working on the streets. I drank several beers and ate chili-cheese dogs with some other officers. Looking at my watch, I noticed it was getting late and decided to go home.

I had too much to drink and shouldn't have been driving. Making my way onto the interstate highway, I almost hit a car with children inside. It was a foolish decision, and I considered myself lucky I didn't hurt or kill anyone. I thanked God that I didn't hurt anyone and made it home safely. That was the last time I ever drove drunk.

I remembered another occasion I was drinking with other agents and officers in a bar after work. A well-dressed young woman sat beside me, and we started talking.

"What kind of work do you do?" I asked.

"I'm a schoolteacher," she replied.

One of the narcotics officers whispered something in the woman's ear. I figured he must know her. She leaned back and started to pull up her dress. She had no panties on and exposed her vagina for anyone to see.

"Is she crazy?" I shouted as I leaped out of the chair. "She is showing me her hairless thing."

The other narcotics officer suddenly burst out in laughter as I stood there in shock.

"No, she's not a teacher. She's a prostitute," he exclaimed like a stand-up comedian delivering a punchline. I quickly moved away from her as the other officers joined in the laughter.

I believe that once an agent or an officer got involved with sex, drugs, or dirty money, they crossed over to the "dark battle" of corruption. Self-control and praying are the only way around it. Sex and dirty money were always available to any agent or officer who wanted to exploit it.

We all have faults, and I saw a lot of crazy stuff working in narcotics. It was up to me to say "No." I was never tempted to have sex with other women or to take a bad guy's money. I did my best to stay away from any kind of corruption.

A few months after the incident with the "schoolteacher," I was at the firearm range. One of the narcotics officers approached me.

"Hey," he said. "That officer who introduced you to the "schoolteacher," shot himself in the but accidentally a few years ago while he was on the range."

"How can someone shoot himself in the butt?" I asked with a laugh. "Especially, his big wide butt."

The officer in question was standing on the firing line, and he quickly started to pull his weapon from its holster.

"Hey, Blue, don't stand next to him. He might shoot you in the butt!" someone shouted.

I looked at the officer standing next to me. "Are you going to accidentally put a bullet in my butt," I asked.

After shooting at the firearm range with other officers and agents, I returned to the office. The officer who had accidentally shot himself in the butt was cleaning his handgun at his desk. A firecracker was in my desk, and my mind raced through the possibilities. This guy had put the "schoolteacher" up to flashing me at the bar. Why not? The incident and my reaction were still the subject of office jokes, although months had passed since it happened. This was my opportunity for payback.

I lit the fuse on the firecracker, then quickly threw it under the officer's chair. The firecracker exploded with a sound like gunfire. The noise echoed throughout the building. Secretaries screamed, and agents and officers jumped with weapons in hand from their seats. Everyone was looking to see where the shot came from. The officer didn't move. His wide butt was frozen to his chair. Everyone was looking at him.

He sat there holding the barrel of his gun in his hands, looking confused. Slowly, he looked up from his desk and stared at the gun barrel again.

"Hardin threw a firecracker under your desk," someone yelled at last.

After two years in the narcotics unit, I volunteered to be transferred to the DEA office on the Southwest border in Arizona.

"For he that soweth to his flesh shall of the flesh reap corruption."
(Galatians 6:8, King James Version)

Chapter 38

Honor Thy Father and Thy Mother

Before Momma could say anything else, I jumped up, pointed my finger at her, and yelled, "Don't move, or I'll blow your f------- head off." Momma seemed startled by the display, and I continued the explanation in a more conversational tone.

"Momma, that's how I stop the bad guys from hurting me. It's not like what you see on TV," I said with a wag of my hands.

I transferred from the San Diego office and decided to go home and see my family in Kentucky. With one chapter of my career ending and another just beginning, it was an excellent time to reconnect with family. Soon I would continue my work as a special agent in Arizona along the Southwest border.

During my first few days back home, I spent most of my time fishing with Daddy and working in his vegetable garden. I decided to spend some quality time with Momma. It was late in the evening, and Momma would be in bed before the sun disappeared behind the water maple trees. I was sitting on the couch with Momma. Daddy was lying back on his worn-out recliner, chewing his last piece of bacco (tobacco) for the day. Daddy hadn't taken off his "sugar shoes" yet, but he would follow Momma to bed when he did.

I was listening to Momma talking about some of her aunts, uncles, and cousins dying from kidney and heart disease. She mused quietly for a few moments and looked up at me.

"Lawrence Raymond, life is going by us all so quickly. Your job is so dangerous. How do you stop someone from hurting you?"

That's when I got up, pointed my finger at Momma just like I would point my gun at a criminal, and showed her how I protected myself.

Momma stared at me like she had seen a headless ghost. "Oh my God," she said.

I glanced over at Daddy. He sat there stoically, not saying a thing, but he was no longer chewing his bacco. I wondered if he had swallowed the bacco with all its juice.

"Lawrence Raymond, you scare me. I'm going to bed, said Momma.

I got up to hug Momma and realized my demonstration was too much for her.

"I'm sorry for scaring you," I spoke. "Momma, it's violent and filthy working on the streets. The streets are very dangerous. You can't be gentle and kind to the bad guys. The bad guys will hurt and kill you if they can. It's street trash talk."

"I'm going to bed," was Momma's only response. My explanation had done nothing to comfort her. She walked towards the bedroom with her head looking down at the floor. Suddenly, she stopped, turned around, and looked at me.

"We are so worried about you. Why that job, Lawrence Raymond?"

I could not give her an answer as to why I had chosen to work narcotics. Only God knows, I thought.

"I love you, Momma. I'm sorry I scared you and Daddy."

Daddy was taking his shoes off, then slowly removed his socks. Before getting up to follow Momma to the bedroom, he turned to look at me.

"I'm going to bed," he said. "I love you. I'll see you in the morning."

Later that night, I entered their bedroom and sat beside the big window in Momma's rocking chair. I was glad to see her. *How often had Momma sat in her chair looking out the window while praying for her family?* I looked at Momma and Daddy sleeping peacefully.

"God," I whispered. "I have to leave soon to go back to the streets. God, please take care of them."

I slowly got up from the chair and looked reverently at Momma and Daddy. I leaned over and kissed them on their foreheads just like I did every night when I was home.

"Honor thy father and thy mother: that thy days may be long upon the land which the LORD thy God giveth the."
(Exodus 20:12, King James Version)

Chapter 39

Enjoy the Good of all His Labor

I walked into the office and quickly realized I didn't want to work there. The office was less than 10 miles from Mexico, and the major cartels had a significant presence along the border. The bad guys and corrupt cops could hurt me quickly, and the Mexican Cartels had a violent reputation. It didn't help that the security outside and inside the office was horrible. 4 000 pounds of confiscated marijuana sat in a side office, all but forgotten. I had barely arrived, and I was ready to leave.

Earlier that morning, I reported to the DEA Yuma office in Arizona. The office was certainly different from what I had expected when I had taken the transfer to Yuma. Two agents and one secretary were squeezed into a room the size of an empty sardine can. The temperature outside was over 117 degrees, and moving around in the heat was miserable. The inside of the office wasn't much better, and I quickly realized that I had made a big fat mistake.

"Hello! Are you the new guy?" the secretary cheerfully asked. I started to respond, but she cut me off. "The boss isn't here. Go ahead, take the desk in the corner of the office."

I went to the corner the secretary had indicated and set my things down on a bent-up grey metal desk with two missing drawers. The armchair was broken, and I wondered whose nasty butt had been sitting on it. I thought the secretary must have found the desk and chair in a dumpster. Curiously I noticed that the younger agents had newer office furniture. I didn't want to be here.

Wiping the sweat from my brow, I tried to get myself situated. My efforts were hindered by the overwhelming smell of confiscated dope that permeated the office.

"Wow!" I exclaimed. Why's it smells so bad in the office? I can't breathe. Are you having problems breathing?"

"Well, we're used to the marijuana storage here in the office, especially when it smells sweet. Maybe you can take it out of the office this week?" suggested the secretary.

"How much marijuana is it in the other room?" I asked, fearing what the answer would be.

"About 4,000 pounds," she replied.

I had been in the office for about a week when the secretary asked me to get rid of the source of the nauseating smell.

"Larry, you need to get the marijuana out of the office. You need to get rid of it today."

I asked one of the younger agents where we were supposed to destroy the marijuana.

"I don't know. I think you can get rid of it in the desert," he responded with a noticeable lack of certainty.

"Okay. Tomorrow morning, let's load the 4,000 pounds in my undercover SUV and your car. I will find somewhere to burn it out in the desert," I decided.

We met at the office early the next morning and loaded the 4,000 pounds of marijuana in the vehicles.

"Follow me to the gas station," I instructed the other agent. I need some gasoline to help burn the marijuana."

We filled up two red plastic five gallons containers with gasoline, and I realized we would need matches to light them.

"Can you go get matches from the gas station clerk? While you're inside, buy a 12-pack of cold beer to drink and a large bag of tortilla chips. We'll shoot the empty bottles while the weed's burning," I suggested. "Maybe we'll get high off the smoke," I joked as he walked over to the small gas station convenience store.

The agent quickly returned with the beer and tortilla chips.

"Did you get the matches?" I asked, and he assured me that he had. "Then let's go before the beer gets hot."

I found a place in the desert near the Arizona State Prison, about one mile North of the Mexican border. It took the other agent and me all morning to open the marijuana packages. We dumped them into a large pile on the desert sand, and I poured the gasoline over the pile.

"Okay Brother, I'll put the gasoline on the weed. You can light it up. While it's burning, we can inhale some of that sweet smoke," I joked. "I'm getting thirsty for a cold one.

"What will we do with the empty bottles?" he asked.

"Brother, don't worry. We can target practice with the empty beer bottles," I replied as I reached for a cold beer.

"Okay. Light it up, Brother. Let's see it burn," I said after emptying 10 gallons of gasoline all over the 4,000 pounds of weed.

He fumbled through his pockets while I waited, realizing he did not have the matches.

"Oops! I can't find the matches in my pocket. I lost the matches at the gas station," he admitted with embarrassment.

"Don't worry, let's do it like the actors in the movies. You know, when the actor shoots into a car gas tank, it blows up, "right?" The other agent nodded in agreement.

"Okay, let's see who's the fastest to draw their guns and shoot into the pile of weed?"

We quickly drew our handguns and opened fire at the gas-soaked pile of weed. We fired and continued to fire until we had emptied our magazines of bullets, but the expected flames failed to materialize. We stared at the pile in disappointment.

"What will we do with all that weed?" asked the agent.

Who else could it be out in the hot heated temperature of the desert firing their guns into a pile of weed? While I pondered that question, two Border Patrol officers drove up to see who was shooting.

They looked at the gas-soaked weed pile and us and quickly surmised that we were DEA agents.

"Do you guys want a cold one?" I asked. "We have some tortilla chips but no hot salsa. Oh! Do you guys have matches?" They didn't, and we were left to find a solution to our problem.

I drank another beer as I tried to come up with a solution. Suddenly a thought occurred to me, and I grinned like a possum at the agent like a possum eating a dead cow. I walked over to my SUV, reached into the backseat, and pulled out an emergency road flare. It worked like a charm.

"Let's have another cold one," I suggested. "I'm ready for target shooting. Line the bottles up in a row. I'm first to shoot."

The 4,000 pounds of Mexican weed had a sweet smell while it burned, which I found enjoyable. We drank the last of our beers and finished eating the tortilla chips. I wondered if the

Border Patrol officers were enjoying the sweet smell of the weed like I was. I considered the prisoners in the nearby prison and laughed while I wondered if they were enjoying the sweet smell blowing toward them.

We lined up the empty beer bottles while the pile continued to burn and reloaded the magazines of our weapons. One by one, the glass bottles exploded as we shot at them under the hot desert sun. The 4,000-pound pile of weed slowly finished burning to ash, and we started to pack up to leave. The other agent offered to show me the DEA "safe house" near the Mexican border before we returned to the office.

The safe house was typically used as an undercover location for the agents and narcotic officers to conduct all-night surveillance operations. Its location was ideal for watching major dope smuggling operations crossing into Arizona from Mexico. Only some of its functions were official, though. It was also a place to eat, sleep, and play poker.

"Behold that which I have seen: it is good and comely for one to eat and to drink, and to enjoy the good of all his labor that he taketh under the sun all the days of his life, which God giveth him: for it is his portion."

(Ecclesiastes 5:18, King James Version)

Chapter 40

God Shall Judge the Righteous and the Wicked

"Are there any case files I can read about how those two agents were almost killed in Mexico?" I asked the secretary.

"Go into the file room. On the bottom of the file cabinet, there's a case file on Mexican Cartel brothers trying to kill two agents several years ago," she replied.

A few days after burning the sweet-smelling weed, I played poker with a DEA agent and three local law enforcement narcotics officers at a safe house. They were waiting to hear from an informant in Mexico and were taking some downtime while they waited. One of the narcotics officers was in the kitchen making spicy Mexican jalapeno chili. The other two officers were lying around on the couches and floor like old flea-infested coonhound dogs.

The informant had information about a vehicle entering from the Mexican border tonight loaded with cocaine from two brothers who belonged to a major cartel family. According to the informant, the car would travel to an unknown residence near the border after it crossed.

We had just finished a hand of poker when the other DEA agent turned to look at me.

"Larry, you are new here. I'm going to explain who the Cartel family brothers are. The family's connected with corrupt Customs officers and Immigration inspectors at the Port-of-Entry (POE)," he explained.

The agent continued to explain that no drugs came across the POE into the U.S. from Mexico without the Cartel family's approval. Three brothers ruthlessly controlled the family's dope business. They had even gone so far as to try and kill two DEA agents in Mexico several years prior.

I was fascinated by what the agent had told me and continued to ask questions while we played poker. The narcotics officer finally got the phone call from the informant he had been waiting for. The trafficker was moving the dope to a residence. The three officers abruptly quit playing and took off to investigate. I kept playing poker with the agent for a while longer. I wanted to stick around and hear more stories about how the cartel brothers tried to kill the DEA agents.

I went into the office the next day and started asking the other agents and secretary a lot of questions about the Cartel family, especially the brothers. It occurred to me that I could learn a lot of additional information from the case file that the secretary kindly directed me to.

I reviewed the material with a growing fascination for several hours. The case file read like a script for a Hollywood movie. Ultimately two agents had been kidnapped, shot, and left for dead on the streets of Sonora, Mexico.

According to the file, corrupt Mexican police had informed the cartel brothers that two DEA agents were working in their territory. The agents were buying black tar heroin from their mules and gathering damaging information about the cartel's activities. The brothers wanted to stop this and devised a plan to kidnap and kill the two agents.

The brothers hired assassins that wasted no time kidnapping the agents. The assassins caught the agents unaware and forced them suddenly and unexpectedly to the ground. They proceeded to kick the agents brutally and repeatedly in the ribs, leaving them injured and stunned.

The assassins quickly jerked the agents off the street and threw them into the back of the agent's pickup truck. In the chaos of the sudden assault, the assassins had failed to thoroughly search one of the agents for weapons. The agent's Smith & Wesson snub nose revolver had avoided detection when it slipped out of his waistband and into his crotch.

The pickup lurched forward, speeding outside the desert town toward the open desert. A bus suddenly stopped in front of the pickup, forcing the driver to hit the brakes and stop behind it. The injured agents saw their chance and jumped out from the pickup truck. Another group of assassins escorting the pickup truck spotted the fleeing agents and started shooting at them. The agents sustained additional injuries from gunshot wounds as they fled through the hail of bullets. Despite their agonizing wounds, they continued to run. They knew that failure to escape would lead to torture and death.

The assassins continued shooting until they ran out of bullets. Defenseless and having brought too much attention to themselves, they jumped into their car and disappeared. The agents survived the brutal attack by the assassins, but they suffered from severe pain for many years.

An informant later reported, "The Cartel brothers were unhappy the agents lived. The brothers wanted to kill them."

As I went through the files, I was surprised that there were so many narcotics cases related to the cartel family and the brothers. A son of one of the brothers was selected and endorsed by an Arizona congressman to attend the Air Force Academy in Colorado Springs, Colorado. Before the son ever went to the academy, he was arrested and released the same day by Immigration inspectors at the POE for smuggling marijuana into Arizona. The son never attended the academy.

According to sources and informants, the Cartel brothers were well connected to an Arizona congressman. The congressman was a Mexican American who supported strong agricultural ties with Mexico. The congressman was supposedly familiar with the brothers' "agriculture business" in Mexico.

Some of the information in the case files was heartbreaking. I read about a trafficker that had to give up his daughter to the Cartel brothers in exchange for missing cocaine. The trafficker's daughter was only 12 years old. She was used by the brothers for sexual pleasure. An informant asked DEA to help the little girl escape from the brothers. The agents working with the informant requested assistance from the

Assistant U.S. Attorney's (AUSA) office. They never got the help they needed and could not bring the girl to the U.S.

"I said in my heart, God shall judge the righteous and the wicked: for there is a time there for every purpose and for every work."
(Ecclesiastes 3:17, King James Version)

Chapter 41

He that Committeth Fornication Sinneth Against his Body

I arrived at the office, tired and bleary-eyed from a late-night poker session at the safe house. The secretary approached me as I entered the office, and I could see that something was bothering her.

"One of the agents was standing too close to the student aide in the file room," she said. "I think he was rubbing her breasts."

There wasn't any room for that kind of behavior in the office, and I wanted to make sure the other agents understood that.

"Be careful what you do in the office with that new student aide," I told them. They just laughed, and I could tell they weren't taking my concerns seriously.

The secretary approached me again a few days later.

"I believe the girl might be having sex with him," she informed me with growing concern.

"I'll take care of it," I assured her.

The secretary looked at me very seriously. "If you don't tell him to stop, that girl will lose her job."

I was getting ready to leave for the night and wanted to think about what I would say. The agent was still in the office, and I wasn't ready to talk to him about the incident.

"Lock up the office and turn on the security alarm when you leave," I said.

Walking out the front door, I suddenly realized that I had forgotten some paperwork I needed. I decided to enter through the back door of the file room, and no one noticed as I walked back into the office. To my annoyance, I saw that the agent was sexually flirting with the student aide.

"Knock that off!" I shouted emphatically.

The girl blushed with embarrassment as she looked suddenly up at me, turning her eyes away. I walked past the agents and the aide, over to my desk, and picked up the papers I needed without saying another word. I turned and got ready to walk out, then paused, knowing I needed to say something more.

"This type of activity upsets me," I told them, "Don't do that in the office anymore!"

Shortly after that incident, the student aide quit working for DEA. There was nothing new about agents having sex with co-workers, attorneys, law clerks, informants, married women, church-going women, or prostitutes. For some agents and narcotics officers, acting like that was just part of the workplace culture. I could never understand how some agents and officers professed to love their wives and children, but they would have sex with any woman who dropped her panties.

"Flee fornication. Every sin that a man doeth is without the body; but he that committeth fornication sinneth against his body."

(1 Corinthians 6:18, King James Version)

Chapter 42

For He that Soweth to His Flesh: Shall of the Flesh Reap Corruption

As I crossed into Mexico, I could see the corrupt cops standing below a large sign warning that it was illegal to carry weapons and ammunition into Mexico. I was crossing into Mexico with my shotgun and automatic machine gun in the car trunk, a 38 Smith and Wesson 5 shot in an ankle hostler, and a 40 Cal Sig Sauer in my waistband. And, of course, my pocketknife. The term "Mexican Showdown" came to mind as I chuckled at the sign.

The Mexican officers at the border and many Cartel traffickers knew I was a gringo DEA agent. The bad guys had no problem coming into the U.S. with weapons. My day had been spent chasing them through the searing desert heat of Arizona and back across the Mexico border. I was exhausted.

I remembered the first time I had crossed the border entry and looked up to see the sign. Two Mexican customs officers were standing next to it, looking bored and disinterested, just like they do now. Traveling into Mexico was not a problem for DEA agents, and the Mexican customs officers never gave us any problems. When returning to the U.S. from Mexico, I was always stopped by the United States Customs officers and the Immigration inspectors at the POE. Some of them knew us, and the ones who didn't ask the typical questions.

"Who are you? What is your purpose in Mexico?"

"I'm DEA. I went to Mexico to eat grilled chicken and drink a couple of beers," I casually replied.

Several months later, one of the Spanish-speaking agents in the DEA office asked me to accompany him across the border.

"Larry, do you want to go with me across the border into Mexico to visit a prosecutor?"

"What's going on in Mexico?" I asked.

"I received a call from the Mexican prosecutor. He wants to talk about the Cartel brothers trying to kill the agents several years ago. He was the lawyer that initiated federal arrest warrants against the brothers for what they did to the agents."

My experience reading the case files about that incident several months prior had stuck with me. I remembered how the agents had been tortured and left half dead on the desert road to die in Mexico.

"Absolutely," I said with enthusiasm. "I'll go with you to see this prosecutor."

I wondered why he wanted to talk after so many years. What new information did the Mexican prosecutor have about the cartel brothers trying to murder the agents he wanted to share with DEA?

That evening, I went with the agent to see the Mexican Prosecutor at his office in Mexico. I asked the prosecutor about the Cartel family, the brothers, and their drug smuggling organization.

"There are criminal investigation reports on the cartel family and the brothers from DEA and other law enforcement agencies in the United States," he nervously said in broken English.

The prosecutor pointed to some opened brown boxes behind the file cabinet in the corner of his office.

"I'm working on several dope trafficking cases involving the brothers," he explained.

"Can I look at the criminal documents in the boxes?" I asked.

"Yes. Go and look."

I was shocked by what I saw in one of the boxes. Nothing was redacted in the investigative reports. The names of DEA agents, FBI agents, Customs agents, Immigration officers, and local law enforcement officers involved in ongoing cases into the cartel were all plainly visible.

The reports also included information about law enforcement agencies methods to learn about the brother's dope trafficking routes. They listed "mules" that were known by U.S. law enforcement to be smuggling dope into the U.S. for the brothers. I even saw DEA identification numbers for informants and the names of witnesses on the reports.

"How did you get the investigative reports?" I asked.

"I received them from the American Embassy in Mexico. The cases are related to Mexican citizens arrested in the States. I think you Americans call it discovery," he replied.

My eyes darted to the other agent. "The cartel brothers are reading the written discovery reports about Mexican defendants arrested in the states."

"Can I take one of the boxes?"

"Those boxes belong to the Mexico government," the prosecutor firmly stated.

"Let's get a beer and something to eat before crossing the border. It's a lot cheaper," I said as we left the office.

I pondered what we had seen while we drank a couple of beers.

"The Cartel family brothers understand how our agency, FBI, and other law enforcement operates in the United States, Mexico, Colombia, and many other counties in Central America, South America, Europe, and Asia," I said to the other agent. "The cartel family brothers are using Mexican defendants' discovery reports to sneak their drugs into the U.S. They are also learning to hide their money entering Mexico. No wonder DEA and cops can't win the war on drugs. Our Justice Department in D.C. knows that. It's a game between our government, the Mexican government, and drug traffickers."

I was worried about what I had seen. The brothers knew the names of agents, cops, informants, and witnesses from releasing discovery documents. It was no wonder that criminals always seemed to be one step ahead of us.

While the agent was driving back to the office, I continued to think about everything I had learned. How had the brothers planned their operation against the two DEA agents? Did they read the reports from the boxes? Did they know that DEA, specifically those agents, were targeting them? Is that how the brothers covered up the ambush of the two DEA agents?

The next day, I told the supervisor and called DEA Chief Legal counsel in Washington, D.C, about the boxes at the Mexican prosecutor's office in Mexico. After listening to my concerns, the supervisor suggested I meet with the Assistant U.S. Attorney (AUSA) about what was inside the Mexican prosecutor's office boxes. The DEA Chief Legal counsel never returned my call, but I did speak with the AUSA.

"The Cartel brothers are behind the attempted murder of the agents in Mexico. Even the DOJ (Department of Justice) pursued U.S. warrants for the brothers to be arrested in Mexico. However, the brothers were never arrested by the corrupt Mexican authorities," I explained to the AUSA.

I went on to tell the AUSA about the meeting with the Mexican Federal Prosecutor. During the meeting, the prosecutor told me that Mexico was very interested in taking another look at the brother's involvement in trying to murder the agents. The AUSA seemed very interested in what I had to say.

"We need to pursue this again," he said. "Larry, let's go ahead and re-open the criminal investigation on the Cartel family brothers."

He said that the U.S. Attorney's Office would coordinate any legal issues with the Mexican Federal Prosecutor's office regarding the extradition of the brothers to the U.S. and the release of discovery reports.

"The discovery reports are released to the Mexican defendants in the U.S. The reports are also sent to Mexico. You need to contact DOJ," I said, explaining my concern. "The Cartel will discover what I'm doing in Mexico and the U.S."

The AUSA shook his head in disgust. 'I'll look into it," he promised. "Do you believe there is corruption at the U.S. and Mexico POEs (Port-of-Entries)?"

"Absolutely," I responded with complete conviction.

Like myself, the AUSA was upset about the probability of corrupt law enforcement working on the U.S. and Mexico border. We agreed that the U.S. - Mexico border was a very dangerous place to work because of the corruption.

"I'm more worried about getting shot by a Customs officer or Immigration inspector than the Mexican police or one of the Cartel brothers," I sadly admitted.

"For he that soweth to his flesh: shall of the flesh reap corruption; but he that soweth t the Spirit shall of the Spirit reap life everlasting."

(Galatians 6:8, King James Version)

Chapter 43

Who Reject Gain from Extortion and Keep their Hands from Accepting Bribes

"Can you summarize the case?" I asked the Customs narcotic agent.

"My informant provided me some great information about marijuana cultivation being grown in the citrus and cotton fields. One of the bad guys was a member of former President Reagan's presidential Staff. The other is a Professor from the University of California in Berkeley," he replied.

A U.S. Customs agent had told me that he was working on a marijuana investigation that he wanted to tell me about. I met the agent at his office a few days later. He said he did not want to work with any other DEA agent.

"Why?" I asked, curious about why he wanted to work with me specifically.

His answer was a simple one "I can trust you."

"Hey, look, I'm really busy with a Cartel Family case that involves the brothers," I said. The case he presented sounded interesting, but the other kept me busy. I could tell that he was disappointed.

"Okay," I offered noncommittally, "let's meet with your informant."

Within a few days of our conversation, I met with a Customs agent and his informant in a lemon grove. The informant explained who the marijuana growers were.

"A professor teaches mathematics at the University of California in Berkeley. He has land in Mendocino and Humboldt Counties. He also has a home in Captain Cook, Hawaii." He continued to explain how the operation worked. "The professor provides his marijuana cultivation expertise and labor force from his properties in Mendocino and Humboldt Counties. His labor force consists of old 'hippies' that harvest and trim the marijuana." The informant said he might be able to identify 36 of the professor's associates assisting him with growing and distributing the marijuana.

The informant saw that we were interested, and he told us about a particularly interesting suspect involved with the case. "A former State Department diplomat that worked for Reagan's Presidential Staff provided citrus farms, cotton fields, vehicles, and water irrigation for the professor to cultivate the marijuana in the cotton fields and citrus groves. The former diplomat went to Amsterdam with the president. He brought marijuana seeds back from Amsterdam. The seeds were cultivated inside cotton fields and citrus groves."

Once the informant left, I spoke with the Customs agent. "Okay. I heard enough from your informant. This marijuana case is awesome. I'm going to get myself assigned to help you," I offered.

A month later, a local Arizona Department of Safety (DPS) narcotics officer came to the office and met with my supervisor. After a few minutes, the supervisor also called me into his office.

"The narcotics officer is asking for help on his methamphetamine investigation," explained my supervisor. "He needs help from DEA." It was apparent that "help from DEA" meant help from me.

"Wait a minute, Boss," I countered. "I'm extremely busy with the Cartel brothers' case and the Customs marijuana case. I don't have time to take off my shoes to get in bed,"

"Larry, the narcotics officer is asking for you. No one else in the office. Only you."

"Why me?" I asked. "There are now three DEA agents in the office,"

"Larry, just listen to the officer. He will explain the case. I really want you to work with him. He also has information on the Cartel family brothers."

I asked the DPS narcotics officer why he wanted me to work with him. I got a similar answer to what the Customs agent had said. "I can trust you. There is corruption at the POE."

"What?" I responded sarcastically. "Okay. Tell me your case and why you want DEA's help."

The narcotics officer had obtained information from his informants that a major Cornbread Mafia methamphetamine (meth) distributor was trafficking in the area near the border. The meth distributor had connections to the Las Vegas Mafia and the Hells Angels in California. His investigation also revealed the Cartel brothers were involved.

"The meth distributor is known to DEA and FBI to be receiving illegal chemicals as well as pounds of meth manufactured in Mexico," explained the officer. "The meth distributor is getting the chemicals and meth across the POE and into the U.S. with the protection of the cartel brother's drug smuggling organization."

"Why didn't you ask the FBI for help?" I asked.

He smirked at the question and answered with a look of disgust. "I did ask an FBI agent, but he refuses to help me. The FBI agent said he was too busy."

We concluded the meeting, and the narcotics officer told us that he would focus on getting authorization from the state of Arizona to conduct electronic communications interception on the meth distributor's home.

I ran into the FBI agent who initially asked to assist with the case a while later. I was curious why he hadn't taken the case, so I asked him. The agent made it clear that he didn't want to work with any local narcotic officer on the case because of corruption.

It disappointed me that the FBI refused to work with local law enforcement agencies. What did the FBI know that I didn't know about corruption? Why had he refused a case like this? The next time I saw the DPS narcotics officer, I clarified that I was there to help him.

As a federal agent, I was responsible for coordinating and directing DEA surveillance teams. I was the only DEA agent working with the local narcotics officer. Several times I followed marijuana and meth traffickers from Arizona deep into California.

I conducted surveillance of marijuana and meth trafficking activities for three months at the POE, and throughout the U.S. With help from the DPS narcotics officer, I identified criminal networks that were moving many pounds of meth to their criminal associates every month. The IRS assisted me with obtaining bank and income statements that detailed the financial activities of the meth distributors. I reviewed the information carefully and found a financial trail that linked the meth distributors to the cartel's agriculture business in Mexico. I also learned that the brothers and their cartel in Mexico were providing the meth distributors with meth and cocaine to distribute in the United States.

While I was working on the case, informants reiterated that there were corrupt Customs officers and Immigration inspectors at the POE working for the brothers. When the meth case finished, I arrested 11 of the meth distributor's criminal associates on narcotics charges. The principal suspect was later released from jail on a $140,000 bond posted by the Cartel brothers.

I found it odd that the cartel brothers had escaped justice for so long, and I wondered if they were receiving help from intelligence elements within the U.S. government (Spooks).

"Do you think the brothers might be connected with the Spooks?" I asked the DPS narcotics officer.

"Yes. The brothers are working with the Spooks," he asserted.

It concerned me that I needed to be worried about elements within my own government. The brothers were a cancer that spread corruption. Hopefully, I would arrest the brothers and end the corruption at the POEs. I remained focused on the brothers and corruption at the POE throughout my time in Arizona.

"Those who walk righteously and speak what is right, who reject gain from extortion and keep their hands from accepting bribes, who stop their ears against plots of murder and shut their eyes against contemplating evil - [16] they are the ones who will dwell on the heights, whose refuge will be the mountain fortress. Their bread will be supplied, and water will not fail them."

(Isaiah 33:15-16, King James Version)

Chapter 44

Evil Men Understand, not Judgment

I remember one occasion when I decided to take a shortcut around the Mexico POE (Port-of-Entry) through the open desert. After I crossed back into the U.S., all hell broke loose. Cars belonging to Customs agents and Immigration inspectors appeared from nowhere and sped up to me with their sirens blazing. I stopped my car, and agents and officers leaped out of their vehicles, drawing their handguns on me.

"I'm DEA," I yelled to them, shocked by the response. "Some of you know I'm DEA. Or do you think I'm "Pancho Villa?" I added sarcastically.

I slowly pulled out my DEA badge and showed it to them. They were clearly unhappy with my shortcut. They asked me to return to the POE with them, and I complied.

Several days earlier, my investigation into the marijuana and meth smuggling operations had come to an end. Wrapping up those investigations left me free to focus on the cartel brothers like a bird dog savagely eating his prey. I wanted them to face justice for the two agents they had attempted to murder in Mexico. One thing I learned from working the marijuana and meth investigations was who I could and couldn't trust on the Mexico Port-of-Entry (POE).

"You know, Agent Hardin, something isn't right at that POE. Customs officers and Immigration inspectors are asking questions about our visit to Mexico," one of my informants had told me.

"What kind of questions?"

"The officers and inspectors asked what was going on in Mexico. Why are we returning to Arizona" I told the officers and inspectors we live in Arizona. We showed the officers and inspectors our Colombian passports with the visas. Also, they asked if we knew the brothers." The informant was clearly suspicious about the motives behind those questions.

With the help of several sources and informants, I finally identified one of the corrupt Immigration inspectors at the POE. She was a niece of the cartel brothers. Without a doubt, there were several more corrupt officers and inspectors at the POE border. Because of corruption in law enforcement at the POE, I was forced to work without support from the Customs agents.

At first, I trusted the agents in my office. Later I learned from the DPS narcotics officer that a DEA agent from my office was telling local law enforcement in the community about my contact with various sources and informants who worked in Mexico. Many lived and worked in Mexico, and I worried because their situation exposed them. The brothers had family members that worked at the POE, and the informants made it clear they had been told that an Agent Hardin from the DEA was going after the brothers.

There weren't many agents or narcotics officers I could trust or count on to cover my back out on the streets. The only one I could trust in my office was the secretary. She kept me squared away with my paperwork, ensuring everything I wrote was completed and read smoothly for the AUSA office. She watched over me like a hen taking care of her chicks, protecting me from agent gossip about why I worked alone on the streets and in Mexico. My sources and informants were the only other people I trusted outside of the office.

At times, I even worked alone across the border in Mexico. I conducted surveillance checks on the Cartel brother's residences and businesses. Vehicles with U.S. plates were frequently parked at those locations, and I carefully wrote them down. Many of those license plates turned out to be registered to known drug traffickers in the U.S.

The brothers had a produce or shrimp business in Mexico. When the employees got off work, I followed some back into the U.S. The employees who lived in the U.S. tended to have beautiful homes in sharp contrast to those who lived in Mexico and lived in houses made of plywood. The employees living in plywood homes were not involved in drug trafficking.

I learned from the sources and informants that the brothers and their family members were behind shipments of drugs coming across the border on produce, shrimp, and furniture trucks to warehouses somewhere in the U.S. I searched a lot of produce and furniture trucks, most of them 18-wheelers, coming across at the POE (Port-of-Entry). Whenever I got information from the sources and informants that there might be drugs on a truck, I'd stop and search it. I wanted the brothers in Mexico to know that I, DEA Agent Larry Ray Hardin, would seize their drugs and trucks at the POE. Despite all my hard work, the brothers and their family members continued making millions off their dope. The damage I was doing to their operations was no more than a drop in a pee bucket.

I never had any problems at the POE until I started to focus on the Cartel brothers and their illegal dope activities in the U.S. The Customs agents and Immigration inspectors at the POE couldn't be trusted. I didn't want anyone to so much as suspect that I was in Mexico looking into the brothers' criminal activities. My sources and informants made it clear that activities were being tracked.

"Some of the brothers' family and relatives seem to know when you're in Mexico," informants told me on more than one occasion.

As a "gringo" in Mexico, I'm sure my face stood out. Perhaps I was the only "gringo" hanging out near the brothers' businesses and residences who weren't doing business with them. More likely, however, the brothers were finding out when I crossed into Mexico from the corrupt cops at the POE.

My growing distrust of the personnel working the POE prompted me to take a shortcut through the open desert and avoid it altogether. My decision had not worked out how I hoped it would, so I accompanied the agents and inspectors back to the POE. When I got there, I was escorted to the office of a Hispanic Immigration supervisor, who glared across her desk at me. She demanded to know why I had failed to enter the U.S. properly at the POE.

"You've got some corrupt Custom officers and Immigration inspectors working here at the POE. I didn't want to identify myself to the wrong agent or inspector." She didn't like my answer.

"You can leave now," is all she said.

After I retired from DEA, I applied for the Customs and Immigration Global Entry card to enter the U.S. without many hassles at Transportation Security Administration (TSA) checkpoints. After about six weeks, I finally received a letter from Customs officials stating that I was not qualified for the TSA Global Entry card. I called the Washington, D.C. phone number provided in the letter and spoke to a customs supervisor.

"Sir, according to our records, you are not qualified to have the TSA Global Entry card," he informed me.

"Why?" I asked, confused why there would be any reason that I should be denied.

"Customs and Immigration records stated you were a "Border Jumper" because you crossed the border illegally from Mexico into the U.S."

I explained that I was working as a DEA agent in Mexico.

"Yes," she acknowledged. "But you failed to identify yourself to the officials when entering the POE."

This led to a long conversation about why I had not entered through the POE. I told the Customs supervisor in Washington, D.C, about the rampant corruption I had encountered at the POE.

I did eventually receive the TSA Global Entry card.

"Evil men understand, not judgment: but they that seek the LORD understand all things."

(Proverbs 28:5, King James Version)

Chapter 45

Violence Covereth the Mouth of the Wicked

The felon came running out the front door towards his car, barefoot and shirtless. The other DEA agent and I stood beside his car with our guns pointed directly at him. He had done exactly what we anticipated he would do.

"Hey, Pancho Villa," I shouted. "DEA. Don't move, or I'll shoot you in the face."

A rookie agent with less than a year on the job had recently reported to our office. We had spent the mid-morning in the desert's scorching heat following cartel family members near the border. We finished our surveillance, and there was some work I wanted to take care of in Mexico. The new agent was driving, so I had him drive us there.

While we were in Mexico, I got a phone call from the supervisor. He had received a tip about a dangerous felon and suspected murderer that he wanted us to arrest. The criminal's sister called the DEA office, explained the situation, and stated that her brother stayed at their parents' home overnight.

"The felon might be armed," the supervisor warned us. "He's extremely dangerous. He's leaving early tomorrow morning. Get the other agents to help you." the sister didn't want DEA agents to go to the house and arrest her brother because the parents were old and sick.

On the way back to the DEA office from Mexico, I was sitting in the passenger seat, staring out the window. I noticed about a dozen sheep strolling out of the lemon grove, crossing the road in front of us. They were followed by a young Hispanic boy doing his best to keep them together.

I waited for our car to slow, but the new agent didn't seem to be paying attention.

"Slow down; you're going to run over the sheep and the boy," I shouted.

He seemed lost and confused as he looked over at me.

"You're going to kill the sheep and the boy!"

He looked out the windshield as though the sheep had suddenly materialized from thin air and skidded suddenly into the oncoming herd of sheep. It was too late; the sheep were spooked and jumping around everywhere. Some of them were even on top of the hood of our car. The agent blasted the horn to disperse the sheep, jerking the car off the side of the road and around the sheep. After traveling along a water canal and missing several lemon trees, he finally drove the car back onto the highway.

"I don't think you killed any sheep," I said. "I saw the boy duck into the canal; he's fine. Speed it up! I need to get to the office now, so I can get out to the felon's parent's house to arrest him before he decides to leave town."

When I got back to town, I arranged to have two other agents go with me to the felon's parent's house. We arrived in three unmarked cars and set up undercover surveillance near the felon's parent's house. According to the supervisor, the criminal's sister stayed inside the house with her parents all night. She would contact DEA early in the morning when her brother was ready to leave the house. Without a doubt, this was going to be another long night.

I knew that we could not let this felon leave the house. He was an armed murderer with a DEA Federal warrant for his arrest. If we didn't arrest this guy, he might hurt or kill a cop during a traffic stop. This bad guy posed a danger to the law enforcement community and the public.

I had asked the rookie agent to park next to the other agent and myself for our mutual safety. We had arranged to take turns watching the house so that we could all get some sleep as we sat waiting through the long night.

"I don't want the felon to sneak up on me while I'm sleeping," I said sternly. "If he does, you are going to regret it. I want you to focus on the felon's house like a night desert one-eyed owl waiting for his first rat."

I told the rookie agent to watch the front door of the house and the felon's car and not to worry. "I will get a call from the supervisor if the felon leaves the house."

"I'll watch the house, and if there's any movement, I'll wake you up," the rookie assured me.

Despite his assurances, I wondered if I could trust the rookie agent not to fall asleep while the other agent and I were sleeping. I closed my eyes and drifted briefly off to sleep. Shifting uncomfortably in the seat, I opened my eyes and checked the time. It was somewhere between 3:00 and 4:00 am. I looked out the car window to see how the rookie was doing. I could see his head on the steering wheel, sound asleep. Wow, after everything I had told him, the rookie was sleeping.

I got out of my car and jumped in the passenger seat with the other agent and touched him on the arm.

"What happened?" asked the other agent with a yawn.

"That rookie agent's sleeping, but don't worry, the felon's car is still at his parent's residence. I haven't received any information from the supervisor about when the felon's leaving his parent's house."

I slowly rolled down the passenger window and pulled out my little sweet-pee .38-revolver snub nose midnight special from inside my pants.

"What are you going to do with your gun," nervously asked the agent.

"Watch the rookie agent jump; he will scream for his momma."

The agent could see that I was aiming roughly toward the rookie's car. I pointed my little sweet-pee .38 out the window and slowly squeezed the trigger, firing a bullet into the dark sky. The rookie agent jumped out of his car, swiveling about to peer into the darkness with his gun in his right hand.

"What happened? He screamed. "What happened?"

"You're supposed to watch the house," I shouted.

He stood there sheepishly without saying a word. The round I fired off had not been so quiet. The sound of the round from the .38 echoed loudly in the early morning darkness. Within minutes, a County Deputy Sheriff's patrol car drove slowly down the street. Its spotlight swept the street, illuminating our undercover vehicles. The Deputy Sheriff recognized us and knew that DEA agents were up to something in the neighborhood. He turned off his spotlight and quietly left the area.

Shortly after my Sweet-Pea, cracked like thunder in the night, I got a call from our supervisor. The sister had called to let him know that her brother was on the move.

"My brother and I heard a gunshot, and he saw a police car going by our house with his spotlight on," she told him. "He's leaving the house now."

No sooner had the supervisor called than the felon came running out of the house. He nearly ran over me, trying to get to his car. He froze when he saw us standing there with our guns aimed at him. Within seconds, the rookie agent had the felon on the ground eating dirt and handcuffed him. After all, I thought the rookie was doing a good job, but he could do a lot better by staying awake.

"Blessing are upon the head of the just: but violence covereth the mouth of the wicked."

(Proverbs 10:6, King James Version)

Chapter 46

Out of the Heart of Men, Proceed Evil Thoughts

I found 539 pounds of cocaine stashed inside the abandoned car's back seat. Sooner or later, I figured the driver would return to their abandoned car. That much cocaine would be missed, and I wanted to make sure the driver reported to the Cartel brothers in Mexico that DEA had taken their cocaine. I also wanted the Cartel brothers to know that the corrupt Immigration inspector at the POE (Port-of-Entry) that allowed the drugs to pass had inadvertently helped me find the cocaine. To my disappointment, the driver never returned to the vehicle, and I figured they probably returned to Mexico on foot.

Throughout the six years I worked in the desert town, I seized a lot of marijuana, cocaine, and heroin from the Cartel and its mules. Sometimes I found large quantities of unlabeled pills on the mules as well. The United States Attorney's office had well-documented procedures for dealing with the prosecution of illegal drugs. The attorneys never instructed the DEA agents or other law enforcement officers in the area about preparing cases involving the illegal distribution of pharmaceutical pills.

Later another source in Mexico told me that a car with cocaine would be crossing the POE that day.

"I know the type of car carrying cocaine from Mexico across the POE into the U.S. The driver will leave the car at a grocery store parking lot. The driver is a mule for the brothers," the source reported. "There is a bad official at the POE helping to smuggle the cocaine for the brothers."

With the source's description of the car and help from a Border agent's narcotic dog, I seized 32 kilos of cocaine. We had found the abandoned car parked in a grocery store parking lot, just like the source said. I wondered where the driver had gone.

"I was hoping to talk to the driver about the cocaine in the car," I later told the source. "I also wanted to thank the bad officer at the POE for helping me find the car with the cocaine." I never got the opportunity.

About a month later, an unknown female speaking broken English called with a description of a pickup truck smuggling drugs. The next day an unknown male who barely spoke English called me with additional information about the same pickup truck. The truck was supposed to cross the POE with drugs in the next few days.

A few days later, I checked an abandoned pickup truck near the POE left in a public parking lot. The pickup truck met the exact description the unknown female and male had given me. A Border Patrol agent with a narcotics sniffing dog assisted me. The dog quickly alerted us to the drugs inside the pickup. I seized 226 lbs. of cocaine from inside the truck.

I wondered what had motivated the unidentified female to report the pickup truck. Was she the angry girlfriend of one of the brothers? Maybe the unknown male was a corrupt official who thought he could balance the scales of his corrupt side income by anonymously reporting cars he let through. Perhaps he sat post on the POE, watching me as I crossed.

Days later, I got another call from the same unknown female that had given me the tip about the pickup truck. She had information about another load of drugs coming across the POE.

"It is the same driver from the pickup truck that had the cocaine," she said. "The driver works at the brother's warehouse. The car is a white Ford with California license plates. I overheard the driver telling another employee that he went through the POE yesterday without any problems from Customs officers or Immigration inspectors. The car will be parked in the same public parking lot as the last time." She ended the call abruptly, as though she feared someone might overhear what she was saying.

I arrived at the parking lot with another agent from my office. A Border Patrol agent with his narcotics dog was already at the parking lot, waiting for me. After I verified the car's description, the Border Patrol agents' narcotics dog immediately alerted me to drugs inside the car. As we opened the doors and trunk of the car, we were assaulted with a disgusting smell like dead seaweed. The odor overwhelmed us, and I could barely breathe. Inside the car, we found 360 lbs. of marijuana, divided into little packages the size of bricks. Tightly wrapped packages covered the front and back seats. It was loaded to the max.

I was upset by the corruption allowing these vehicles to cross the border. I couldn't believe that a Customs officer and Immigration inspector at the POE weren't bothering to check them. The pickup truck had crossed with 226 pounds of cocaine; now, this car had 360 lbs. of marijuana. I wondered if I was being set up by the brothers and the corrupt officials at the POE. How did the unknown female in Mexico know so much about the driver of the car? Who was she?

One day, my informant called, "The brother's female mule says she can smuggle a kilo of cocaine, a pound of heroin, or pills across the POE without any problems from U.S. Customs officers and Immigration inspectors." I listened as he continued. "She won't charge me for bringing a kilo of cocaine or heroin across the POE. She can get anyone or anything across. She said the brother's niece and nephew work at the POE. She can also get information on what the DEA is doing at the POE. She can find out who is working for DEA."

"Where did you meet the mule?" I asked.

"We were at the brother's Oompa party in Mexico," replied the informant. "The brothers were laughing about how some of the Mexican police target "gringa" women in Mexico. They were saying that when the police detain an attractive "gringa" woman, they take her to a private location. They start touching the gringa.

The brothers were laughing about it. They said that sometimes the "gringa" would freak out, and other times the "gringa" would just be quiet while the cops enjoyed themselves with her body. One brother said, "When the "gringa" cries, the police tell her not to scream or they will hurt her or the ones with her. After the police finish with the gringa, they strongly encourage her not to mention what happened to anyone in the U.S., or she and her gringo husband or boyfriend will disappear in the desert. They can even charge her with a serious crime in Mexico."

"This is just a way of life," the informant continued to quote what the brothers had said. "This is just how it is for the gringa women and the young girls when the police want them. Mexican women are smarter than the gringas. Many Mexican women carry a bottle of Vaseline with them for lubrication to their vaginas. The women never know if they will be forced to have sex with a bad police officer or two. American gringa women never carry Vaseline. That's why they bleed a lot.'

It shocked me to hear how callously the brothers were talking about the sexual abuse of women in Mexico. The informant had overheard one of the brothers bragging about the DEA agents he tried to kill. I could feel the anger burning inside me while the informant talked about the things the brothers had said at the party, which fueled my desire to bring them to justice.

It was shocking to hear how much influence the brothers wielded on the U.S. side of the border. Besides having family members working on the POE, the informant told me the name of another of their relatives who worked in the U.S. as a schoolteacher. She oversaw the school's Drug Abuse Resistance Education (DARE) program.

"For from within, out of the heart of men, proceed evil thoughts, adulteries, fornications, murders."

(Mark 7:29, King James Version)

Chapter 47

Stand Against the Wiles of the Devil

The DEA was aware of my investigation targeting the brothers and their Cartel family drug business. They provided me with information about a drug defendant who was squealing like a rat. He was providing information to DEA on the Cartel brothers and their trafficking organization in Mexico with the hope of cutting a deal.

The defendant told the DEA that the brothers had more than 500 kilos of cocaine waiting to move into the U.S. through the POE. He said he could arrange for DEA undercover agents to purchase 15-20 kilos of heroin every 15 days from the brother's traffickers. According to the cooperating defendant, there would not be any problem for the cocaine to cross the POE into the U.S.

Not long after receiving this information, I received a call from the informant.

"The brothers are ready to sell me 30 kilos of cocaine for $14,500 a kilo. The brothers have a lot more of it and can sell it to me real cheap," he said.

I told the informant to purchase a one-kilo sample before he negotiated the price for the other 30 kilos with the brothers. I wanted one kilo of cocaine from the brothers so that I could provide evidence to the AUSA and start the prosecutorial process.

The informant called me on the day we were scheduled to buy the one-kilo sample of cocaine.

"I can't meet with the brother's mule alone. Can you find someone to help negotiate with the mule to buy the one kilo?" asked the informant.

"I can't speak Spanish fluently with the mule," I told him. "But I do have someone that can help you negotiate the buy. She is from Europe. She knows how to negotiate the price for the sample kilo and the other 30. Hopefully, the 500 kilos later. She will have the rest of the money to buy 30 more kilos if the price is low enough to move it to Europe."

I called the woman from Europe later that day. "Can you help me buy a kilo of cocaine and hopefully negotiate 30 kilos more with a mule? After you buy the 30 kilos, I want you to talk to the mule about getting another 500 kilos."

She assured me she could negotiate the buy and even offered to meet the mule in Mexico if necessary. We met the informant the next day in a parking lot behind a grocery store.

The woman didn't go easy on the informant. "Don't be a sissy when you talk to the mule," she insisted. "Do you want me to talk to him, or can you set up the purchase for the sample kilo of cocaine with him?"

The informant shuffled his feet nervously and seemed indecisive. The woman was growing irritated with him. "Don't you have the guts to make the buy with the mule? I need you to set this up. Can you handle it? Call him!"

The informant called the mule and passed the phone to the European woman. She set up the time and place to meet the mule and buy the one-kilo sample. After a bit of haggling, she convinced the mule to sell it to her for $14,500.

"Okay. I can deliver the kilo of cocaine," he acknowledged. "Then, I'll deliver the other 30 kilos when you are ready for the same price."

"No," she insisted. "I want the other 30 kilos for less than $12,000."

The mule paused to think about that. "I have to talk to someone."

I arranged for the mule to meet with a DEA undercover agent. The following day the undercover agent purchased one sample kilo for $14,500 from the mule. Later, the mule agreed to $12,000 a kilo for the

30 kilos if she committed to follow up with a purchase for the other 500 kilos.

I got a call that the informant had been arrested for DUI (Drunk Under the Influence). He was useless to me in jail, and I would have to get him out to continue the investigation. Several days later, I met a local Judge that could help release the informant from the county jail. The judge listened as I explained that I needed the informant to help me buy 30 kilos of cocaine and later another 500 kilos. I said,

"Judge," I addressed him respectfully. "The brothers who own the cocaine tried to kill two DEA agents." The judge was sympathetic to my request and agreed to release the informant.

I told the FBI I had bought a kilo of cocaine for $14,500 from a mule working for the Cartel. I would need a lot of money to purchase 30 kilos of cocaine. The DEA couldn't provide me with all the cash I needed to make the buy, so I would have to reach out to other agencies.

"The kilo of cocaine is a sample," I said. "We have a deal for 30 more kilos of cocaine and a follow-up sale for 500 kilos. The brothers are ready to sell the rest of the cocaine for $12,000 a kilo to the informant.

"Will you help me buy the 30 kilos?" I asked. "I need $360,000. Can the FBI help to pay half?"

I was hoping the FBI could help me. If I could make this buy, I might learn how the brothers successfully moved cocaine across the border at the POE and into the U.S. To do that, I was going to need help from the FBI. After I bought the 30 kilos, I could arrange to purchase the remaining 500 from the brothers and follow up with the arrest warrants for the mule and the brothers.

"Put on the whole armor of God, that ye may be able to stand against the wiles of the devil."

(Ephesians 6:11, King James Version)

Chapter 48

They are Greedy dogs Which can Never have Enough

I was waiting to find out if the FBI would pay half of the $360,000 for the 30 kilograms of cocaine. Their cooperation was critically important to move the case forward in a meaningful way, and it felt as though my investigation was coming to a standstill. That's when I got the call that the informant was getting on a plane to Los Angeles with one of the brothers to conduct business in the Chinatown district.

When they got on the flight, I called the Asian Gang Task Force to follow the informant and the Cartel brother to Chinatown. The brother and the informant were met by two Asian men at the Los Angeles (LA) airport and, after a brief exchange of pleasantries, got into a car together. Their destination was a Chinese Seafood Company in Chinatown, where the informant met with an older Asian man. They shook hands and exchanged greetings, then cut the meeting abruptly short. The two Asian men took the brother and informant back to the LA airport.

Later, the informant told me that nothing had happened in Chinatown. The planned discussion about a business arrangement between the informant's shrimp business and the Asian Seafood Company never occurred. The two Asian men might have observed the DEA surveillance team following the informant from the LA airport to Chinatown. My gut feeling was that the Asians knew the informant might be working with the government.

I initially didn't see the connection between the brothers and their interest in Chinatown. There weren't any indications from the law enforcement community that Chinese and Mexicans were working together to move drugs from Mexico into the United States.

When the Chinese trafficked white heroin, they dealt strictly with their own group of people. The idea that the Chinese had gotten involved with the Mexicans was new to me. Recent events indicated that the Mexican cartel gave the Chinese access to the brother's drug trafficking network in Sonora, Mexico. It seemed unlikely that could happen without the support of high-level officials within the Mexican government.

Serval days later, I got another call from the informant, stating that shrimp containing white heroin was being shipped to the Chinese Seafood Company in Chinatown.

"The white heroin is in the Tiger shrimp tails," he said. It is inside the truck. I saw it with my own eyes."

I told my supervisor what the informant had said and described how white heroin was hidden in the Mexican shrimp tails.

"I need to stop the shrimp truck and search it," I asserted firmly. I will find the white heroin."

The supervisor paused to consider what I was saying. I could tell that he wasn't entirely comfortable with what I wanted to do.

"If you don't find the heroin, it will cost DEA a lot of money. You are going to destroy all that shrimp," he warned me as he reluctantly approved my idea.

I watched as the brother's shrimp truck entered the POE from Mexico. It was undoubtedly loaded with the white heroin the informant had told me about. The prospect of catching the Mexicans and Asians working together to smuggle white heroin into the U.S. filled me with the excitement of the hunt. I and some other agents from my office waited patiently as the truck passed through the POE. It hadn't gone far when we swarmed it with our vehicles, lights flashing, and stopped it.

The border patrol provided three narcotics dogs to assist with the search. They quickly alerted to the presence of drugs as they searched outside the shrimp truck. I told the truck driver to follow me to a cooling facility company in town.

At the cooling facility, I had the shrimp unloaded from the truck. The boxes of shrimp were carefully searched, but I could not find the white heroin. We also searched the tails, but a long and exhaustive search did not reveal anything. I stood there looking at the pile of shrimp on the floor with a profound sense of disappointment and tried to understand what had gone wrong.

One of the Border Patrol agents tapped me on the shoulder. "Hey," he said. "We want the shrimp lying on the floor." I heard that Border Patrol agents had a nice shrimp barbecue feast at their homes.

A close friend of mine worked at Border Patrol in the Office of Personal Responsibility (OPR). It was part of his responsibility to investigate wrongdoing by Border Patrol agents. He later said that two Border Patrol agents were suspected of getting money "under the table" from narcotics traffickers in Mexico. The Border Patrol agents were the two dog handlers I used on the shrimp truck.

"Yea they are greedy dogs which can never have enough, and they are shepherds that cannot understand: they all look to their own way, every one for his gain, from his quarter."

(Isaiah 56:11, King James Version)

Chapter 49

A Prudent Man Foreseeth the Evil

After destroying the Cartel brother's Tiger shrimp, I wondered why they never filed a complaint with the DEA for stopping their truck. At the very least, I figured they would want to file a claim for the $70,000 or more in damage to their shrimp shipment. The brothers undoubtedly knew the reason I searched their truck. I'm sure that a corrupt cop at the POE (Port-of-Entry) reported the entire incident to them.

Earlier in the investigation, the sources and informants told me about a computer at the maquiladora furniture business in Mexico. They said the computer had information related to the brother's drug business and their Chinese connection. I shared that information with the FBI, hoping to encourage them to assist me with purchasing the 30 kilos of cocaine.

Several days later, an FBI agent and an unidentified female from Washington, D.C., met with me and my sources just after midnight at the POE. She identified herself as an Information Technology (IT) Specialist and just smiled when I asked her name. She wouldn't communicate with me. Her lack of communication made me wonder if she could be trusted. Did she work for the FBI, some other agency, or was she a contractor? I would have felt more comfortable knowing who I was dealing with.

A source and I stayed near the POE. The FBI agent, the IT Specialist, and another source went into Sonora, Mexico, to search for the computer at the maquiladora furniture business with permission from the Mexican government.

"The IT Specialist downloaded a lot of great information from the computer about the brother's connection with the Chinese," said the FBI agent when he returned to the U.S. "She will provide you with copies of everything she took from the computer."

Several days later, I visited the FBI agent and asked him about the copies of the data retrieved from the computer.

"The IT Specialist has the copies," he assured me. "There's nothing there, and I can't tell you anything else. It's just a bunch of numbers."

More time dragged by as I waited to find out if the FBI would help fund my purchase of the 30 kilos. At last, the agent came to see me at our office, and I was hopeful they had decided to help us move forward with the operation.

"FBI no longer wants to be involved with the brothers' case," he stated.

The cold finality of his answer stunned me. "Why the sudden change?" I asked. He refused to explain.

"Please tell the FBI I need their help to purchase the 30 kilos from the brothers," I pleaded.

"My boss says, 'NO.'" He firmly stated.

Whatever happened down in Mexico had changed things. The FBI's tentative support had turned suddenly cold, and the case had changed in ways I couldn't understand.

"A prudent man foreseeth the evil, and hideth himself; but the simple pass on, and are punished."

(Proverbs 27:12, King James Version)

Chapter 50

A Wise Man Feareth, and Departeth from Evil

While I was at the Mexican police station, I observed a young man being repeatedly slapped in the face by the federales. Blood was slowly dripping out of his nose as he bore each slap without daring to make a sound. I couldn't believe that he wasn't begging the cops to stop. A young woman was trying not to cry as she watched them beat him, and it seemed like they were together. The federales eventually marched her off to another part of the facility.

Another DEA agent had asked me to go with him to meet with the Mexican Federal Commander in San Luis, Mexico. The commander had called about a stolen American Cessna aircraft that crashed in the desert near a fishing village.

According to the commander, the small plane was loaded with cocaine. I knew from the informants and sources that he was corrupt and worked closely with the brothers. The other agent, who was Hispanic and spoke fluent Spanish, said he had met the commander before. He had given him several boxes of 45-caliber ammunition, and on another occasion, he had given him an apple pie in exchange for information about drug traffickers in Mexico. I didn't trust what the corrupt Mexican official had to say. His motives were suspect as far as I was concerned, and I didn't want to be there. It surprised me that the other agent put any trust in him at all.

When we arrived at the Mexican Federal Police station, the commander greeted us with the feigned warmth of a used car salesman. He told us about the plane and said he would take us to where it had crashed near the fishing village. I waited quietly while the other agent exchanged small talk in Spanish with the commander. After a short time, a federale entered the commander's office and informed him that we were ready.

"Let's go," the commander announced as he stood up and slapped his palms on the desktop.

I took another look at the young man as we left. The expression on his swollen face seemed to be one of hopeless defeat. I feared for what the young man and woman were about to experience. Informants and witnesses had told me that corrupt Mexican cops would take advantage of a woman for sexual pleasure.

The Hispanic agent and I jumped into the back seat of the commander's black SUV. We quickly left the city behind and turned onto dirt roads. The driver was traveling very fast, and clouds of dust billowed out from behind us. Several black SUVs with armed plainclothes federal police followed closely behind.

We finally arrived at an isolated desert where the stolen Cessna had crashed. I noticed that the small plane was burned down to the metal.

"The American plane carried cocaine, but someone must have unloaded it before we arrived," laughed the commander.

I caught the commander's smile as he talked about cocaine disappearing from the plane. It didn't surprise me; I was sure the corrupt official knew exactly where the cocaine was and who had it. I wondered why they had really called us.

The commander had a small black camera in his hand and told the other agent, in Spanish, that he wanted to take a picture of me. No one else, he insisted, just me.

Here I was at a desert crash site in the middle of nowhere, looking at a burned-out plane with a corrupt Mexican official. I was irritated with the blusterous, self-satisfied commander and his self-serving federales. I couldn't speak Spanish fluently, and the Mexican slang eluded me completely. How dumb had I been to agree to this meeting?

I looked directly at the Commanders bulging black eyes as I considered how to respond to his request.

"I want the commander to understand that if he wants a picture of me, then his officers, all 12 of them, are going to take their shirts off, and we'll all take a picture together, like a big family. Like a big happy family in the middle of the 120° F desert."

The agent nervously translated what I said to the commander. A wave of laughter erupted from the Mexican, and the commander smiled. He ordered his officers to remove their shirts and indicated that the other agent and I should do the same. The officers complied gleefully. Reluctantly I peeled off my own polo-red shirt and joined them. My light skin shined like a beacon in a sea of golden brown.

The commander bellowed with laughter as he put the camera to his face and pointed it towards the group. He focused mainly on me standing next to the crashed, stolen plane.

There I was in the middle of the desert, surrounded by armed federales without their shirts. After he snapped several photos of me, the commander invited us to a Cantina bar in the fishing village for lunch – the only restaurant in the small village. As much as I would have liked to have declined his invitation, it didn't seem like the prudent thing to do. It didn't seem like poking the commander's fragile ego by declining his invitation was in my best interest.

"We are all eating tiger shrimp!" announced the commander when we arrived at the cantina.

I wondered who was paying the bill, it wasn't me, and it didn't appear to be the commander. The poor proprietors would likely be expected to bear the cost as an operational expense.

I drank a Corona beer and ate two of the biggest shrimps I'd ever seen.

"The shrimp is tiger shrimp. The best!" bragged the commander.

At the very least, I wanted to pay for the Corona beer I drank with lunch, but the commander told me, "No." It was all "free."

The other agent and I finally crossed the POE border late that night. I was so excited to be back home. It was a beautiful feeling to be back on the U.S. side of the border. I thanked God for being alive, but it bothered me that the brothers undoubtedly had a picture of me.

At the POE, an Immigration inspector told me that an underage Mexican boy had just been arrested for having a kilo of cocaine hidden inside his pants.

"Why are you telling me?" I asked.

"The boy said he is working for DEA," stated the inspector as though he expected me to acknowledge it.

"That is bull crap!" I insisted. "All the traffickers tell you guys at the POE the dopers are working for DEA. Inspector, listen very carefully to what I'm saying to you. You take care of the Mexican boy and give the kilo of cocaine to the other Customs agents at the POE."

Did the commander have something to do with telling the corrupt Immigration inspector about the kilo of cocaine? For all I knew, it could be one of the kilos stolen from the crashed plane. I had the feeling that the inspector was evil and corrupt.

The brothers and their dope traffickers now had a photo of me without my shirt on, standing next to the accursed crashed plane. They would undoubtedly be able to recognize me when I followed them in Yuma and near the Mexican border. The existence of the photo made it extremely dangerous for me to go back to Mexico. I could be kidnapped and killed.

My biggest concern was not the corrupt cops in Mexico or the brothers but my people in the law enforcement community. I wasn't afraid of the brothers and or the other criminals. They were indeed a threat that called for caution, but I was more cautious working with other agents and law enforcement that might be corrupt.

"A wise man feareth, and departeth from evil; but the fool rageth, and is confident."

(Proverbs 14:16, King James Version)

Chapter 51

I will not Fear: What can Man do Unto Me

It puzzled me that a Marine hero would be working as a guard for the cartel brothers. "According to military records, he was an enlisted Marine promoted to a field commissioned Lieutenant," The DoD (Department of Defense) official said in response to my query. "He was a real hero wounded twice in Vietnam while on patrol and once by a sniper. He saved the lives of his Marine buddies."

I had found out about the Marine several days earlier from a source. "I met a Marine working for the Mexican Cartel," he said. "He is guarding the brother's business in Mexico. Do you want to meet him?"

I did want to see him, but first, I needed to know what I was walking into. "Before I meet this guy, give me his real name," I told the source.

I called the DoD and identified myself as a DEA agent. They confirmed that the person the source named had served in the Marine Corps and provided me with some background from their service record. I called the source back after I finished the call. "I want to meet the Marine."

Working undercover, the informant and I met with the former Marine officer near the POE. He clearly had no interest in talking to me about working as a drug guard for the brothers. After the introduction, he looked at me as though he had seen a mortal enemy. He abruptly gestured for us to stop by holding his palm out in front, turned, and walked away without saying another word. The meeting had come to a sudden end as quickly as it had begun.

"That guy you were with is a CIA agent. I saw him several times in Sonora, Mexico," the Marine later told the source.

It disappointed me to hear that. I wondered why he thought I was a "spook."

"The Lord is on my side; I will not fear: what can man do unto me?"

(Psalm 118:6, King James Version)

Chapter 52

I will Fear no Evil: for Thou art With Me

I was leaning back in my office chair with my feet up on the desk when the phone rang. I answered.

"I represent a client in LA (Los Angeles)," said the voice on the other end of the call. "While working for them, I learned you're targeting their furniture trucks coming across the POE (Port-of-Entry) at the Mexican border."

I found Public Defense lawyers to be particularly despicable. There weren't many lawyers that I liked, even when they were on my side. The worst lawyers of all were the ones working for the dopers. They tended to lie a lot and could be brutal in the courtroom. They would go to great lengths to convince juries that cops and agents were liars. It was a game of chess with a lot of them.

"Who are you?" I asked.

"Robert Bonner, I'm a former DEA administrator," the voice said pleasantly, without the arrogance I had come to expect from people in such positions.

"Sir, why are you calling me?" I asked with a touch of suspicion.

"I'd like to meet with you," said the former administrator.

I agreed to meet with him soon. Dutifully, I went to my supervisor and informed him about the meeting with the former DEA administrator.

"No, you're not going to meet a former DEA administrator alone. Instead, you'll meet with him at the DEA office," insisted the supervisor. The supervisor was adamant that he would not let me meet with the former DEA administrator alone in Yuma. He was overly cautious as far as I was concerned, and I wondered what he feared would happen.

Eventually, the meeting was scheduled at the DEA office in Phoenix. I drove up to Phoenix and arrived for the meeting. Getting on the elevator, I noticed two guys not wearing suits I didn't know. As we rode the elevator up together, they looked at me as though they knew exactly who I was. I returned their stares but said nothing.

One of the secretaries greeted me as I got off the elevator. The two men walked down the hallway.

"Who are those guys," I asked once they were out of earshot.

"CIA from Los Angeles," she replied.

I found it odd that the CIA was here meeting with the big bosses. At the time, I wondered if they related to the former DEA administrator. Or were they here for something else? I couldn't shake the feeling that there would be a problem with these guys. My "gut" told me that the spooks learned I was focusing on the Chinese Seafood Company in Chinatown and its connection with the Cartel in Mexico.

At the time, I was unaware of the role that the former administrator, Judge Robert C. Bonner, had played in revealing illegal drug trafficking on the part of the CIA. In November of 1993, shortly after ending his tenure as administrator, he gave an interview to the weekly news show "60 Minutes" regarding illegal CIA activity. Utilizing the Venezuelan National Guard, the CIA smuggled 1.5 tons of cocaine into the United States. The CIAs justification for allowing the shipment was to protect a source within the Cartel. Per federal law, any such operation required the approval of the DEA, which they had tacitly refused. The decision was made by CIA assets to conduct the operation without the required approval. The drugs found their way onto American streets without tracking or oversite. (Wallace, Mike. Nov.1993, 60 Minutes Interview. Retrieved Feb. 20, 2023, from https://www.youtube.com/watch?v=IF-IYdsFGrw)

I ran into the former DEA administrator standing near the secretary's desk. He quietly whispered that we should meet later to talk privately about the brothers' case. He undoubtedly understood that the local bureaucracy had a vested interest in keeping one of its agents from speaking privately with a former administrator.

Later, I saw him outside, smoking alone in the secure parking lot. This might be an opportunity to speak with him privately, so I joined him.

"I am disappointed that we haven't had a chance to discuss the investigation, but we'll talk later." He said, insinuating that this was not the time or the place he wanted to have that discussion.

"Yes, sir!" I acknowledged.

We briefly talked about my career with DEA. He deserved my respect as a former DEA administrator, even though he was now a private attorney. I figured entertaining him with a summary of my career wouldn't do any harm. Eventually, we met again at the United States Attorney's office.

Besides the spooks, many people from other law enforcement agencies were involved in the meeting. It was not just about the brothers. It was also about the Chinese. I thought about the two spooks and wondered what their involvement was. They had listened intently at the meeting but said very little. Their unknown involvement in my case bothered me on a personal level. This case had taken some strange twists and turns between the spooks and a former Marine, a real American hero working for the cartel.

"Yea, though I walk through the valley of the shadow of death, I will fear no evil: for thou art with me; thy rod and thy staff they comfort me."

(Psalm 23:4, King James Version)

Chapter 53

So Run, That Ye May Obtain

The meeting had not gone as we hoped. The AUSA (Assistant United States Attorney) was uncooperative and had managed to elevate rudeness to an art form. He had gone so far as to tell the former DEA administrator that there was not enough evidence to present the case to a Federal Grand Jury to indict the brothers. The investigation clearly showed that the brothers were dangerous and that there was rampant corruption at the Mexico POE, but he dismissed the facts of the case out of hand.

"There is no evidence of law enforcement corruption at the POE," he insisted dismissively.

In spite of my earlier reservations the former DEA administrator was trying to move my case forward. He sat at a large mahogany table and tried to convince the U.S. Attorney and her staff of AUSAs that I had a good case against the brothers and the corruption at the POE. I was deeply invested in his desire for the U.S. Attorney and her AUSAs to prosecute the brothers.

I was fuming with anger. It was insulting that the AUSAs would tell the former DEA administrator that the brothers and the corruption at the POE are only a conspiracy case. How could they say that there was no evidence the brothers tried to kill two agents, sold narcotics in the U.S., and that there were corrupt officers working at the POE. The investigation had clearly showed that all these things were true.

I had been working quietly with DEA Chief Legal Counsel in D.C. and I knew the brother's case was ready to be presented to a federal grand jury. The two agents who were almost killed by the brothers in Sonora, Mexico deserved to have a grand jury review the evidence. It seemed strange to me that DEA Chief Legal Counsel was convinced that there was enough evidence for a Federal Grand Jury, but the AUSA would go so far as to call it a conspiracy case. *What did they want from me?*

The case was undoubtedly ready for the AUSA to indict the brothers. If they were too lazy, corrupt, or gutless to prosecute the brothers, I knew that there were other lawyers that would. I suspected that the Yuma County attorney's office would take on the case if the AUSA wouldn't. I was confident that with help from my sources and informants, we could take the brothers down. I had the Cartel in my gun sights.

"Know ye not that they which run in a race run all, but on receiveth the prize: So run, that ye may obtain."
(1 Corinthians 9:24, King James Version)

Chapter 54

If God be For us, Who can be Against us

"I want you to tell me the truth. Have you ever snorted cocaine with the brothers in Mexico?" That's how the AUSA started the meeting with my informants.

"Yes sir," they replied truthfully. "We had to sniff the coke up our noses."

The AUSA mechanically proceeded to the next question. "Okay. Did you ever have sex with any underage girls in Mexico?"

"In Mexico, there are no underage girls," they replied with sad, brutal honesty. "If they start bleeding, their women."

Although the meeting with the AUSAs a week earlier had gone terribly, the former DEA administrator had convinced them to meet with my informants. I told the informants to dress in suits and not look like they were homeless street guys.

"You guys are working for DEA. I want you to look professional," I insisted. "You're going to go in front of the Federal Grand Jury to testify what you learned about the brother's dope trafficking business, the agents they tried to kill, and the corruption at the POE."

At the appointed time, we met with the AUSA at his office. I was hopeful, and despite a few reservations, I felt like the meeting would prove to be a productive one. The informants looked great in their clothes, smelled good, and were well-groomed.

The informants looked at me as the AUSA launched an attack on their credibility while showing a noticeable lack of interest in what they had learned or how they had learned it. They seemed hurt and confused by the line of questioning, as was I. I had expected questions about the brother's drug business, the attempted murder of the two Agents, and corruption at the POE, not an attack on my informants.

"Much of the time, we could not call Agent Hardin," the informants tried to explain. "The brother's bodyguards watched us very carefully. Later one of the brothers pointed a .45 automatic handgun at us and asked, 'Are you DEA?' Then he laughed out loud and said, 'I'm joking. We know DEA can't do drugs, and they can't have sex with young girls.'"

"We were locked up in the brother's house in Mexico. We had to snort cocaine with them," the informant continued to explain. "Older women and younger girls come and go from the brother's house."

The AUSA tapped his finger impatiently on the table as the informants tried to explain their actions. "Stop! He blurted out rudely. "I do not want to hear about you guys shoving coke up your noses. I do not want to hear about the girls."

It had become clear to me that he didn't want this case. I found it unlikely that a man of his experience and position would be unaware of the brutal realities in Mexico and those faced by DEA informants. He shouldn't have been surprised the informants had snorted cocaine with the brothers or by any other things they felt pressured to do.

"Another brother pointed his .45 caliber handgun at us and accused us of being DEA agents," one of the informants said. "The more the brothers snorted cocaine, the more they ran their mouths about how they could never be arrested because of their relationship with the CIA. One of the brothers told us they tried killing two DEA agents. After snorting cocaine, he shouted, 'We will make sure the DEA agents are dead!'"

Another informant told the AUSA what the brothers had told him on another occasion. "Do you know our cousin?" the brother had asked. "He owns a car dealership," they had said, laughing. "You should buy a car from him, but don't bring your wife, daughter, or girlfriend around him. He will rape them."

I looked the AUSA in the eyes and emphasized the importance of what the informants were trying to tell him. "The brothers have a cousin selling used cars in the United States. He was once a mayor of a small town along the Southwest border with Mexico. He has a lot of relatives working in law enforcement at the POE."

"Look!" I continued to defend the informants and overcome his reluctance to accept their testimony. "The informants are involved in the criminal world of the control. They are given cocaine to snort with the brothers, and they are expected to indulge. With the help of the informants, I'm building a case against the brothers who tried to kill two DEA agents."

I addressed the corruption issue at the POE that the AUSA had dismissed as a conspiracy theory. "When the informants met with the brothers in Mexico, they were often stopped at the Southwest Port-of-Entry (POE). Customs agents and Immigration inspectors asked if the informants met with the brothers in Mexico. Of course, they said nothing to the POE officers about meeting with the brothers."

One of the informants chimed in. "The brothers have a lot of protection from corrupt law enforcement at the border. The brothers bragged about their niece and nephew working for customs and immigration at the POE."

"I'm excited the informants are inside the brothers' homes in Mexico," I said. "We know things about their operation that we couldn't otherwise know."

The AUSA paused to consider his next words; lacing his fingers on the desk, he leaned forward in his chair. "Larry, you don't have enough to prosecute the brothers for conspiracy to transport narcotics into the U.S. nor for the attempted murder of two agents." I was stunned; how could he say such a thing after everything he had heard.

"How about the brothers' relationship with Chinese Seafood Company?" interjected one of the informants.

The AUSA looked like he had never heard about the Chinese Seafood Company.

"How were you so successful in penetrating the brothers' family?" the AUSA asked the informants. It felt as though he were trying to change the immediate subject.

He quickly segued into another attack on the informant's credibility. "How did you know for sure if the girls were 18 years old? Did you ask the girls their age?"

"No," they replied.

The AUSA clearly didn't want to be put into a position where he would have to address the informant's use of drugs or sex with young girls in Mexico.

The informants had tried to defend their actions, but the AUSA didn't want to hear it. "We had to snort cocaine. Sex with the young girls was normal whenever we met with the brothers. The brothers knew DEA agents can't do drugs, and they can't have sex with young girls."

"I never told the informants they could use cocaine in Mexico," I explained. "Unfortunately, it was necessary for them to stay alive."

The first time I discovered that the informants were doing cocaine with the brothers was during that meeting. Before then, I had not known they were snorting cocaine with them. It especially bothered me to hear they were having sex with young girls.

The informants had mentioned having sex with girls from the brother's shrimp business, but they said the girls were over 18 years old. Despite these revelations, I understood the pressures the informants faced and the real threats to their lives. This case was too important to be derailed by such revelations. The AUSA didn't see it that way.

"I can't prosecute the case," he spat out with disgust.

Another informant had purchased a kilo of cocaine and set up deals for 30 kilos with another 500 kilos to follow. He was afraid of corruption. It was his duty to prosecute this case, but he stubbornly refused.

"This is bull crap!" I blurted out.

One of the informants commented on my frustration and used the opportunity to vent their own.

"Why did I go to prison for five years for helping a DEA undercover agent buy an ounce of cocaine?" he shouted. "I was charged with conspiracy but never saw any cocaine." It wasn't smart for the informant to talk to the AUSA like that, but I understood his frustration.

"You can't do this!" I insisted. "You've got the brothers. There is corruption at the POE. The brothers told the informants how they tried to kill two DEA agents in Mexico. It's on the tape recordings. I have evidence. We have a kilo of cocaine from the 30 kilos pending purchase from the brothers. What else do you want?"

"This is at least a conspiracy case!" I stated with firm resolution. "Let me arrest the brothers. I'll put them in jail for a few days, and I can start squeezing them about the corrupt cops, their dope business, and who the corrupt officials are working at the POE (Port-of-Entry)."

"You can get the brothers indicted with the Federal Grand Jury," I insisted.

He looked at his watch. "I am not going to present the case to the Grand Jury! I cannot prosecute this case."

"Let's leave," I spat out angrily. "He isn't going to prosecute the brothers."

"Larry. The AUSA was looking for an easy excuse to get out of indicting the brothers," said one of the informants as we left the office.

He's right, I thought. For reasons I could not hope to understand, I was sure the AUSA was trying to sabotage my case.

"What shall we then say to these things? If God be for us, who can be against us?"

(Romans 8:31, King James Version)

Chapter 55

Trust in the LORD with all Thine Heart

I drove back to the office alone, feeling defeated. The informants stuck their butts out, risking their lives to target the brother's drug activities. The AUSA, on the other hand, was gutless. It infuriated me that he had told the informants he didn't have enough to prosecute the brothers and me. Not even the attempted murder of two DEA agents had been enough to get him off his butt and do his job. I feared the brothers would learn that the informants worked for me and the DEA.

I was confident about the case. I'm the kind of a guy who can separate facts and evidence from conspiracy and present a case for federal prosecution based on facts. I don't deal with the types of hearsay and lies spread by the good and bad guys alike. You give me the bits and pieces of evidence, and I will pull them together so the AUSAs office can prosecute.

When I arrived home, my wife asked me how the meeting had gone. She could see that I was feeling down.

"I feel very comfortable with the information the sources and informants are providing me," I told her. "They have my back, and I have theirs."

I couldn't understand why I constantly had to fight battles within my own office and with the AUSAs office. When I got a chance to arrest the brothers and have them prosecuted, I knew the sources and informants would be great witnesses.

The long hours I spent working this case and others were taking a toll. The informants could not believe I was the only DEA agent working this case. My supervisor saw that I was becoming burnt out and no longer wanted me to focus on other narcotics cases.

The case against the brothers had reached the stage where we should make arrests and prosecute those involved. That had not happened, thanks to weak, frightened attorneys who were too lazy to do their job. A great former cop and source encouraged me. I was tired of fighting the legal system and the political hypocrisy.

"Stay focused, man. You're doing this for the American public and the common good. You must stop the corruption at the POE (Port-of-Entry) Mexico border."

"Trust in the LORD with all thine heart; and lean not unto thine own understanding."

(Proverbs 3:5-6, King James Version)

Chapter 56

I will Render to the Man According to his Work

After the meeting with the AUSA, the informants didn't want anything further to do with the case. They feared their lives were in danger because of the corruption at the POE. The informants continued to work with me where they could, but they refused to subject themselves to the types of risks they had previously taken. They no longer wanted to go to Mexico and especially did not want to meet with the brothers.

My informants had risked everything in Mexico with the brothers. On the other hand, the AUSA lacked the guts to prosecute the brothers and wasn't willing to risk anything. The corruption at the POE, which the AUSA refused to acknowledge, and the Chinese connection had left the informants paralyzed and unwilling to act.

Despite their reluctance, I continued to push for federal prosecution. Eventually, I got a call from U.S. Attorney's office,

"We're assigning you a new AUSA to help you with the Cartel brothers," the attorney's office relented.

The third AUSA was young and inexperienced. His ideas about prosecuting drugs were very liberal, and he was very naïve about the damage that illegal drugs did to our society. He thought the federal drug charges were too harsh on traffickers, especially the poor mules. I wasn't sure I would have any more luck with the third AUSA than I had with the previous two.

Our prior AUSA had gone back to prosecuting low-level cases. He stayed away from the investigation into the brothers, which suited him just fine. He was afraid to do anything about the corruption in law enforcement and at the POE and too squeamish about dealing with the harsh realities of prosecuting a major narcotics case.

I invited the new AUSA to travel across the border into Sonora, Mexico, to see the brothers' homes. I wanted him to clearly understand the brothers' opulent lifestyle. I wanted him to see their luxurious white houses with marble pillars imported from Italy. I wanted him to realize that their wealth was built on a culture of violence and that the victims had overdosed on their drugs. After he saw the brother's homes, he started to get excited about the case.

As it turned out, his views had not changed as much as I had hoped. I thought the AUSA was beginning to understand why this case was so important. He didn't understand why the charges against the brothers and their traffickers for trafficking cocaine would be so severe. I explained to him that federal drug laws were that way for every State, but each State played its own way in prosecuting drug cases.

In a state like California, the public took a liberal view toward narcotics distribution. This meant that most state and federal attorneys no longer enforced sentencing guidelines to prosecute drug traffickers. There was also much more cocaine being sold and moved throughout California, so prosecutors prioritized more prominent cases. California's state and federal jury selection was also a significant problem for attorneys. Many liberally minded jurors hesitated to find a poor mule guilty of drug trafficking violations.

It became apparent that the new AUSA did not want anything to do with prosecuting the brothers. He wanted to take on simpler cases like charging the mule that sold us the one kilo of cocaine. That completely missed the whole point of this case as far as I was concerned, and I wasn't going to let the brothers get off that easy. There was plenty of evidence to indict them.

The AUSA wanted me to meet with agents from other regions involved in the brother's case. He explained that he wanted to see additional evidence before charging the brothers for trying to kill two agents and their dope trafficking business.

Within a few days, DEA agents from Los Angeles, Washington, D.C., and Hermosillo, Mexico, expressed interest in meeting with the AUSA in Yuma. The agents were assigned to gather intelligence that targeted Asian drug trafficking groups. They wanted to know how I gathered evidence showing the brother's connection with the Chinese Seafood Company.

At the meeting with the AUSA, I summarized the case for criminal conspiracy against the brothers and the evidence we obtained. After summarizing the case, I showed how the brothers were connected to the Chinese Seafood Company. The agents felt, as I did, that there was ample evidence to prosecute the brothers. They also thought that additional evidence was needed to prosecute their Chinese connection. It seemed clear that that was their primary reason for wanting to be at the meeting.

The other DEA agents at the meeting seemed uninterested in the case against the brothers. They were interested in gathering information about related cases they were working on, which I could understand. However, their primary interest in the meeting appeared to make sure that my case did not negatively impact their own cases. They wanted to isolate my case against the brothers so that it did not touch on Asian trafficking organizations or the Chinese Seafood Company. The AUSA remained quiet for most of the meeting. He wanted to see what I would share about the brother's criminal activities with the other DEA agents, but he didn't want to do anything about it. That was my last meeting with the agents.

"Say not, I will do so to him as he hath done to me: I will render to the man according to his work."

(Proverbs 24:29, King James Version)

Chapter 57

Vengeance is Mine; I will Repay said the Lord."

The agent worried that the pregnant Mexican girl would lose her baby. She was crying and rubbing her belly. It was clear that she would have her baby at any moment. I was sickened by the thought that the baby of the heinous assassin would be born a U.S. citizen.

Earlier that day, Arizona Highway Patrol officers had stopped and detained the killer's pregnant wife and her brother as they traveled Southwest toward Sonora, Mexico. The DEA agent had been killed during an undercover operation in Arizona. A Mexican citizen had planned the cold-blooded killing of the agent. Thanks to the information the informants provided, we knew that the assassin's wife and his brother-in-law were fleeing to Mexico in hopes of evading capture by the DEA.

A younger DEA Hispanic agent and I took custody of the assassin's wife and her brother from the Highway Patrol officers.

"She's practically a kid and nine months pregnant," I said with surprise as I looked at her. "Her brother's a kid. Do you officers know their ages?"

The DPS officers shrugged. "They don't have any ID."

"We don't have any information from DEA that the pregnant girl and her brother were directly involved with the agent's death," said the other officer as we took custody of the suspects and left.

"Then why are they trying to get out of the United States? Why are they running back home to Mexico?" I snapped angrily at the officers.

The other agent drove while I attempted to question the assassin's wife and her brother. They refused to answer any questions about where her murderous husband was hiding. When I asked about his whereabouts, she would start to cry out loud and rub her huge belly, complaining of sharp pains. I thought about the agent's death, his family, and their pain. Her own attestations of victimhood only served to fuel my growing anger.

"Shut up! I'll slap you and your sick-looking brother in the mouth," I shouted angrily. "You know your husband killed a DEA agent. The agent has a beautiful family. He was a friend to us.

I wanted to slap the evil out of her and her brother. He needed someone to remove the remaining teeth that meth had not already taken from him. "Please stop," he pleaded in Spanish as he sobbed, tears flowing from his eyes. He was breaking under the anger-fueled intensity of my questioning.

I saw an isolated area next to a lemon grove as we drove down the road to Mexico. "Stop," I told the other agent. He hit the brakes and pulled the SUV gently to a stop on the dirt shoulder next to the lemon grove.

He watched as I reached into the glove compartment for a leftover packet of ketchup and stepped out of the car. The agent got out as well and walked over to me.

"What will you do with the ketchup?" he asked nervously.

"I'm taking the freaking girl into the lemon grove," I said. "I'm going to handcuff her hands to a tree. Then I'll shoot one round from my little Sweet Pea .38-revolver into the air. The boy will hear a gunshot and freak out. After I shoot a round off in the air, I'm going to smear the ketchup on my face and chest. It's going to look like her blood is all over me. When I return to the car without her, the boy will see blood on me. He will think I shot his sister, leaving her in the woods to bleed to death. While the boy's begging for his life, I will grab him by his scruffy neck and jerk him out of the car. Once I get the boy on his knees, I'll point my Sweet-Pea between his eyes. He'll be pissing in his pants. He'll tell me where the killer is," I insisted.

I reached for the handle to open the passenger door, as the other agent put his hand on my arm to stop me.

"Don't, Larry," he whispered. "The girl could have a miscarriage and lose the baby. The baby could die. The girl could die."

I swung around to glare at him angrily. The only thing I could think of was how her husband had planned the murder of a fellow agent.

"Her husband murdered our friend like a dog on the streets," I spat out. "His family is suffering. She and her brother helped kill our friend."

I opened the passenger door and grabbed the girl's arm to pull her out of the SUV. Her brother screamed in terror, pleading for help.

"Stop screaming, or I'll shoot your sister between her evil eyes now, right now," I shouted. The thing that scared me was that I really wanted to. My hurt and anger over losing a fellow agent, a friend, drove me to lose control.

Reluctantly, I pushed her back into the seat next to her screaming brother. Taking a moment to put my anger aside and regain control, I returned to the car. They were still crying as I sat back down.

"Stop screaming," I said without anger and without shouting. "I'm taking you and your brother back home to Mexico. My friend, the commander, is waiting for you. He can get the answers I need from you both."

When we reached an abandoned trailer near the border, they stopped screaming, and their tears ceased. She finally admitted that her husband was already in Mexico, hiding from DEA. We left them at the trailer and told them they could make their way back across the border from there, but we continued surveillance. The next day the assassin's wife and her brother disappeared into the dark Mexican night.

We waited anxiously to hear what would happen when the assassin's wife and brother returned to Mexico. A few days had gone past when I received word from my informants. The brothers had told the informants that a DEA agent had been killed in Arizona. They knew the killer's wife and brother were in Mexico, but her husband was not with them.

"Who killed the DEA agent?" the informant had asked the brother.

"We don't want DEA to focus on us," the brother replied. "The assassin's wife and her brother are no longer around. We don't want him or them anywhere near us. We don't want DEA to focus on our family. The DEA might think it was us behind killing the agent."

The assassin became one of the FBIs most wanted fugitives. With DEA pressure on the Mexican government, the killer was captured and eventually extradited for prosecution in the United States.

The assassin's wife and her brother were never seen again, and I have no idea what happened to them after they returned to Mexico. Perhaps one of the cartel families made them disappear into the hot Mexican desert near the mountains called "Path of the Devil." Or, perhaps, they simply went on to lead quiet lives in Mexico or back in the U.S. once pressure to apprehend the killer had ended.

"Dearly beloved, avenge not yourselves, but rather give place unto wrath: for it is written, Vengeance is mine; I will repay said the Lord."

(Romans 12:19, King James Version)

Chapter 58

He that Justifieth the Wicked

"Larry, the case is already done – whoever gets it at the US (United States) Attorney's office, they don't need to do anything! It's ready to go! It's all written out, and you've got the evidence to back it up." The Chief Legal Counsel in Washington D.C. assured me, "You need to indict these brothers with all this evidence."

I had prepared to show the AUSA, and the agents from D.C., Los Angeles, and Hermosillo the Chief Legal Counsel's review of my case. It clearly laid out the federal charges and the indictments against each of the brothers. I wanted the AUSA to read the official letter from the Chief Legal counsel stating:

"This is the best case ever on the Cartel family brothers. Keep up the good work. You have enough to prosecute the brothers. You can go after the corruption at the POE border."

The DEA Chief Legal counsel also stated that I had some great evidence from the sources and informants. He specifically cited the tape recording in which the brothers had bragged to the sources and informants about having tried to kill the agents. The case was already prepared! It was ready for the Federal Grand Jury, based on the evidence and information provided. It was unbelievable that the AUSA would not move to prosecute the brothers for the attempted murders and their drug activities in the U.S. given the mountain of evidence that had been uncovered.

A new supervisor had recently been assigned to the office. I proudly showed him the letter from the DEA Chief Legal counsel.

"You have the brothers indicted," he said supportively.

"I want to do this for the two agents," I responded with heartfelt sincerity. Their story had touched something deep inside me since those earlier days when I had first arrived at the office. My heart burned with a desire to see justice done for all that they had suffered.

My new supervisor's support was soon tainted by complaints from upper management. The AUSAs office was growing tired of my insistence that they do their job and made their feelings known to DEA management. They responded by telling my supervisor to tell me that I had to back off and stop pushing the AUSAs to indict the brothers. The AUSAs could not really tell me to start closing the case or I would force them to explain national security issues involving corruption at the POE.

The AUSA wanted to close my case against the brothers, and they were putting pressure on DEA management. One day the supervisor asked me if I wanted to be transferred to another DEA office. They hoped that by sending me away they could sweep the whole thing under the rug.

The AUSA's involvement with the case ended one day when they called me in for a meeting. I was still upset by their continued lack of support, and I wasn't expecting much from the meeting. There were a few attorneys sitting stiffly around a conference table as I stepped into the room. The meeting was short and to the point. An attorney that I'd never met before took the case file and slapped it on the table.

"The AUSA office can't do anything else," he stated.

The attorney, whom I assumed to be in a managerial role, instructed me to put the case to rest. If management within the AUSAs office was blocking the case, it would explain why the former two AUSAs were removed for unknown reasons and no longer worked the case against the brothers. The AUSAs office had everything I provided them on the brothers. I knew in my heart that I had everything that was needed to prosecute them. The review of my case by the DEA Chief Legal counsel in Washington D.C. made that clear.

"You've got the brothers!" He had clearly stated.

The latest AUSA that I had been working with asked me to come to his office when the meeting had ended.

"We can indict the mule for the sale of the kilo of cocaine to the DEA undercover agent, but nothing else," he offered.

"Who is we?" I asked. After all the late nights, the constant battles, and the danger that my informants had faced the word "we" seemed insulting. I had gathered the evidence, made notes, and gotten a review from the Chief Legal Counsel and the AUSAs office had done nothing.

I wasn't ready to let go. I deserved better, my informants deserved better, and the two agents that the brothers tried to kill certainly deserved better. If the AUSA wouldn't help me, I would find someone who would. I abruptly stood up and walked to the door.

"I'm going to take the case to the Yuma County prosecutor's office. The County Attorney wants to process it. He'll indict these brothers and expose the corruption at the POE if you won't!" I shouted as I left.

"Larry, you can't take this case to the County, it's a federal investigation, not a state investigation," he yelled back.

"Not anymore," I said defiantly as I spun around to look at him. "I'm going to take it to the County attorney's office because they're going to do it. They are going to indict the brothers and everybody on that list."

"It won't happen!" he shouted. People in nearby offices could hear us as we shouted at each other, and someone poked their head outside of their office to see what the commotion was.

"The brothers tried to kill two DEA agents. That's a no-no. You don't get to do that! Those agents are part of my family." With that, I walked away and didn't look back.

What a letdown, I thought as I jumped into my car and slammed the door shut behind me. The idea that they would indict the mule for a kilo of cocaine, but let the brothers distribute several hundred times that amount on a regular basis and go unpunished for trying to kill two DEA agents was a slap in the face. I had become emotionally involved in the case, it was personal to me, and I wasn't going to back down.

I was going to keep pushing for an indictment of the brothers. It didn't matter that the AUSAs office didn't want me to continue the case. *Who were they to me to back off the brothers? How do you do that without explaining the reason?* The new AUSA didn't care, that much was for certain.

Despite my firm resolution to keep fighting, I was worried that nothing was going to happen with this case! I felt with conviction that I was doing what was right, but it seemed like everyone was against me. The AUSAs office certainly was, corrupt law enforcement at the POE, and even my own office. The CIA was even involved in ways that I didn't understand because of the Chinese connection with the brothers. My mind swirled with the firm resolution of my convictions and doubts like an Arizona dust devil.

It goes without saying that I had lost all trust in the AUSAs office, but I was certain that the county attorney's office would help me. With their help, I was confident that the brothers would be indicted for attempting to kill the two agents.

"He that justifieth the wicked, and he that condemneth the just, even they both are abomination to the LORD."

(Proverbs 17:15, King James Version)

Chapter 59

Deliver me From the Deceitful and Unjust Man

I had encountered a lot of opposition as I fought to get the brothers indicted and a crackdown on corruption at the POE, but I needed allies. One of my staunchest allies was Lieutenant Danny Elkins, who worked for the Yuma police department. His co-workers called him the LT. He frequently accompanied me when I traveled to the POE. We had worked well together on several drug cases when I supervised the office.

When the AUSA refused to handle the case, I turned to the LT. The LT wanted to put the brothers in jail as much as I did. He was shocked to learn that the brothers were connected to Asian organized crime and the Chinese Seafood Company. He knew that I was dealing with corrupt cops at the POE and within the law enforcement community. As a local police officer, his help getting the case against the brothers moved to the county attorney's office would be invaluable.

"If the AUSA doesn't prosecute the brothers, then I want you to talk to the County Prosecutor," he assured me. "She's in charge of the narcotics unit. I've already called the County Prosecutor about your case. She's as excited as I am. If she can charge the brothers on State crimes, maybe we can stop the corruption at the POE."

He couldn't understand why the AUSAs would indict the mule but didn't want to prosecute the brothers. He embraced my plan to move the case to the county attorney's office.

The next day, the LT and I met with the County Attorney. The County Attorney knew about the brothers and their criminal activities. She knew how dangerous it was working so close to the border and learned about the corruption in the law enforcement community. I presented her with the case review from DEA Chief Legal counsel. She was speechless when she read that the Chief Legal counsel had recommended the case should be submitted to the Federal Grand Jury.

After a long and productive meeting, the County Attorney was excited to start. She assigned one of her assistants, a young but ambitious attorney, to prepare the case for presentation to a State Grand Jury. If the AUSAs office didn't want to prosecute the case federally, she was more than happy to present it to the state.

"I'm ready now to meet in front of the Grand Jury," I assured her.

Based on the evidence, the County Attorney's office was sure the Grand Jury would indict the brothers on State charges for the attempted murder of the two DEA agents and their drug activities. The young County Attorney's assistant was from the East Coast. He was a clean-cut guy who bristled enthusiastically and wanted to make a name for himself. This was the kind of case that he had always wanted. It would be a big feather in his cap, the sort of case that he could build his career.

I continued to work closely with the LT. We met regularly to discuss our work together on the brothers' case. After all the time I had spent fighting alone, struggling with the system, it finally felt like I had allies I could rely on.

"Judge me, O God, and plead my cause against an ungodly nation: O deliver me from the deceitful and unjust man."

(Psalms 43:7, King James Version)

Chapter 60

An Unjust man is an Abomination to the Just

The County Attorney called me. The excitement she had expressed when I presented her with the case had been replaced by a new emotion, fear.

"The Police officer came to our office today and said there would be threats against us because we are targeting the Mexican brothers and their family members."

Several days earlier, I had been approached by my supervisor.

"Larry, you need to talk to the Police officer about the Mexican brothers' case. He has been assigned to help with your investigation. You have got to bring the officer on board. He's going to be working the border with you," he explained.

Corruption was rampant along the border and within the local law enforcement community. I met with the police officer and summarized my investigation into the brothers. There were things that I intentionally didn't mention, such as my informants. I didn't know this police officer, and if I didn't know him, I couldn't trust him. *What guarantee did I have that he wasn't corrupt?* I resented that my supervisor was pushing me to work with someone I had no basis of trust.

A few days later, I got a message from my supervisor late at night that he wanted to talk to me right away and that he needed me to come into the office. As I pulled into the parking lot, I wondered, *what was so urgent that he wanted to talk right away, yet so sensitive that he would not discuss it over the phone.* I noted the concern and urgency in his voice, so I wasted no time returning to the office.

The supervisor called me into his office when I walked into the building. He sat behind his big oak desk with the County Attorney and the assistant prosecutor. We had a meeting scheduled for the next morning, so it was odd that they would be here now. What's going on? I wondered. I was sure it wasn't good.

"Larry, you need to sit down," said my supervisor.

"No, I'm going to stand up," I insisted.

I wondered if the AUSA had stepped in to block the county attorney's office from taking the case. The very thought of that possibility angered me. I had just been driving for three-and-a-half hours to be here, which gave me ample time to reflect on my years of struggling with the system. I braced for news I was sure I didn't want to hear.

"The Police officer you were assigned to work with went to the County Attorney's office," the supervisor announced.

I thought about what he said for a moment. "I have been working the brothers' case for several years. I've found corrupt cops. Let's think about what just happened today."

"The officer went to the Attorney's office," he continued. "Behind my back, behind everyone's back in this office, and told the County Attorney, 'If you take this brother's case, there's a chance you and your assistant attorney will get killed.'"

I paused to let them consider the ramifications of that statement. Their faces told the story; the corrupt police officer had scared them! I was as angry as a rabid dog.

"The reason he scared you," I said, acknowledging their fear, "Is that he knows the brothers. He must be one of the corrupt cops working for them. He is either corrupt or crazy."

"I will contact the FBI tomorrow and report the police officer's threat," said my supervisor, taking the situation very seriously. We wrapped the meeting up, and the attorneys thanked us for our time.

It was clear that our reassurances had done nothing to diminish their fear.

"Larry, I have a wife and a newborn baby," the assistant attorney said nervously as they left the office. His eyes were pleading for understanding as he said it.

I watched them leave and then turned to my supervisor. "It is too late. The corrupt officer did his job threatening the attorneys. The case is done."

My sources and informants shared my suspicions that the police officer was corrupt. Now I had to prove it, but I would have to be cautious when I met the corrupt officer again. I warned the other DEA agents in my office to avoid the police officer.

"You don't want to meet or talk with the officer; he's corrupted," I said.

The supervisor shared my concerns, and by the next morning, he had made sure that the police officer was removed from our office. The corrupt officer was not surprised that he had been asked to leave. He left quietly, never asked why he was removed from the case, and could no longer enter the DEA building. The County Attorney's office did not move forward to indict the brothers, and the case went downhill. The damage had been done.

Within a week, two FBI agents interviewed the police officer for corruption and threatening the County Attorneys. After questioning the police officer, the FBI agents wanted to meet with my supervisor. I was not invited.

"I should have been involved in meeting with the FBI agents," I complained to my supervisor. "I'm the case agent, no one else. I want to know why the officer made those threats. Who encouraged the officer to go to the Yuma County Attorney's office? Was it the brothers? Someone at the FBI, CIA, or the AUSAs?"

"You know what, Larry," the supervisor sighed. "The FBI agents can't do anything with the officer. The FBI agents told me that he is mentally deranged and sick."

"Yes, but he's corrupted, too," I insisted. "You wanted him to work with me on the brother's case. What the FBI said about the officer is a lie, and you know it." The supervisor gave me one of those wordless looks that said, *what do you want me to do about it?*

How the FBI agents handled the Police officer threat against the County Attorneys worried the supervisor. The supervisor realized that something might be stopping me from indicting the brothers. *Perhaps the supervisor was worried about his safety?*

The supervisor had to know that the corrupt police officer's threats signaled the end of my investigation against the brothers. He would have passed that information to the FBI agents, but despite that, they failed to take the incident seriously. I didn't know whom I could trust, and I wondered if someone on the inside was protecting the brothers. *Could someone at the AUSAs office have convinced the FBI to sweep the incident under the rug to protect the brothers?*

"I think the FBI put the officer up to threatening the County Attorneys," suggested a source.

My mind was swimming with questions. Why did the Police officer threaten the attorneys for working the brothers' case? Why didn't my supervisor and the FBI do anything about the corrupt cop? If the police officer was mentally deranged and sick, why was he still working on the streets?

"An unjust man is an abomination to the just: and he that I upright in the way is abomination to the wicked."

(Proverbs 29:27, King James Version)

Chapter 61

For he that Soweth to his Flesh Shall of the Flesh Reap Corruption

I was about halfway into my run and meditating on prayers. The frustration of recent events slowly faded, and I found a sense of peace that had eluded me in recent weeks. The sounds of a bicycle approaching from behind interrupted the silence, and I realized that the rider was calling out my name.

I turned to see a Deputy U.S. Marshal riding up to me on his bicycle.

"Lieutenant (LT) Danny Elkins and Sergeant (Sgt.) Mike Crowe were killed last night at their office by Yuma County deputy sheriff Jack Hutchinson," he breathlessly announced.

On the morning of July 5, I decided to go for a three-mile run along the water canal next to the orange and lemon trees and enjoy the desert landscape. I ran there regularly to reduce stress from work and focus on how blessed I was to be alive. Then, I learned that my two co-workers and friends from the narcotic law enforcement community were murdered.

I turned around, ran home, and quickly changed. No time was wasted as I rushed to the crime scene where LT and Sgt. were murdered. When I arrived, I found the drug and weapons evidence custodian, who appeared shaken and distraught. He had been with the narcotic officers last night when they were murdered in cold blood by the deputy sheriff. The evidence custodian struggled through his grief to summarize the events leading up to the LT's killing and the Sgt.

Drugs and weapons that had been confiscated were stored in a secured evidence vault. A few of us knew someone inside the building was stealing drugs and weapons from the evidence locker. Lt. Elkins and Sgt. Crowe had arranged to meet at the office to investigate the missing items.

Video from the evidence locker showed that a deputy sheriff assigned to work narcotics was stealing the seized drugs and weapons.

To their surprise, they found the deputy sheriff in the building with a red bandanna wrapped around his head, wearing black pants, a black shirt, and carrying bolt cutters. The deputy turned to leave the building, walking quickly down the narrow hallway to the back parking lot. Suddenly, as though he had decided he could not leave any witnesses, the deputy reappeared in the narrow hallway and opened fire with his automatic handgun.

The deputy was a retired staff sergeant in the Marine Corps. Everyone knew that he was the kind of guy that, once having started something, didn't stop until it was finished. The LT. and the Sgt. hadn't expected any problems when they arrived at the office and had certainly not seen any reason to enter the building with their handguns. They were trapped and weaponless, and their assailant blocked their only way out.

Lieutenant Elkins and Sergeant Crowe took cover as the deputy opened fire and continued shooting. The loud crack, crack, crack of ammunition being expended suddenly stopped as the weapon jammed. The trapped officers got up and bolted for the temporary safety of an adjoining room within the larger office. The deputy knew that his prey had nowhere to go, and the room offered little more than the illusion of safety.

The evidence custodian did not appear to be as fortunate at first. Their assailant had him trapped in the hallway at close range. He took aim with the pistol and mercilessly pulled the trigger with the intention of ending the man's life. The explosive round of life-ending gunfire never came, click, click, that's when the gun jammed. The deputy turned around and walked out to the back parking lot to clear the round, coldly and mechanically.

The LT. and Sgt. left the cover of the room to see if everything was okay.

"Let's go out the front door," shouted the evidence custodian. That said, he ran for the door as fast as he could. He had barely made it out the door to the public parking lot in front of the building when he heard gunfire resume from inside the building. Knowing that the unhinged deputy could emerge at any moment, he hid behind a nearby trash dumpster. Peeking around the dumpster, he saw that the Sgt. had also exited the building and was running towards the dumpster. The deputy followed close behind, with the muzzle of his pistol flashing thunderously in the night. Struck by gunfire, the Sergeant fell.

When the deputy had walked out to clear the jam in his pistol, the LT. had decided to remain in the front office reception area and call the local police for backup. The deputy coldly put several more rounds into the Sgt. to make sure he was dead. Having finished the job, he returned to the building to look for the LT and the evidence custodian, whom he did not realize was hiding behind the dumpster.

The LT. undoubtedly knew that the deputy would return. He was waiting in ambush as the deputy returned and grabbed him by surprise. The evidence suggests that a fistfight ensued. LT's watch was found on the floor, and bullets were sprayed throughout the partitions and into the ceiling.

LT knew that his only chance for survival was to quickly wrestle the weapon out of the deputy's hands. He successfully took the weapon as both men tumbled to the floor, and the assailant's weapon skittered out of reach. Unfortunately, the deputy had a second weapon, a .45 automatic, hidden behind his back. As the LT tried to pull himself up from the floor, the deputy reached for the hidden weapon and fired a bullet into the LT's spine. Coldly, the deputy fired another round to make sure the job was finished. That round nearly blew the LT's head off. The LT dropped to the floor, dying bravely, just as he had lived.

Sirens were flashing, and guns were pointed with deadly intent as the deputy stepped into the night. The local police had just arrived, having wasted no time after receiving the call from the LT. Unfortunately, it was too late to save his life, and the Sgt's.

"Get your hands up!" shouted the officers. The deputy knew he didn't stand a chance and surrendered.

The corrupt deputy never got the death penalty for murdering his supervisor and his boss. He was found under the influence of methamphetamine and sentenced to life in State prison.

The tragedy left me sickened with grief and rage. The Sgt. was my neighbor. His wife was pregnant and ready to have a baby. The last time I saw him, he held his wife's hand as they walked past my house.

LT was married with a son and daughter. The last time I saw him alive, he proudly told me about a fishing trip he would take with his son. Their deaths were a tragedy to all of us in the law enforcement community and to me personally.

"For he that soweth to his flesh shall of the flesh reap corruption; but he that soweth to the Spirit shall of the Spirt reap life everlasting."

(Galatians 6:8, King James Version)

Chapter 62

He Devises Mischief Continually

When I looked at the IRS (Internal Revenue Service) agent, he was waving both hands over his head, trying to slap away the menacing black bees.

"Stop fighting the bees," I yelled.

Thousands of stinging black bees were buzzing around the agent's head.

"Help me! Help me!" He screamed as he flailed about helplessly.

That morning the IRS agent told me some information he had learned from his informants. The brother's warehouse across the border in Mexico had been severely damaged in a fire during the early morning hours.

My case against the brothers had reached a dead end, but my desire to see them face justice remained strong. I was working with an agent from the IRS who was investigating their finances for business they were conducting in the United States. The IRS agent established that the brothers were making millions of U.S. dollars selling produce and shrimp in the U.S.

The DEA and IRS offices were in the same building on the second floor with the FBI. The DEA office was overcrowded, and I got permission to move into the same office as the IRS agent. It made sense, considering our close working relationship.

"Let's go look at the warehouse. I'll drive into Mexico," I suggested.

He agreed, and before long, we crossed the border into Mexico. It didn't take long to arrive at the burned-out warehouse. Exiting the car, we walked into the ash-covered, skeletal remains of the warehouse structure. I scanned the damaged floor for any criminal evidence I might find. I only noticed several black honeybees buzzing around hundreds of broken and burned pieces of honeycombs. I had no idea why they were there, and it certainly wasn't what I expected to find.

I remembered my earlier fight with the big black bumblebees while cutting tobacco on the farm in Kentucky. My crazed swatting had only enraged the bees who stung me in the butt. They continued to sting me as I ran home, and I realized the battle was far from over. Nothing deterred their relentless attacks until I reached the safety of home.

Due to my allergy to bee stings, I could not afford to be stung now. I remembered the red hives that covered my skin and how I had struggled to breathe. Only the quick intervention of Momma and the old country doctor had saved me from the potentially deadly consequences of those stings.

"Be careful stepping on the broken honeycombs," I shouted. "Whatever you do, don't fight the bees even if they sting you." As a country boy, I could only imagine how mad these bees were that a fire had destroyed their honeycombs inside the warehouse.

I quickly walked away and reluctantly sought the safety of the car. My allergy to bee stings made it dangerous for me to remain outside.

"Larry. Help me!" cried the IRS agent as I reached for the car door's handle.

I had hoped he could return to the car on his own, but I couldn't leave him there. Without another thought, I charged back into the buzzing black cloud surrounding him. Bees covered his head, stinging through his hair. With my left hand, I reached for the top of his head, grabbed a handful of bees, and squeezed them to death. They stung my hand defiantly as they died. I grabbed his hand with my right hand, and we moved quickly into a vacant building.

After the bees flew away, the agent and I quickly returned to my car.

"We must get across the border to a hospital now. I am allergic to bee stings," I said with urgency.

The experience had left him in shock. He sat there trembling and said nothing. I drove at high speed and crossed the border to the hospital emergency room.

"You were both stung several times all over your bodies," said the doctor that attended to us. "You are lucky these were not the deadly brown bees."

The next day, the agent told me he was in trouble with his IRS Supervisor for not getting approval to leave the United States and enter Mexico.

"I needed an IRS supervisor's approval to enter a foreign country," he said with the humility of a child chastised by his parents.

"I don't need DEA's approval to work across the Mexican border," I said with a cavalier sweep of my hands. "I just let someone at my office know I'm going to Mexico. Once in Mexico, I drink a few Corona beers and get some barbequed chicken to eat. If I have time, I look at the brother's residence to see if there are U.S. license plates."

"Larry, you are DEA. You can go anywhere, but I am in trouble with IRS and the supervisor. I might lose my job," the IRS agent said with a hurt expression.

I quickly learned that the IRS was much different from the DEA. Several days later, as I rummaged through my desk, I found some firecrackers my nephew gave me. Some of the firecrackers were very small, but they made a loud bang, like a gunshot.

I smiled as I remembered the day my nephew had given them to me during a visit. As a California Highway Patrol (CHP) officer, he had confiscated several boxes of firecrackers and bottle rockets during traffic stops near the Mexico border. He showed them to me as we chatted.

"Let's buy a case of beer and pick up our friend," I suggested. "We'll drive out to the open desert and have fun with the firecrackers and bottle rockets."

As the sun set, we picked up our friend in my wife's little green Mazda. We drove out into the desert night, popped open some beers, and unloaded the confiscated fireworks. Our friend had a huge bottle rocket in his left hand and a beer bottle in his right.

"Let it fly up into the dark sky," shouted my nephew dramatically as he lit the fuse.

Our friend happened to drop his beer as my nephew lit the fuse. The intended trajectory of the bottle rocket was altered drastically as he reached down to pick it up. The rocket shot forward in a crackling shower of sparks, not skyward, but into the open rear window of the little green Mazda. The Mazda's back seat exploded in red sparkles and white smoke.

"The boxes with the firecrackers are in the car. They're going to explode," I screamed. "Run!"

I reminisced about when my brother threw a firecracker under the bus driver's seat on the school bus. Fortunately, the boxes did not burn or explode inside the car as I had feared. We laughed about the incident and drank a few more beers. They chuckled, and I told them about the other time I put a firecracker under a narcotics officer's chair while he was cleaning his gun.

Thinking about those incidents, about the good times, brought a smile to my face as I rolled the firecracker over in my hand. The IRS office was far too quiet. I quietly lit the fuse and let go, thinking about the sound the firecracker would make when it went off inside the building and how the people would react.

It went off with a big bang that echoed loudly through the quiet office. People jumped from their chairs while others ducked behind their partitions. Some of the IRS employees thought I had shot my gun off accidentally.

"It's just a firecracker, not my Sweet-Pea .38-Revolver," I told the agent beside me. Laughing as I patted the revolver. He wasn't laughing.

After that incident, I was strongly encouraged by the IRS supervisor to move back to the DEA office. The supervisor was still upset that her agent had accompanied me on my side trip to Mexico. The incident with the firecracker inside their IRS office had put her over the edge.

"Forwardness is in his heart; he devises mischief continually; he soweth discord."

(Proverbs 6:14, King James Version)

Chapter 63

Man Should Eat and Drink, and Enjoy the Good of all his Labor

I pushed the old undercover Mercury hard as we drove west on the Interstate highway. The needle on the accelerator edged steadily upward to 120 miles an hour.

"Highway Patrol and Border Patrol are going to chase us down like bandits," the agent next to me shouted over the engine's roar.

"Don't worry, Buddy," I shouted back. "Their cars aren't fast enough for this old Mercury."

That morning, I had received information from my sources that a load of "dope" was being transported in an 18-wheel semi-truck hauling furniture. The truck had left town and was traveling west on the Interstate Highway. With the description of the furniture truck and the driver, I jumped into my old grey Mercury with the young agent. The truck had a big head start, but I was focused like a runaway bloodhound dog and determined to catch up with the truck.

I was wrong about how fast the old Mercury would go. It was fast but needed to be faster to outrun the Highway Patrol and Border Patrol. I saw a Highway Patrol car and several Border Patrol cars rushing in behind me as I looked in the rearview mirror. Behind them were several pickup trucks struggling to catch up.

"I must stop. If not, the cops might spike the tires up the road," I reluctantly told the young agent at my side.

Stories and rumors spread quickly within the DEA. I did not want to be remembered as one of two crazy, out-of-control cowboy agents that were shot and killed for not stopping at a cop's roadblock. I knew the story would grow with each telling as it traveled from agent to agent and division to division.

"Those DEA agents had pounds of marijuana in their car. They even had underage Mexican girls in the back seat with a case of Corona beer on the floor," people would say before the rumor ceased spreading.

I decided to slow down and pulled over to the side of the road. The cars behind me braked suddenly to a stop behind us. In my rearview mirror, I watched as the officers swung open the doors of their patrol vehicles and took cover behind them. A female Highway Patrol officer and several Border Patrol agents drew down on the old Mercury with handguns and rifles.

"Driver, exit your vehicle with your hands up and over your head," demanded the amplified voice of the female officer.

"Hey Brother, stay cool, don't swing your hands," I advised the young agent. "I'll take care of it, just like telling the supervisor only what he wants to hear. Just watch how a country boy handles this."

I put my DEA credentials in my left hand and slowly exited the car. The Highway Patrol officer stood behind the door of her patrol vehicle, pointing her gun at my chest.

"I'm DEA, credentials in my hand," I shouted back, keeping my hands visible and above my head.

"Don't you face me! Turn around now and slowly walk backward until I tell you when to stop," she commanded authoritatively. Her gun remained unflinchingly pointed at me. I walked back slowly, just as she had ordered.

"Larry, hurry up! We'll lose the dope truck! Quit talking with the girl and hurry up."

My mouth was agape as I struggled to believe his words. Did he want them to shoot me? In case he had failed to notice, I had many guns pointed at me. Now was not the time for him to shout, "Let's go!"

"Stop! Turn around slowly with your hands in the air," the officer commanded.

"I'm a DEA agent," I repeated as I turned to face her. I could see that some of the Border Patrol agents were snickering unbelievingly. *Sure you are, Buddy,* I could hear them thinking sarcastically.

The Patrol officer slowly took the credentials from my hand.

"I'm so sorry," she apologized. "I should have known you're DEA. Your license plate on the Mercury is Mexican."

I smiled, reassuring her and the Border Patrol agents that had stepped forward from the cover of their vehicle doors that I understood.

"I was down in Mexico following a furniture truck loaded with dope," I explained. "When the truck crossed into the U.S., I forgot to take off the Mexican license plate on the Mercury. I'm sorry to scare you and the Border Patrol guys."

"What happened?" asked the young agent as I returned to the old Mercury. "What took you so long? The girl was beautiful," he added, referring to the highway patrol officer.

"Nothing much. The patrol cop was doing her job," I acknowledged. "You know the furniture truck's too far away for us to find. It's hot out here in the middle of the desert. Let's go back into Mexico, drink a cold Corona and get something to eat before we return to the office."

"Okay," he agreed with a smile. I smiled back at him as I thought about the day's misadventure. It was another great day on the job.

"I know that there is no good in them, but for a man to rejoice, and to do good in his life. And also that every man should eat and drink, and enjoy the good of all his labor, it is the gift of God."

(Ecclesiastes 3:12-13, King James Version)

Chapter 64

The Fear of Man Bringeth a Snare

The DEA supervisor shot one round from his .38 Smith & Weston five-shot revolver into the big black, four-legged beast that had charged at him.

"I shot a wild hog! I killed that ugly thing," he yelled triumphantly.

Before the supervisor had shot the hog, I had been out on another long day following drug traffickers around town and down into Mexico. I got back to the office late in the afternoon, and I was casually chatting with the supervisor. We decided to go catfishing on one of the canals connected to the Colorado River near the Mexican border. In the past, while working nights, I caught some giant catfish out of the river canal while looking for dope smugglers.

It was late at night, and the supervisor and I weren't catching catfish or anything else. Off in the distance, I could hear Border Patrol agents yelling at illegal immigrants to stop running, but for the most part, things were quiet. Suddenly there were rustling sounds in the bushes behind the supervisor, and I heard a noise behind him in the bush. He jumped to attention and reached for his pistol. "It's a wild black hog," he screamed.

"It might be an illegal immigrant hiding in the bushes," I whispered, urging him to be cautious. There was a brief flash and a sound like thunder as the weapon fired.

"What hog did you shoot at? I said, scanning the area. There were no hog's that I could see, but I did see a large black beaver moving slowly near the riverbank as though it were injured.

"Shoot it again before it crawls into the river," I said, pointing at the beast. It was too late, and the injured animal disappeared into the murky water.

The bushes in the nearby vicinity had suddenly come to life. Illegal migrants were running around past the supervisor and myself.

Some of them were traveling south, back to the Mexican border. I guess the gunshot scared them.

Border Patrol agents followed the illegal migrants in close pursuit.

"I'm DEA. Do you guys need any help?" I shouted as they passed.

"Nope," one agent responded. "Did you catch any fish?"

"The fear of man bringeth a snare: but whoso putteth his trust in the LORD shall be safe."

(Proverbs 29:25, King James Version)

Chapter 65

God Hath not Given Us the Spirit of Fear

"You know I always carry a backup gun in my ankle holster, a snub nose five-shot revolver? My little Sweet-Pea .38," I said, patting my ankle. "A .38-revolver saved the agents from being killed by the brothers down in Mexico."

I had spent the day with another DEA agent, roasting in our pick-up trucks under the hot desert sun. The temperature was hovering near 111°, unbearably hot. Word was that a load of drugs was supposed to come across the border into an Arizona Indian tribal land from the POE. The Tribal Police were nowhere to be found and didn't seem interested. It wouldn't have surprised me to learn that they knowingly allowed the shipment to pass.

The supervisor met us in his new undercover government car, a beautiful grey Mercedes. He wanted to convince me to stop focusing on the brothers and spend my time focusing on other major dope traffickers. I resented that he tried to tell me what I should and should not do with the case.

"How about the two agents who almost died in Mexico because they happen to be DEA agents. The brothers wanted to kill the agents," I said indignantly as I kicked at the dirt. "You know, Boss, I'm a senior agent. I was in the office as an acting supervisor before you arrived at the office. I knew the investigation was going to be difficult. I kept going because I wanted the brothers to face justice for trying to kill those agents."

The hours I spent suffering in the relentless heat had made me irritable. That he would so casually toss aside the years I had put into this case, my heart, soul, blood, sweat, and tears, was more than I could take. My mouth ran freely without bothering to engage my brain.

"Boss, I can take the little Sweet-Pea from my ankle holster. I can stand next to you and play with the .38, and you know what? I might drop this thing, and a round could accidentally go off. Boss, it's hot out here in the desert on the Indian reservation," I said irritably. "Do you know that?"

I looked at the supervisor, laughing. He probably thought I was crazy. He smiled nervously, got back into his Mercedes, and drove off.

"Do you think a shot from that 38 could hit the boss?" asked the young agent.

I probably shouldn't have said what I said, but the heat was getting to me, and I resented what he was trying to do. I didn't understand why the supervisor couldn't let me do my job. His timing couldn't have been worse, either. He knew the young agent, and I were waiting on a group of traffickers moving drugs across the reservation.

"For God hath not given us the spirit of fear; but of power, and of love, and of a sound mind."

(2 Timothy 1:7, King James Version)

Chapter 66

For all Flesh had Corrupted His way Upon the Earth

I had spent six long years targeting the brother's drug operations. It had finally dawned on me that they had become untouchable by the Department of Justice and other federal law enforcement agencies.

"Do you see what's going on here?" I told my sources and informants. "I can't stop the corruption at the POE (Port-of-Entry) Mexico border. The abuse and corruption in our law enforcement are in the hands of wicked men and women. They have no understanding of God's justice. They call themselves cops and agents, but they are no different than the brother's corrupt niece that works at the POE border as an Immigration inspector."

"Once I end the case, no one is going to target the niece or any other friend or family member that helps the brothers," I explained to them.

Most AUSAs would "die" to have a major narcotic trafficking case with as much evidence as I had provided. I had all the pieces of factual evidence for the AUSA. In addition to the information from the informants, we had a buy from a mule that worked directly with the brothers. We had a deal to make larger buys. The informant had everything recorded on tape. We even had the brothers bragging about trying to kill two DEA agents.

The informant was upset as well. "I went to prison for calling a guy to meet with a DEA agent. The agent wanted me to help buy some cocaine."

"My hands are tied," I admitted reluctantly. "Everything I have is discovery. The brothers and the Chinese Seafood Company will view everything in the discovery documents that happened in this investigation. It will be released through judicial due process to indict the mule. The mule has the right to see the evidence against him. Then he will give it to the brothers."

My remaining hope was that once the corrupt cops at the POE discovered that DEA had evidence on the brothers, they would squeal like "pigs in slop." I hoped the day would come when they would fight to talk with DEA. I felt in my heart that justice was coming. My work produced all the factual evidence needed to prosecute the brothers. Hopefully, the AUSAs would indict them one day. Then they could shake out the corrupt officers and inspectors at the POE.

It had become widely known that I was investigating the brothers, and I began to experience acts of personal retaliation. One morning when I went to the office, I had a flat tire on the SUV. Someone had put a spike into one of the tires. On another morning, I found chicken guts in a plastic bag in the backyard. Later I found the window of my undercover SUV had been smashed.

I was not the only one to experience retaliation. My sources and informants were reporting that they were being harassed by officers at the POE. The attacks against myself had angered me, but I was infuriated that the corrupt cops wouldn't leave the sources and informants alone.

The local police set up temporary surveillance on my home to see who was behind the incidents against me. There was no guarantee that the surveillance officers weren't themselves corrupt. It almost seemed like a sick joke.

"It's time to go. You need to be transferred somewhere else," insisted my supervisor. "You are too close to identify the corrupt cops at the POE."

The supervisor wrote to upper management that things were getting worse for the office due to corruption in the local law enforcement community. He stated there were a lot of corrupt cops and agents involved with the brothers' smuggling organization. The DEA office had identified a few corrupt Customs officers and Immigration inspectors at the POE.

According to the informants and sources, the brothers were learning from the corrupt cops that DEA was determined to arrest them. The informants suspected the brothers knew what I looked like from the photo taken by the Mexican Commander at the plane crash site. It was becoming too dangerous for me to stay.

The former DEA administrator heard what was happening and called me personally.

"Larry, where would you like to go?"

"I'd like to go to Madrid, Spain," I said. After six long years in the Arizona desert, I knew my wife would welcome the chance to return home.

"Okay, let me see what I can do. Larry, I never knew what the agents had to go through dealing with the AUSAs. I was always isolated from the problems you agents had."

I appreciated his remarks.

"And God looked upon the earth, and behold, it was corrupt; for all flesh had corrupted his way upon the earth."

(Genesis 6:12, King James Version)

Chapter 67

Let not Your Heart be Troubled

I met the Arizona United States Attorney (USA) and her aide in the DEA Yuma conference room. They were shown photographs of the extravagant white houses owned by the Cartel brothers in Mexico. I told them about the tunnel between the brother's homes.

I was moving on to the next point in my presentation when the aide said, "Oh, I've been to this home with the former Congressman."

I was scheduled to leave soon for six months of Spanish language school in Arlington, Virginia. I recently received a phone call from DEA Headquarters offering me a choice of three different positions. The first two were Instructor positions in Quantico, Virginia, one for Domestic Training and the other for International Training. The third offer was a special agent position in Bogota, Colombia. I chose Bogota.

"How can I resolve this case before you leave for language school?" asked the U.S. Attorney. How long had I struggled for their assistance? And only now that I was leaving did they show any real interest.

We looked at each other across the table, and I could see the political lies reflected in her eyes. The idea that my ability to do my job might be based on political whimsey infuriated me. What political realities had changed that had suddenly made this case palatable to the U.S. Attorney?

I was trying to wrap my head around that idea when the aide casually mentioned that he had been to the brother's home with the Congressman.

"You are telling me you've been to the brother's houses in Mexico?" I asked in disbelief. "A person doesn't go in those houses without seeing the brothers snorting cocaine."

"Yeah," he responded as though the comment had no real relevance.

I focused in on the aide like Grandpa's old Bluetick coonhound dog Blue, getting ready to bite him. He grew increasingly nervous under my gaze. Why must he and the Congressman be inside the brother's homes?

"Why did you go into those houses?" I asked slowly and deliberately.

"Well, it was part of my work with Congressman Ed Pastor. I went there for a conference connected to agricultural production in Mexico."

The U.S. Attorney saw that the interaction between her aide and I was growing tense. She slowly distanced herself, stepping to the back of the conference room. The aide suddenly became aware of my accusatory tone and ended our conversation. The U.S. Attorney didn't mention the brother's case again. I knew that any hope of reopening the investigation had died.

My anger over learning that the U.S. Attorney's aide and the Arizona Congressman had met with the brothers in their home led me to decline my transfer. Now I understood why the brothers said DEA could never arrest them. The supervisor insisted that I stopped working on the investigation and begged me to take the transfer.

"Let not your heart be troubled: ye believe in God, believe also in me."

(John 14:1, King James Version)

Chapter 68

Let Thine Eyes Look Right on; and Let Thine Eyelids Look Straight before Thee

DEA management and my supervisor encouraged me to take the transfer I had been offered.

"If you go to Bogota, Colombia, for three years, you could get your supervisor position when you return to the States. But Hardin, you've got to keep your mouth shut. It's very political there at the American Embassy in Bogota.

You might see things in Bogota that are morally wrong but stay away from it. Go to the Embassy, stay out of trouble, and just do your job. Don't get involved with the politics."

DEA had offered me one of three different positions to get me out of Arizona, and they expected me to take one of them. I knew that my career would be finished if I stayed any longer. My only chance to be promoted was to take the transfer they offered me.

"It's time for me to go," I reluctantly told my wife. "The brothers' case is over!"

I had briefly been an acting supervisor, and my career was headed on an upward track. My case against the brothers had been important to me, and I had stood on my convictions. The arguments with the AUSAs and DEA management because of those convictions derailed my hopes of promotion. There would be no more promotions for me. Three junior agents with less time on the job later received their promotions, jumping past me to become group supervisors.

I had done a lot of hard work on that case, and it disappointed me that it had gone unappreciated. Worst of all, I felt I had failed to find justice for the two agents that were almost murdered in Mexico. I felt ashamed that the brothers were never indicted. My mind pondered what could have been if I had gotten the needed support for the case. The informants and sources had been the only ones to stand by me.

Later DEA Headquarters' office in Washington D.C. formalized my selection for Bogota, Colombia. I had struggled to accept the post-change when it seemed like so much had been left undone. The only chance I could see to jumpstart my career was to take a new post outside the U.S. Any hopes of being promoted to group supervisor or Special Agent in Charge (SAC) at a major office would require a fresh start. My supervisor assured me that if I worked well in Bogota, I'd get my supervisor's promotion.

I knew it would be difficult for me in Colombia because I could not keep my mouth shut when I saw corruption or lies. When I see a cop or an agent doing something wrong, I speak my mind and tell them, but not necessarily to the DEA supervisors and management. That is who I am.

Before transferring to Colombia, I attended Arlington, Virginia, for six months of Spanish language training. After training, I returned briefly to the Yuma office to prepare for my transfer. Unfortunately, nothing had happened with the case against the brothers in my absence. In the absence of external pressure, the case was quickly shut down by the AUSAs office.

Only one arrest was ever made in the case. Eventually, the mule that had sold 1 kilo of cocaine to my informants was apprehended by agents. All the evidence from the case became discovery. It almost certainly found its way into the hands of the brothers and any other trafficker interested in knowing what it revealed.

While in Colombia, I learned that the brother's mule served less than a year in federal prison for the kilo he had sold the informants and the additional 30-kilo and 500-kilo shipments he had negotiated. The mule was the right-hand man of the cartel brother's drug smuggling organization. Given his position within the cartel and the additional shipments he had arranged, it was hard to understand why the AUSAs office had imprisoned him for less than a year.

Looking back on the incident, I find it difficult to believe that "the war on drugs" was ever real. It appears people were turning a blind eye toward corruption. Some dangerous criminals were getting away with little or little consequence for their actions. Where was the justice for the two agents left to die on the desert street of Mexico?

"Let thine eyes look right on; and let thine eyelids look straight before thee. Ponder the path of thy feet, and let all thy ways be established. Turn not to the right hand nor to the left: remove thy foot from evil."

(Proverbs 4:25-2, King James Version)

Chapter 69

So Do not Fear, for I am With You

It became more apparent that people in the DEA, AUSAs office, and others did not want the brothers indicted. At times it felt as though they wanted me to fail. I had stood on my convictions to find justice for the two DEA agents kidnapped and assaulted, and I had stood alone.

I reflected on things that happened during the investigation. The first AUSA had encouraged me to go after the brothers for their actions toward the agents. We hit it off and worked well together. He left the office without a word, and there were rumors he had gone to the CIA.

The closer I got to getting the brothers indicted, the more obstacles were thrown in my path. The FBI and the other two AUSAs seemed "freaked out" whenever I mentioned corrupt officials at the POE. This had never happened before I came to Yuma. My focus on border corruption made me a threat to some in the law enforcement community. They did not want the public to discover the truth about corruption at the POE border.

It was clear to me that management wanted me to take a transfer because my investigation had become a political liability to them. I realized that things were becoming more dangerous for me due to the corruption and the widespread knowledge that I was taking steps to stop it. My supervisor and management had urged me to transfer based on concerns for my safety, but I knew that was only part of the story. I had started to keep to myself because of the corruption. It had helped to build integrity, but it had also isolated me from the internal political influences that could have helped to build my career.

There was no justice for the brother's victims, only a long trail of heartbreak, pain, and for some, death. I have never forgotten the two agents I fought so hard to find justice for. I continue to pray for them and hope to meet them in heaven someday. It broke my spirit when I had to let the case go and decided to accept a transfer. I had given the battle my all, and it was over. A second chance at promotion awaited me in Colombia and an opportunity to live my life not as the man I had been but as the man I had become.

I later got a phone call from the Chief Legal counsel attorney's office at DEA headquarters in D.C. He wondered how things had gone with the Mexican Cartel investigation.

"It's not going to happen, and I'm still not sure why the Cartel's family members will never be indicted for trying to kill two DEA agents," I sadly admitted. "If you can do something to get the Cartel family members prosecuted, that would be great."

"What happened?" He asked in surprise. "We did the work for you at the Chief Legal counsel office. All you had to do was take the indictment packet to any Assistant United States Attorney or the County District Attorney office."

I never heard from DEA Chief Legal counsel again about the brothers. He knew that there would be no justice for the attempted murder of the agents in Mexico.

The weeks before my departure were times of great reflection. I thought a great deal about life and my career. Some truths revealed themselves.

Live your life now. It is important to do the right thing, but we must experience what life offers and be grateful. There is a time to be born and a time to die. With the grace of God, I was still alive.

There was never a war on drugs. It hurt me to admit this, but it was the truth, and I needed to acknowledge it.

"It's time for me to go," I told my wife as we boarded a plane for the next chapter in our lives.

After arriving in Columbia, it did not take long before I realized that the tentacles of corruption had found their way there. Many of the DEA agents and supervisors at the American Embassy had succumbed to it in various ways. A few of the other agents and I struggled to stay away from it.

The office's investigations and reports contained n falsehoods about DEA's success in fighting the war on drugs in Colombia. I took the advice of my previous bosses in the U.S., who said, "Hardin, if you want to get promoted, keep your mouth shut."

So do not fear, for I am with you; do not be dismayed, for I am your God. I will strengthen you and help you. I will uphold you with my righteous right hand."

(Isaiah 41:10, King James Version)

Chapter 70

Be Not Afraid; Neither be Thou Dismayed

Informants told me that some Colombian police officers were reporting that Pablo Escobar Junior was moving back and forth from Spain to Argentina. I quickly learned that Pablo Junior, his mother, and his sister did not fear the DEA and Colombia law enforcement. The real threat, as far as they were concerned, was Pablo Escobar's remaining enemies in Colombia. The Cali Cartel and the Medellin mafia wanted to wipe the slate clean, eliminating anyone and anything associated with the notorious former head of the Medellin Cartel. That included his family. Many within the Colombian government wanted Pablo Escobar Jr. alive or dead, preferably dead.

Soon after arriving in Colombia, I began focusing on Pablo Escobar Junior's whereabouts. He was the son of the infamous Pablo Escobar. Under Pablo Escobar's leadership, the Medellin cartel gained an international reputation for brutality and murder. They had dominated the drug trade in the United States.

The day Pablo died, he talked to his son, Pablo Junior, on his cell phone. DEA knew that Pablo Junior was in Spain, and his father would continue communicating with him as he fled justice.

I heard from a Colombian Police source that Pablo had taken a personal interest in training his son. He wanted to show his son how to survive in the criminal underworld of the cartel. One lesson that Pablo Junior learned at a young age was how to kill. A Colombian Police officer showed me a photo of Pablo Junior pointing a handgun at the head of a sicario (hired killer) while Pablo stood proudly beside him.

"Have not I commanded thee? Be strong and of a good courage; be not afraid; neither be thou dismayed: for the LORD thy God is with thee whithersoever thou goest."

(Joshua 1:9, King James Version)

Chapter 71

A Man that hath Friends must Shew Himself Friendly

The Spanish Guardia Civil introduced my wife and me to the other Guardia Civil officers. We were welcomed warmly at the Spanish Embassy. I had brought a DEA hat for the Guardia Civil to thank him for the invitation. As we were introduced to the ambassador, he saw the hat and grabbed it. Apparently, he thought the gift was intended for him.

Soon after arriving in Bogota, Colombia, I visited the Spanish Embassy with my wife to meet with the Spanish diplomatic staff. My wife's first contact at the Spanish Embassy was with a Guardia Civil, Julio Gomez Franco. She told the Guardia Civil that her father was also a Guardia Civil after serving in Franco's military during the Spanish Civil War.

"My husband is a DEA agent," she said when she had first visited the embassy.

After we had visited the embassy together and the ambassador had mistakenly taken the hat, I turned to the Guardia Civil to apologize.

"The hat was for you. I'm sorry your ambassador took it. I'll give you a better DEA hat if you get me six beers. I like "Cruzcampo."

While attending a party at the Spanish Embassy, I finally met a Spanish narcotics officer. I invited him and the rest of his agents to the American Embassy to meet the DEA agents I worked with.

The Spanish narcotic officer gave me an odd look, then chuckled at the remark. "What other agents? I am the only one working narcotics in Colombia. I want you to come to my party next week."

"A man that hath friends must shew himself friendly: and there is a friend that sticketh closer than a brother."

(Proverbs 18:24, King James Version)

Chapter 72

Envy the Rottenness of the Bones

The U.S. senator looked me straight in the eyes. Here comes the political question.

"Agent Hardin, what do you think about the drug trafficking problems and the billions of U.S. dollars that would be given to Colombia to fight the war on drugs?" The question had come as though on cue.

I looked back at the senator and answered with the type of honesty that my bosses tended to frown upon. "The Colombians don't care about our culture or way of life. They only care about our money and what they can take from us."

The Hardins don't like corrupt politics like most Kentuckians back home. The senator knew my family and our reputation for telling the truth. He had expected an honest answer, and he had gotten one.

Several weeks earlier, my little brother in Kentucky told me that Senator Mitch McConnell and his wife would travel to Bogota. The Senator was scheduled to meet with the American Ambassador and Colombian government officials about several billions of U.S. dollars being provided to the Colombians to fight the "war on drugs." The senator had expressed that he wanted to meet with me when he was in Bogota.

After hearing that the Kentucky senator wanted to meet with me, my boss called me into his office to ask about my connection to him. My boss was clearly uncomfortable with the proposed meeting and told me it might not happen. I had gained a reputation at the American Embassy and DEA as someone who would not lie. They frequently found my honesty to be politically inconvenient. I refused to repeat the mandatory rhetoric about our amazing success in the "war on drugs." The truth was that the "war on drugs" was lost in Colombia and back home in the United States if there was ever a war in the first place.

Shortly after meeting with my boss, I received another call from my little brother.

"Someone at the embassy is causing some problems," he informed me. "They don't want you to meet with the senator."

Despite the objections of the American Embassy in Bogota, Senator McConnell was determined to hear what I had to say. The objections of the embassy were quickly shot down, and I received another call from my brother the next day. He said that the meeting with the senator was on, and it would be set away from the American Embassy.

My boss at DEA reluctantly told me I would meet with the Senator at a local restaurant in Bogota for lunch. He seemed surprised that the embassy's objections to the meeting had been dismissed.

"What kind of connections helped you to meet with Senator McConnel?" he asked with a subtle note of concern. I just smiled and remained purposely silent.

My wife and I arrived early at the restaurant. Within a few minutes, the senator and his wife appeared. They were accompanied by a contingent of security personnel who entered the large dining area and scanned for threats. The American Ambassador, the Ambassador's staff, and two DEA supervisors followed closely behind.

Senator McConnell and his wife warmly greeted my wife and me as they entered the dining room. The senator and I discussed life in Colombia as we entered a private dining area. We had begun to take our seats at the large dining table when one of the DEA supervisors rushed over to direct my wife and me to a spot at the end of the table, away from the senator. No sooner had we finished speaking with the supervisor when a member of the ambassador's staff nervously rushed over to offer the same directions.

We obediently did as we were asked and moved to the end of the table. As we were taking our seats, the senator's voice rang across the room.

"Agent Hardin, come sit across from me," he said just loudly enough so everyone in the room could hear.

The room went suddenly quiet as a cacophony of private conversations ended abruptly. The senator had seen through their attempts to isolate us and shrewdly deflected them.

His wife, who had skillfully learned to pick up on political cues turning their career in politics, moved to sit at the end of the table next to my wife. My DEA supervisors and the Ambassador labored to hide their scowls behind fake smiles as the seating arrangements were adjusted. I knew they would be listening to everything I said, and I would need to be careful with my words during lunch.

Senator McConnell smiled as I took my seat. I returned the smile, communicating unspoken recognition of how he had masterfully handled the situation with the seating arrangement.

"How are your dad and family?" he asked. He had kind words about them and talked warmly about how my little brother had helped him win the Kentucky election. As the senator continued to talk about my family, I glanced toward my wife at the end of the table. She and the Senator's wife were laughing, enjoying their conversation without a care for what was going on at our end of the table.

At last, Senator McConnell asked the question he was really here to ask. The ambassador, his staff, and the DEA supervisors went quiet as they waited to hear what I would say.

I could hear my former supervisor's words as I considered what to say next. "Hardin, keep your mouth shut if you want to get promoted."

That is when I told Senator McConnell what I really thought about the "war on drugs" and the intended funding for the Colombian government. I could hear the silent, agonized gasp from those assembled at the table. I had done the unthinkable, what they had feared all along; I had spoken the truth. The decision to speak truthfully would undoubtedly cost me the second chance at a promotion that I had desired. I didn't believe that the Colombian government should get our hard-earned tax dollars, and I couldn't bring myself to say otherwise for a chance at promotion.

Senator McConnell smiled approvingly at my bold statement of truth. As adept as he was at navigating a world of politics, he appreciated honest candor. I smiled nervously back at the Senator, knowing the ramifications that my decision would have for me.

The DEA supervisors rushed into damage control mode. They practically tripped over themselves as they interrupted our conversation to tell the Senator all the wonderful results. They had dismantled the cocaine labs and disrupted the drug transport to the U.S. The Ambassador echoed their reports of glorious successes and mentioned our excellent working relationships with the Colombian government.

The Senator continued to smile politely as he looked through their lies. He looked at me knowingly as the ambassador continued singing the praises of the DEA and the great job they were doing in Colombia. I was thankful the senator did not ask me any more questions about the war on drugs in Colombia. I never said another word at lunch.

Senator McConnell and I looked down toward the other end of the table, where our wives continued to talk and laugh. They had remained intentionally oblivious to the conversation between the senator and me. My wife was unaware that I had just ended my chances of ever being promoted to a DEA group supervisor.

The Senator and I walked outside with our wives when lunch was finished. He asked me to stay in touch.

"I'll never forget this meeting," I said. It was true. On the one hand, I would not forget the senator's kindness and generosity. On the other hand, it was the day that I had chosen to be true to myself at the cost of ever getting a promotion. I do not regret that decision.

Senator McConnell and his wife were a great couple. Later that year, my wife received a Christmas card and a photo of us all together at the luncheon.

"A sound heart is the life of the flesh: but envy the rottenness of the bones."

(Proverbs 14:30, King James Version)

Chapter 73

Wealth Gotten by Vanity Shall be Diminished

Once a corrupt attorney receives the discovery documents showing evidence against his client, those documents are passed on to the cartel. The cartels use written reports to gather intelligence about the methods law enforcement uses to target them. Utilizing that intelligence, they change the method of moving drugs into the U.S.

After several weeks of investigation, the Colombian police identified the location of a former associate of Pablo Escobar.

"We located a cocaine trafficker who was a former smuggler for Pablo Escobar," they reported excitedly. "We are going to search the smuggler's home. Do you want to come with us?"

The Colombian police knew that the DEA wanted to assist in searching any cocaine trafficker's home to document criminal evidence seized by the police. The police understood that I would gather additional criminal intelligence at the house related to drug activities into the U.S.

Once we arrived at the drug trafficker's home, police interviewed the former smuggler. He denied ever having transported cocaine into the U.S. for Pablo Escobar. The interview went nowhere, but I noticed Colombian prosecutors were reviewing documents inside two large filing cabinets in the bedroom.

"Agent Hardin. Do you want to look at the documents in the filing cabinets?" they asked as I entered the room.

I began thumbing through the files, scanning them individually, and looking deeper at anything valuable. To my amazement, I began to find investigative documents written by U.S. federal agents and State officials. The documents contained detailed descriptions of how drug traffickers were smuggling their drugs across the border into the U.S.

The reports dealt specifically with Colombian drug cartels and how they moved drugs from South America into Central America and, ultimately, the United States. Some reports had been written by state and local law enforcement agencies that dealt with ongoing investigations in their local communities. To my horror, the names of agents, officers, inspectors, police, and informants were clearly documented with no redaction whatsoever.

"These reports are called discovery," I told the Colombian prosecutors. "They are released through due process to the defendant's attorney before trial. According to U.S. law, the defendant's attorney has a legal right to know what evidence there is against their clients." I asked the Prosecutors if I could take the reports back to the American Embassy.

"No," they insisted.

I remembered a similar incident when I was working in Arizona. I had reported my concerns about sensitive case information being leaked to the cartels via these documents. Similar documents

were in the custody of the Mexican prosecutor and would have gone to the defendant's attorney as well. Despite my warning to the AUSAs office and the DEA Chief Legal Counsel's office, nothing happened. Now, I was looking at the same problem in Colombia.

"Wealth gotten by vanity shall be diminished: but he that gathereth by labor shall increase."

(Proverbs, 13:11, King James Version)

Chapter 74

Many Foolish and Hurtful Lusts, Which drown Men in Destruction and Perdition

The Colombian police reported that the Fuerzas Armadas Revolucinarias de Colombia (FARC) and the Colombian military were unloading the cocaine and destroying the stolen American planes. By the time DEA could arrive to investigate, it was too late. There were no pilots left on the scene to arrest and no cocaine left to seize.

Not long after arriving in Colombia, I was assigned to help follow stolen planes loaded with drugs. The planes were leaving Colombia en route to the United States, full of cocaine. If a pilot discovered that DEA was following their stolen American planes, they would land immediately. They would not even wait to find an adequate runway; any open spot on the ground with enough clearance would do.

I remembered one plane we had followed somewhere over the jungle-encrusted Colombian mountains. We followed the cocaine-laden plane in an aircraft owned and operated by the Colombian military. The pilots traveled low at high speeds, banking to avoid the treacherous mountains and the strong winds at higher altitudes. It felt like riding a roller coaster as the small plane jostled and bounced unexpectedly in the turbulent skies. I prayed that the pilot could land me safely on the ground.

The Colombian military plane was an Otter. It had a flexible wingspan for traveling around and through the mountains and valleys. After several hours of thinking the Otter would crash into a mountain or a river, it finally landed in an open field. When the plane door opened, I jumped out, fell on my knees, and kissed the ground. I didn't care who was laughing at the ridiculous "Gringo" on his knees kissing the ground. Apart from my sincere desire to stand on solid ground, I wondered why we hadn't landed earlier.

There was plenty of time for the stolen American plane to land and the traffickers to remove the drugs before we landed. I was left feeling that no one really had the guts to fight any "war on drugs."

"But they that will be rich fall into temptation and a snare, and into many foolish and hurtful lusts, which drown men in destruction and perdition."

(1 Timothy 6:9, King James Version)

Chapter 75

But woe to Him That is Alone When He Falleth

I squinted my eyes in the darkness as I was awakened from a sound sleep by the ringing phone.

"A DEA agent was killed in a firefight," the voice on the other end reported with cold professionalism.

"Who's this?" I asked, snapping suddenly to wakefulness. It was a Marine at the American Embassy.

While in Colombia, I was assigned regular turns as the duty agent. Any significant activity after normal business hours that affected our office would be routed to my attention. It was about 1:30 a.m., during one of my turns as a duty agent, when the Marine called to report that an agent had been killed. When that occurred, I was expected to handle or route the matter appropriately.

"What? Is this a joke?" I asked reflexively. It clearly wasn't.

"An agent has been killed. The agent's name is Frank Moreno."

I quickly thanked the Marine and ended the call. My fingers moved quickly over the keypad to dial my boss so that I could tell him what had happened.

"Son-of-a-b----!" he exclaimed. "Larry, give me a few minutes to get the details. Call me back." His voice reflected the time-sensitive urgency of the situation.

I decided that I should call the agent's wife. Flipping through a list of numbers, I found the home phone number for the agent and nervously dialed. I was about to give her the tragic news when she voiced her concerns.

"I don't know where he is! He's not answering his cell phone or pager," she said with a hint of panic. "I'm worried about him."

It was clear that she wanted my help finding her husband. I couldn't bring myself to tell her that he was dead.

"When he gets home, have him give me a call. I need his help with something." I felt guilty about ending the call like that, but I didn't know what else to say.

I called my boss and told him about my conversation with the agent's wife. My wife was sitting up in bed, instinctively awakened by the urgency of my voice and listening intently.

"You need to get to the hospital. You're going to meet the Embassy nurse. When you get there, go with the nurse," my boss instructed me. "The agent has been shot."

I jumped quickly out of bed as the call ended. My wife was following me, grabbing her clothes.

"Stay home," I said, not wanting to bother her.

"No, the agent's wife needs my help," she insisted.

The agent had been killed by a 9mm bullet to the chest. After entering his chest, the bullet had cut through his aorta and exited his back, hitting a young Colombian boy in the side of his neck. The agent died quickly. The boy passed away the next day.

I watched four people examine the agent's body at the hospital. The medical examiners moved his body from side to side on the table, locating the gunshot wound, and taking photos. His body lay there naked on the table while they moved him around mechanically, looking for other bullet holes in his body.

It filled me with sorrow as I watched the medical examiners carefully examine the body. Frank had been my buddy, and I remembered him fondly. My memories drifted to all the occasions he had walked up to my desk with a sly smile. He would tell me everything that was going on in the office, much of which I had been unaware of. Then, while I sat there distracted by his stories, he would casually swipe an apple from my desk. This agent always had my back, and he would defend me whenever gossiping agents spoke ill of me. I would miss him.

The Colombian Medical examiner finished his external examination and moved the agent's body to another location for a more detailed autopsy. I accompanied the body to the autopsy room, lost in thought and my memories of Frank. Another Medical Examiner was waiting in the room, wearing a large black leather apron, black rubber gloves, and black rubber boots up to his knees.

"Do you want to observe the autopsy while I examine the agent's body?" he asked professionally.

"No," I responded.

That was the body of a human being, a living being I had fond memories of. I didn't want to watch when the examiner cut him up like butchering a hog back home on Grandpa's farm.

I waited quietly in a chair outside the autopsy room. My eyelids hung heavy with sleep, and my head bobbed as the hours passed. At last, the Medical Examiner immerged and asked me to look at the body. Reluctantly, I did as I was asked. Blood and other fluids streamed down the skin from incisions in the chest, legs, arms, and skull. It was a mess, and I cringed at the sight of it.

"Can you wash his body and his face? Comb his hair? I asked out of a desire to give Frank some final piece of dignity.

The examiner later put a white Styrofoam cooler next to the body. At the time, it didn't occur to me to ask about the purpose of the cooler. I later learned that it contained the agent's brain and organs. The image of that white Styrofoam cooler is still burned into my brain.

My wife joined me once the agent's remains had been covered. His feet poked out from underneath the sheet, and a big white tag was tied to one toe. She had no words as she looked in horror at the white tag.

That night, one bullet had killed two people, the agent and a young Colombian boy. The killer, a Colombian national with alleged ties to money laundering, would eventually turn himself in and be sentenced to 30 years in prison. He served only 5 years before being given an early release.

I helped take care of the agent's body for three days until transport could be arranged to his home in Texas. The coffin had an American flag draped over the lid. The macabre white Styrofoam cooler went with the coffin.

A meeting was held at the American Embassy to discuss the agent's death.

"His death was a bump in the road, an end that could happen to any DEA agent," another agent privately commented to me.

My growing belief that the "war on drugs" was a big political lie surged within my thoughts upon hearing the comment. I contemplated the cost of that lie. Privately, I cried over the agent's death. I wondered if that life that had suddenly been snuffed out after only 37 years meant anything to the people who waged that war.

"For if they fall, the one will lift up his fellow: but woe to him that is alone when he falleth; for he hath not another to help him up."
(Ecclesiastes 4:10, King James Version)

Chapter 76

There Shall be no More Death, Neither Sorrow, nor Crying

Less than a month after DEA Agent Frank Moreno was murdered, my wife received word that her friend, Guardia Civil Julio Gomez Franco, was killed in a gun battle on the streets of Bogota. I had not known Julio well, but I liked him immediately when we met. My grief was still fresh, and hearing of yet another murder of someone I learned about on the streets of Bogota left me distraught. I had just finished caring for the body of a buddy and fellow agent until it could be flown back to the United States. Although Julio was not a U.S. citizen and not a DEA agent, he was a brother-in-law enforcement.

A week after his death, my wife and I attended the funeral Mass for Guardia Civil Gomez. I met his son and his wife and saw the sorrow and loss in their eyes. His wife was crying, and his son held his mom's hand. I looked down at Julio's son and gave him the DEA hat I had for his daddy. The boy proudly donned the hat. I had gotten another DEA hat for Guardia Civil Gomez but never had the chance to give it to him.

There was no room to sit at the Catholic Mass, so my wife and I stood in the back of the church. Most of the people began to sing a song I had never heard. Although I couldn't really understand the words of the song sung in Spanish, something about it touched me.

"What's the name of the Spanish song?" I asked my wife.

"Salve Rociera," she whispered quietly.

I found myself saying with the rest of the mourners, "Ole, Ole, Ole, Ole."

"And God shall wipe away all tears from their eyes; and there shall be no more death, neither sorrow, nor crying, neither shall there be any more pain: for the former things are passed away."

(Revelation 21:4, King James Version)

Chapter 77

He Shall not be Visited with Evil

The Consular officer told me she had Pablo Escobar's sister and brother-in-law in her office.

"Don't let Escobar's sister and the brother-in-law know they will be meeting a DEA agent," I said excitedly. "I'll be there in the next few minutes."

I developed a good working relationship with some consular officers I trusted. The State Department's consular officers at the American Embassy in the Visa Section knew I was looking for Pablo Escobar Junior. It wasn't unusual for them to call me if someone came into the office, they thought I would be interested in.

I walked into the small interview room alone. Pablo Escobar's sister and brother-in-law's Colombian passports were in my hand. They sat quietly behind a small table, waiting for me, unaware I was a DEA agent.

I consciously tried to control the anger I felt boiling up inside of me. This was Pablo Escobar's family. They seemed like a nice-looking couple, yet they were devils in disguise. Pablo Escobar had left a trail of terror, murder, and bloodshed across Colombia. That didn't even begin to account for the victims of the Medellin Cartel outside of Colombia. This was his family, and more than that, they were his associates. I could not believe their gall to go to the United States to visit family and relatives.

A U.S. Marine Embassy guard was standing in the doorway. I told the Marine he could leave the room. At the small table, Pablo Escobar's sister and the brother-in-law thought I was a consular officer who would provide them their visas to travel to the United States.

"Hello," I said politely, that I did not feel.

Reviewing their passports, I noticed they had traveled to a few other countries in South America, along with several trips to Spain. I can't believe I have Pablo Escobar's sister and brother-in-law sitting before me, I thought. This is my golden opportunity to find Pablo Junior.

"Are you related to Pablo Escobar," I asked, getting straight to the point.

I watched as they stiffened nervously in their chairs at the mention of the name. Reaching into my breast pocket, I pulled out my DEA credentials and identified myself as an agent.

They appeared to be very humble and polite, unshaken by the revelation, but I noticed their hands were shaking. They started to shift uncomfortably in their chairs and glanced nervously at each other. I got the impression they wanted to leave.

I asked again, "Are you the sister of Pablo Escobar?"

"Yes," she acknowledged in perfect English.

"I am her husband," her partner chimed in.

She did not wait for me to ask anything else before launching into an eloquent defense of her bloodthirsty brother.

"Pablo was a very good brother," she insisted. "He helped our family, the poor people of Medellin, the churches, schools, and the police."

I looked at her husband and paused before asking my next question. "What did you do for Pablo?"

"I was his bookkeeper and lawyer. I took care of his business," he said proudly.

They both denied that Pablo was a drug trafficker.

"Where is Pablo Junior?" I asked at last.

They dropped their heads without making eye contact and said they didn't know where he was.

"Why do you want to go to the United States?" I asked, knowing that they would not provide me with any information on the whereabouts of Pablo Jr.

"To see family and friends," they responded.

"Where do your friends live in the United States?"

The question was designed to get additional information about their associates in the United States, and they knew it. They slowly got up from their chairs.

"We want our passports; we're leaving now," they announced.

I was still determined to find Pablo Escobar's son. The husband was a lawyer and a bookkeeper for the Medellin cartel. The humble-looking lawyer knew I had no authority to arrest either of them. I had to return their passports and let them leave.

"The fear of the LORD tendeth to life: and he that hath it shall abide satisfied; he shall not be visited with evil."

(Proverbs 19:23, King James Version)

Chapter 78

To Fight for you Against Your Enemies

The DEA Diversion Investigator and I were forced to take refuge in the hotel for two days. Loud gunshots rang out in the distance as we lounged by the pool, eating banana splits. We could hear people screaming outside the hotel windows, especially at night when the situation intensified. The fighting continued from one day into the next as we ate our banana splits and watched the taxi canoes transporting people down the river.

"If we don't leave, we are going to get fat," I told the DI as we downed another one of the decadent concoctions.

I was assigned to help the DEA Diversion Investigator (DI) and the Colombian Police search for chemicals illegally entering Colombia from Venezuela, Ecuador, Peru, and China. DEA and the intelligence communities knew that the chemicals were being smuggled into Colombia to be used in the production of cocaine. Most chemicals were used at cocaine labs hidden throughout the dense Colombian rainforest. The labs were particularly common in Ipiales, Manizales, Medellin, and Cali.

The DI and I were investigating the illegal importation of precursor chemicals when violence erupted between the Colombian Army and the drug traffickers. The violence became quickly widespread, and the Colombian Police forced us to take shelter in the hotel for our own protection.

"For the LORD your God is that goeth with you to fight for you against your enemies, to save you."

(Deuteronomy 20:4, King James Version)

Chapter 79

For the Love of Money is the Root of all Evil

"You're not carrying any guns, knives, a hand grenade, or a large amount of money on you?" I asked the young Hispanic man.

"No, Sir. Only this cash I have in my pocket," he replied.

"Let me see your cash," I insisted.

The young man slowly pulled a large wad of cash from his pocket. It was not from his wallet or a stack of bills neatly folded like people typically carry money, but a big wad, neatly wrapped in a rubber band.

"How much do you have?" I asked.

"$5,000," he slowly replied.

"My partner is going to take a quick look inside your shoulder bag," I informed the boy.

We waited quietly as the narcotics officer on duty with me reached into the bag and began to search the contents methodically.

"We'll need you to come with us to the office," I instructed the young man as the officer completed his search.

My tour of duty in Colombia had come to an end. After leaving South America, my duties took me back to San Diego, California, where my career began. I was assigned to a group that targeted gangs distributing methamphetamine, heroin, and narcotic pills in the San Diego County area. I quickly learned from informants and medical professionals that opioid pills were favored by heroin addicts for their heroin-like effects. According to the informants, the heroin addicts were receiving their pills, not from violent gangs but from the medical community. Some of them were even receiving the pills free of charge.

I received an assignment to work for the San Diego International Airport narcotics group. During my first week working in that capacity, I received a phone call from an informant at the Miami airport.

"A Hispanic boy paid in cash for a one-way ticket to San Diego," stated the informant. "He did not have any checked luggage. He will have one stop in Houston, Texas, before arriving in San Diego."

I jotted down the flight number and arrival time, thanking the informant for the information. Another agent and I were waiting at the arrival gate when the flight arrived in San Diego. The passengers from Miami scrambled off the plane in small groups as we watched for the lone young man that matched the description we were given. I grew concerned that we might have missed him when he stepped off the departure ramp and into the terminal. We followed him as he walked quickly toward the luggage area. The informant in Miami reported that he didn't check luggage, but we needed to be sure.

The young man looked nervously around the luggage area and pulled a cell phone from his pocket. I watched over his shoulder as he tapped his fingers on a black unpowered screen and pretended to make a call. I approached.

"Excuse me. I'm a federal narcotics agent," I said, showing my DEA badge. "How are you doing today? How was your travel from Houston, Texas?"

"It was okay," he replied nervously in broken English.

"How did you get to the Houston airport?"

"My parents took to me to the airport," he lied. It was stupid for him to lie to a federal agent. He would know that the question was a trap if he had been smarter.

"Do you have cash?" I asked.

I was surprised by the neat wad of bills, exactly $5,000 in cash, neatly wrapped with a rubber band. He had continued to arouse a long chain of suspicions since his departure from Miami. I thought he was very inexperienced as I led him like a sheep to slaughter into the trap set for my questions.

Once we arrived in the office, another agent conducted a more exhaustive search of the young man's shoulder bag while our drug-sniffing dog prodded at the bag with its nose. As he went through the bag's contents, the agent pulled out a plastic bag with a shampoo bottle inside and unscrewed the lid.

"Something is floating around inside the shampoo bottle." He announced.

"What's in the bottle?" I asked, staring intently into his eyes. "If there's something that hurts my dope dog, you're going to jail."

"Sir. I don't know what is in the shampoo bottle," replied the boy. I couldn't shake the impression that he was telling the truth. He had to have known something was in the bottle, but I believed he didn't know what it was.

The agent slowly fished five rolls of tightly wrapped bills from the neck of the bottle. Each roll was wrapped with a rubber band, just like the one in the young man's pocket. He slowly counted out $25,000 in 100-dollar bills in front of the boy and me.

"Is this your money? Is this your shampoo bottle?" I asked.

"No, Sir," responded the young man politely. "The bottle belongs to my grandma in Guadalajara, Mexico."

"Okay. Give me grandma's name and address in Guadalajara; I'm going to call DEA in Mexico to talk to your grandma about the shampoo bottle," I told him.

The boy looked at me with wide eyes, then dropped his head as though he were about to cry.

"It is not my bottle and money. It is not my grandma's either," he confessed.

"Okay. You can leave my office. But before you leave, tell me who owns the shampoo bottle," I insisted.

After the young man answered my question, I let him go. He left the DEA office like a dog running after a whipping by his owner.

A few weeks later, I got another phone call from the Atlanta airport. The informant on the other end of the call reported that a black male had purchased a one-way ticket in cash to San Diego. I waited for someone who matched the description to leave the plane. It wasn't long before I spotted him.

"Sir. I am a narcotic agent. Can I talk to you?" I asked.

"You are stopping me because I'm a black man," he shouted angrily.

I gently tried to assure the man that I had not stopped him due to his skin color. The more I tried to assure him, the angrier he became. The man started walking away as he continued to yell defiantly. The man's voice echoed loudly throughout the terminal, and waiting passengers stopped what they were doing to watch the escalating interaction between us.

"Leave me alone. You're mistreating me because I'm black," he insisted.

My supervisor saw the interaction. He could see that I was struggling to deal with the situation in an authoritative yet tactful manner. He approached the suspect, who watched his approach and renewed his angry assertion.

"I'm black. You cops are stopping me because I'm black!"

"Hey, Sir! No one is calling you the "N" word. We want to ask you about your flight from New York," said the supervisor in a ham-fisted attempt at de-escalation.

"The flight from New York is none of your business," shouted the man as he continued to walk away.

Almost 20 years had passed since I joined the DEA, and I would soon be eligible for retirement. I had imagined that I would settle into my assignment with the airport group, and it would be my last. That wasn't the case.

"Larry, you have been reassigned to DEA Diversion Investigations. They decided to move you to Diversion to support their group," my supervisor told me after calling me into his office.

"Why me?" I asked suspiciously, recalling the recent incident. I had acted professionally, based on information from an informant.

The thought that I was being reassigned to another group as punishment seemed unjust.

"It's a great job," insisted my supervisor after seeing my obvious disappointment. "You will be working with the Diversion group to revoke DEA registration numbers from corrupt practitioners in the medical community that are illegally distributing narcotics and pain pills to their patients. Also, the pharmaceutical companies fail to realize that some of their clients are using the products they sell them to manufacture meth."

I remembered the nurses I had arrested for manufacturing meth early in my career as a DEA agent. I couldn't help but ask myself if I would find doctors, nurses, and other medical workers addicted to illegal drugs like cocaine, heroin, methamphetamine, and marijuana. I wondered what I would find in doctors' offices and pharmaceutical companies. Were corrupt doctors and their staff pushing pain pills and other narcotics to their patients? Were they releasing those pills to bad guys who were trafficking them on the streets?

One thing I learned throughout my career was that people were easily corrupted by the blinding influence of cold hard cash. As the quantity of money at stake grew, so did the strength of temptation. As a boy, I learned to trust those in positions of power or responsibility. As a man, I knew that wasn't true. Just because someone had a stethoscope around their neck did not mean they could be trusted. For many who take the Hippocratic Oath, "Do No Harm" has significant meaning. For others, they are only words.

"For the love of money is the root of all evil: which while some coveted after, they have erred from the faith, and pierced themselves through with many sorrows."

(1 Timothy 6:10, King James Version)

Chapter 80

The Lust of the Flesh, and the Lust of the Eyes, and the Pride of Life

DEA had to know about the corruption. I was starting to wonder if the drug Cartels and the medical community were all that different. The Cartels were distributing chemicals in the United States. Pharmaceutical companies in the United States and other countries were manufacturing opioids and other narcotics that the medical community distributed liberally. The Cartels loved the money they received for smuggling their products over the open Southwest border. The medical community and the pharmaceutical companies enjoyed their profits from over-prescribing pills. I asked myself why there was so much corruption between the Cartels and the medical community. Were they driven by the lust for power, money, and sex?

Soon after beginning my assignment in DEA Diversion, I was learning some physicians and nurse practitioners were providing false medical prescriptions (primarily for a narcotic called OxyContin). I was receiving reports regularly from informants that this was occurring. In some cases, they were supplying known dope traffickers. Were medical community members so easily corrupted by the allure of money? Was their desire for worldly wealth so great that they would toss aside all concerns for their addicted patients and the public good?

While working in the Diversion program, I frequently had to interview patients addicted to narcotics. Their stories were heartbreaking. I started focusing like a 'bird dog' on corruption in the pharmaceutical and medical communities.

I frequently found doctors, nurse practitioners, nurses, nursing home workers, and other medical employees pushing narcotics to their patients and diverting them to drug traffickers. They received large sums of cash and sometimes sexual favors from their addicted patients and customers in exchange for pills. It was not unusual for a close friend or family member of the suspect to provide me with information that nurses working in major hospitals were manufacturing meth and frequently addicted to it as well.

The things that I saw made me sick to my stomach. I wanted people to be able to trust medical professionals in white lab coats with stethoscopes wrapped around their necks. Unfortunately, many were pushing narcotics on their patients without physical examinations. I found it unbelievable that I had to arrest nurses for cooking meth.

I asked a DEA Diversion Investigator (DI) if he could provide me with a list of people in the medical community suspected of selling pills. One of the names he gave me was a doctor under investigation for pushing pills to the homeless and heroin addicts.

A week later, I met an informant with a heavy Caribbean accent near a bus station in downtown San Diego.

The man's speech was colorful and expressive. "Where are you from?" I asked.

"Man. I'm from the Caribbean islands."

"How is your health?" I asked. "You don't have any medical illness?" I was not trying to offend the man, but I needed to know these things before I could use him as an informant.

"Man. What's your problem? Why ask me that, man? You think I look sick, Man? Come on, Man. I don't have problems with nothing. Look at me move my feet and legs. Come on, Man. What do you see, Man?"

I laughed as the man moved his arms back and forth as though he were dancing. His movements were as joyful and expressive as his speech. I struggled to understand what he was saying while his arms waved like a skinny black bird learning to fly for the first time. I sensed this guy's disarming and spontaneous manner would make him a good informant for buying pills from corrupt doctors, nurses, and street dealers.

"I want you to see a doctor tomorrow to get a prescription for narcotic pills," I said. "Can you meet me at the pharmacy tomorrow? I want to check your blood pressure. I need to ensure you have no medical issues before visiting the doctor."

"Come on, Man. Why are you going to check my blood pressure, Man? How come you want me to see a doctor tomorrow?"

"DEA will give you $100 in cash to see the doctor. Plus, you'll get a free health checkup."

"Okay, Man. I'll see the doctor for $100. I get what you want from the doctor. But man, I'm not sick. Who's paying doctor?" asked the informant.

"Don't worry. DEA will pay your medical bill," I replied.

The next day I drove to the pharmacy parking lot with another agent. We saw the Caribbean informant skipping on his feet like he had broken both legs.

"Hey, you! Are you okay? Why are you walking like that?" I asked out the window. "Jump in the back of the van."

"This is another agent," I said, indicating the man beside me in the van. "He will give you a ball cap with a microphone listening device. Now don't drop it in the toilet." We waited while he put on the cap and flashed a toothy grin.

"Don't worry," I reassured him. I can listen when you are talking to the nurse and the doctor. You can't hear us in the van talking but remember, we will hear you talking and anyone else talking to you."

"You don't have any money, pills, or dope on you?" I asked. "What is the large bulge in your left pocket?" I asked.

"It's my clean underwear," he said as though the answer were obvious. No man. I have nothing in my pockets but my underwear."

He looked at me quizzically for a moment. "Why you asked what's wrong with my feet?" he asked.

"You are walking like 'Happy Feet,'" I said, referencing the movie about dancing penguins.

"Who is Happy Feet, Man?" asked the informant with a puzzled look.

"I want you to empty your pockets," I said after explaining the reference. "Let me see your underwear."

The informant jerked out what indeed appeared to be underwear.

"Why are you carrying underwear in your front pocket? Is it dirty?" I asked, puzzled as he had been by the Happy Feet reference. "You don't have anything else in your pockets?"

"You crazy, Man? Momma always said to have clean underwear before seeing the doctor," replied Happy Feet.

"Okay. I'm sorry," I said with a laugh. "My momma said the same about seeing a doctor. Let's go inside the pharmacy to check your blood pressure."

"Your blood pressure is excellent," I said as we returned to the van.

"Man, I told you, I am okay."

"You did," I acknowledged, "Now I want you to go across the street to the medical office. You ask for this doctor only," I insisted as I slowly spoke the name Doctor Decker and then repeated it to make sure he would remember it. "The girl at the front desk will ask if you are a new patient. Don't say anything else. Give her the $100 for the doctor's visit. Don't answer any questions from the girl," I said, emphasizing "any." "If she asks you why you want to see this doctor tell her you are homeless. You need to see this doctor." I handed the informant the $100 to give to the girl at the front desk.

"Do you have any questions? I asked.

We watched as the informant crossed the street, skipping on his feet until he entered the front office. I heard him talking on the microphone located inside the ball cap. He was telling the girl he wanted to see the doc.

"What doctor do you want to see?" the girl asked.

"Doctor Pecker," he said incorrectly.

I suddenly burst into laughter like a schoolboy watching someone embarrassing themselves.

"Who is Doctor Pecker?" I asked as my laughter died down. "Why is the informant asking for Doctor Pecker?"

I could hear the girl in the doctor's office laughing as well. It made me feel a little less juvenile.

"No Doctor Pecker is working here," she said at last.

I couldn't figure out how he had gotten Doctor Pecker from the name I had given him. Maybe he was thinking about the soda drink called "Doctor Pepper."

"You want to see Doctor Decker," the girl said with another laugh. "Why do you need to see the doctor? Who told you to come to see the doctor?"

"Man. I'm homeless. A friend said the doctor could help me. Here's $100," the informant replied. The girl seemed to understand and asked him to take a seat.

Within a few minutes, I heard another girl's voice on the microphone ballcap.

"I need to take your blood pressure and your weight. Follow me," she directed. I heard intermittent movement for a few minutes, but nothing was said. "Sit here in the chair. The doctor will see you soon," she said at last.

After several more minutes of silence, I heard a man speaking to the informant. "Okay. Why are you here?" he asked.

"Are you Doctor Pecker," asked the informant hopefully.

The doctor chuckled. "What do you want?"

"I need some pills. I have pain in my arms. My friend said you can help me," the informant said dramatically.

"Well, your blood pressure is high. Here take this blood pressure medication. It will help you," said the doctor.

"Come on, Man. I don't have blood pressure problems," the informant responded with exaggerated dismay.

I waited patiently to hear a response, but there was no other sound from the informant's microphone. Suddenly, I noticed the informant returning to the van, skipping on his 'happy feet.' He was carrying a large brown paper bag.

"Who is Doctor Pecker? What is that in the paper bag?" I asked after the informant got back in the van.

"Man, I forgot the doc's name. He gave me pills for my blood pressure. Where's my $100, Man?"

Soon after, I met another informant that could buy "street pills" from homeless people, prostitutes, and drug dealers.

"I know this woman being treated for stomach cancer by four doctors," he reported. "The doctors give her narcotic pills each month to help her with the pain."

"How do you know this woman?" I asked.

"She is my friend," the informant replied. "She has stomach cancer. She is on Welfare, Social Security, free medical, food stamps, and other free stuff."

"Once a month, she visits four doctors in different locations throughout San Diego for cancer treatments," he continued. "Each doctor gives the woman a prescription for 30 Oxycodone pills (50 milligrams each) for the month to help her with the pain from cancer. She goes to a pharmacy to get the 30 pills. The doctors and pharmacies are clueless that the woman is selling the pills to street dealers or exchanging the pills for heroin in Mexico."

"If the woman is getting 30 pills of Oxycodone from each doctor, then the four doctors are giving her 120 pills a month," I said. "How much does the old woman sell one pill for?"

"She gets about $50," replied the informant.

I quickly did the math in my head. "She is making $6,000 a month for selling the pills."

"If she doesn't sell the pills, she goes to TJ (Tijuana, Mexico) and gives the pills to the pharmacies in exchange for heroin. The pills are free. The heroin is free," replied the informant.

"Nothing is free," I replied.

If only the taxpayers knew how corrupt it was. The taxpayers were the ones paying for these pills. The pharmaceutical companies encouraged the doctors to write prescriptions, sometimes with gifts and other financial incentives. The pharmaceutical companies and pharmacies were then profiting from selling the pills. Taxpayers were paying a heavy price so the woman could make $6,000 a month in illegal drug sales.

"What does she do with the heroin?" I asked.

"Well, she doesn't use the Oxycodone pills to help with her cancer because she prefers the 'high' of heroin. She's scared of taking the pills because they are very addictive. She also makes a lot of cash every month selling the pills even after she gets the heroin," explained the informant.

"I want to buy one pill from her," I said. "Call when she is 'Doctor Shopping' again. You and I can follow her to each doctor's office and the pharmacies. Do you know anyone else selling their Oxycodone pills or exchanging the pill for drugs?"

"I know a lot of friends are getting prescriptions from Doctors and Nurse-Practitioners for Oxycodone," he said.

The following week, the informant and I followed his cancer friend to her first doctor's visit. The woman left the doctor's office and immediately entered a nearby pharmacy. I gave the informant $50.

"When she leaves the pharmacy, walk up to her and buy an Oxycodone pill," I said.

The informant waited outside the pharmacy for his friend. Soon, I watched the informant talking to the woman. After a brief exchange, the woman left the area, and the informant jumped back into my car. He reached out his hand and gave me one Oxycodone pill. We continued following the woman to the other doctor's offices and pharmacies.

"For all that is in the world, the lust of the flesh, and the lust of the eyes, and the pride of life, is not of the Father, but is of the world."
(1 John 2:16, Kings James Version).

Chapter 81

They that Will be Rich Fall into Temptation and a Snare

"What about the garbage dumpsters and trash cans," said the two new Diversion Investigators as they returned to the DEA office. They were covered in filthy poop all over their faces, hands, clothes, and shoes, and at least one of them had what looked like a streak of blood. The Diversion supervisor stepped out of her office and looked at them with a frown.

"They look homeless, like they've been living under a bridge," she yelled.

"I told them to go home to take a shower. Get that nasty poop off them before they return to the office," I explained.

"Larry Ray! What in the f------ are you doing to them? They are new. I want you to train them how to investigate these corrupt doctors. I don't want them digging in trash full of blood and sh----. How come you didn't have anything on your face and hands?" the supervisor demanded to know.

The next morning, I returned from buying a piece of Mexican black tar heroin for $60 from an addict on the streets.

"Hey, Larry, the supervisor wants to see you right now," said the secretary as I walked into the office.

"Now. Why right now? Can she wait until tomorrow morning? I'm busy," I asked.

"No. She wants you in her office now. She's worried about the two new guys working with you."

I breathed a sigh of annoyance, then did as requested. The supervisor waited for me to take a seat with an angry frown.

"Why do you have my two DIs climbing telephone poles?" she yelled. "Why are they playing inside garbage dumpsters and trash cans? You're treating them like homeless dogs." She paused with an angry glare to let the statement sink in before continuing her rebuke. "Are you trying to get these new guys killed? They have been on the job for less than a month."

"Wait a minute," I shouted back defensively. "You told me to teach these two new guys how to find evidence against medical practitioners diverting prescription pills to the traffickers."

She breathed an exasperated sigh as I continued. "Who is telling you the two new guys are climbing telephone poles? I have only one telephone pole with a video camera looking at a house near the Mexico border. If someone's climbing the pole, it will be a DEA technician. Anyway, one of the new guys is too scared to get his feet off the ground. The DIs only review the video camera tapes inside a secure Trailor about two miles from the house."

The accusation that I told the DIs to climb the telephone poles upset me. "I want to know who said the two new guys were climbing telephone poles?"

I continued without waiting for an answer. "The telephone pole camera is recording an older Hispanic woman and two young girls coming and going from home carrying postal packages, envelopes, and boxes. The camera shows the women removing what looks like money orders from the envelopes. The girls sometimes will open the postal envelopes outside in front of their garage. Then they put the envelopes into the trash cans."

"I didn't crawl into the dumpster. I'm not the dumpster diver swimming in the trash. The new guys are doing their job pushing the trash. I only showed them what to look for in the garbage. You know, garbage is a great location to find evidence. The brown poop and black blood can be washed off their faces and hands," I laughed dismissively.

"The garbage has all kinds of good stuff like pill canisters, empty postal packages, envelopes, boxes, gas receipts, utility bills, and receipts. They even found some cash receipts from the Pharmacies in Tijuana, Mexico."

"With the telephone pole camera and the garbage searches, those two new guys identified the older woman as a long-time narcotic trafficker moving cocaine, heroin, and pills. The younger girls are the woman's daughters. The woman and her daughters are working out of their home sending a lot of narcotics in packages at the postal office in several locations," I emphasized with several jabs of my finger and an emotional sweep of my hand.

"The video telephone camera, the trash dumpsters and cans, and the tracking devices on the woman's SUV Mercedes and her two daughters Mercedes show the women using the postal office to distribute the pills. The two DIs have enough evidence for the AUSA (Assistant United States Attorney) to review for criminal charges on trafficking narcotics throughout the United States.

The explanation did little to assuage her anger, but she couldn't argue with the results that had been achieved.

"What about last week's incident when the two DIs were with you at the Mexican border? You almost shot four Mexicans in a car. You could have gotten those new guys killed in a shoot-out," she stated, daring me to explain satisfactorily.

"I needed to provide security for the DEA tech to place a tracking device under the mom's Mercedes SUV. I took the two new DIs to help watch the woman's house. They didn't do anything except sit in my SUV eating gummy bears," I stated.

"But Larry Ray at 3:00 a.m.?" she asked.

"Well. That's the best time to work when the women are sleeping. The guys need to know how to track a car without following it," I explained.

"It's not about the tracking device," she insisted with frustration. You almost got them killed when you stopped some kids throwing rocks at cars."

"Wait one moment," I said, interrupting her. "I can tell you exactly what happened that night."

The supervisor stood up and glared at me. "Okay. Tell me," she said. The statement was phrased as a challenge.

"The technician put a tracking device under the woman's SUV Mercedes early in the morning. I noticed a car traveling by the house twice near where the technician hid the device. I decided to follow the car. Suddenly the car started to follow me. I quickly turned my car around to face the car that was now chasing me. I immediately told the DIs to call the police. I blocked the car from going around me, then I got out of the car. I told the DIs to get out of the car and stand in the rear. If the people in the car start shooting, you both run away for help.

With help from two agents from U.S. Customs working in the area, they stopped behind the car. The car was no longer able to move forward or backward. I slowly approached the car. With my "sweet-pea" 40 caliber sig handgun in my right hand pointed to the ground, I walked up slowly to the passenger side of the car. I quickly glanced inside the car. I immediately see two Hispanic boys in the back seat and two boys in the front. I noticed the passengers had small rocks in their hands.

After seeing the rocks in their hands, I asked, "What are you doing out here driving up and down in the neighborhood? Are you guys having fun busting out car windows with rocks? Do you have guns and knives in the car? You all need to drop the rocks now! Does anyone understand English? Drop the rocks now!"

I stared at the passengers in the car with my gun pointed down to the ground. The front passenger seeing my sweet pea beside me, immediately said, "No one else speaks English. Why did you stop us? Who are you? You can't do this. You stop us because we are Mexicans."

Lucky for the passengers and the driver, the police arrived, followed by Border Patrol agents. The police officer said, "We have been looking for these boys. These juveniles have been breaking car windows in this area for several days. Thank you for catching them."

"There's nothing we can do. Only arrest them, and later today, they will be released from jail," replied the officer.

"How about the car windows they broke over the last several days? Where's the justice for people using their cars to go to work and school?" I asked.

I leaned over to the front passenger and said quietly, if it was several years ago when I was working out in the desert, I would have slapped you all in the mouth if I didn't shoot you in the face first." The front passenger laughed, followed by the others smiling.

"You can't do anything. We did not do anything wrong," smiled the passenger.

"That's what happened with the rock throwers. No one got hurt. The new DIs did a great job listening to me," I said to the supervisor.

"But they that will be rich fall into temptation and a snare; and into many foolish and hurtful lusts, which drown men in destruction and perdition."

(1 Timothy 6:9, Kings James Version)

Chapter 82

He Deviseth Mischief Continually; He Soweth Discord

"I want you to go with the two new DIs and one of the other senior DIs," the Diversion supervisor reluctantly said. She was still upset about my earlier outings with the new DIs. "The DIs need to do an inspection for the Methadone clinic site. The clinic is due for an update to stop anyone from stealing the medication."

The next day I jumped in the backseat of a government car with one of the new guys. The other new DI was driving, and a senior female investigator was in the front passenger seat.

"Larry, I hope you don't get us in trouble today," joked one of the new DIs. The other passengers responded with muffled laughter.

"Don't worry; it's a security check at the clinic," I assured them. "I don't think anyone at the clinic will be throwing rocks."

A few hours later, we were at the Methadone clinic doing a routine security inspection. My role was to provide security and assist the DIs in any way I could. I was looking for ways to be useful when I noticed the front desk area had a clear bulletproof window that separated the Heroin addicted customers from the employees. It was the location where the administration staff would hand out the Methadone tablets to the former heroin users.

"Do you have a silent alarm button near you when giving out the Methadone tablets to the customers?" I asked the woman at the desk.

"Yes. It's under the desk," she replied.

"What happens if you push the button when an addict points a gun at your face?" I asked bluntly.

"Well, the window is bulletproof. If I push the alarm button, within five minutes, the police will be here to help us," she replied.

"Five minutes is a long time. One minute can be a lifetime." I knew from experience that a lot could happen in just a few seconds.

"So, you think if I push the alarm button, the police will arrive in five minutes," I asked?

The new DIs were nearby, reviewing their checklist, when they heard me asking about the alarm button. I noticed they were listening very closely.

"What do you think about the alarm?" I asked, glancing in their direction. "Are we here for a security inspection?"

The new DIs looked at each other and shrugged, not knowing what to say. They watched nervously to see if I would push the alarm button.

"Okay, let me push the alarm button to see how long it takes the cops to get here if there is an emergency," I suggested as my finger moved toward the red button.

"Let's ask the senior investigator what she thinks about you pushing the alarm button," nervously suggested one of the new DIs.

"Too late," I said with a mischievous smile. "I have already pushed the alarm button."

We watched the clock as time passed. The five-minute window came and went, but no cops arrived. The woman at the desk always believed in the security the button would provide. She was visibly upset that whatever security provided was less than reliable.

By this time, the senior DI had wandered over, and she was aware of the dilemma with the alarm. "You're doing the security inspection. You need to push the alarm button yourself," she told her young DIs.

"It might be broken," one of them suggested.

The other DI reached under the desk and fumbled around until they found the infamous button. He pushed it several times and then looked at the time.

"You know the alarm button is probably broken," he suggested. "It has been over 15 minutes, and the cops haven't arrived."

He had barely uttered the sentence when I looked out the clinic's window and saw a patrol car arriving in the parking lot.

"Here come the cops," I announced with a chuckle.

Two uniformed police officers entered the Methadone clinic with serious expressions.

"Hey, officers. We are DEA doing a security inspection at the clinic. The investigators are checking the silent alarm system," I informed them.

After seeing my credentials and observing that everything in the clinic appeared as it should be, they accepted my explanation and left. I was not surprised when I saw them returning a few minutes later.

"My Sergeant wants your name. He also wants your DEA supervisor's name," said one of the officers. It appeared that I was in trouble again.

"Larry, the supervisor wants you in the office now," said the secretary when I arrived. She gently shook her head from side to side with a little smile suggesting a laugh.

"Who me? For what?" I asked.

"Close the door behind you," the supervisor said as I entered the office. "What happened at the Methadone clinic?"

"The staff at the clinic said their silent alarm system works. If they had an emergency and pushed the alarm button, the police would arrive within five minutes," I said.

"Okay. So, what happened?"

"I only pushed the alarm button once," I replied.

"So, who continued pushing the alarm button several times?" the supervisor asked. She had already convinced herself that it was me.

"The new DIs thought that the alarm was broken. I guess they pushed it a few more times." I didn't want to throw the young DI under the bus. "It's not his fault," I added. "I told them I thought it was broken."

"Larry Ray, you embarrassed the police for arriving at the Methadone clinic after activating the silent alarm," she emphasized.

I might have been more sympathetic to that argument had the police not taken so long to arrive.

"What?" I exclaimed. "The cops were over 15 minutes late showing up at the clinic. You know how many employees and customers would die by a crazy addict in 15 minutes?"

A week later, the senior investigator and one of the new investigators wanted me to go with them to another Methadone clinic. Most heroin addicts had criminal records for buying and selling heroin on the streets. The customers were former heroin addicts coming to the clinic for Methadone treatments.

After we arrived at the clinic, the investigators started interviewing a beautiful Hispanic female about the security at the clinic. I decided not to push any alarm buttons or ask the staff any questions. The boredom of sitting around in the clinic left me pining for the days of chasing down bad guys in the streets and across the border.

I sat down with the DIs as they asked a beautiful Hispanic woman routine questions. As I sat there struggling with boredom, I couldn't help but notice that the woman was wearing a low top that displayed most of her large breasts. I tried to look away, but I couldn't help but notice that they looked different and deformed somehow. One had escaped and was nearly hanging out the poor woman's blouse. I glanced at the senior DI to see if she noticed the other woman's predicament.

She quietly acknowledged my glance with a nod, and we looked at the new DI. Despite his best efforts, he was obviously struggling. He was trying not to fixate on the woman's breasts, and act professionally, as he went through the list of questions he needed to ask.

"I'll ask her the remaining questions," the senior DI offered. The younger junior DI seemed relieved.

We finished the inspection and walked back to the car. I couldn't resist the urge to rib the new Diversion Investigator once we got outside the Methadone clinic.

"What did you think about the woman's large hooters?" I asked with characteristic blunt forwardness.

"What hooters? I didn't see anything," replied the DI with a wink.

Forwardness is in his heart, he deviseth mischief continually; he soweth discord."

(Proverbs 6:14, King James Version)

Chapter 83

It is as Sport to a Fool to do Mischief

I couldn't help but notice the beautiful Hispanic woman with the overstretched t-shirt. The image of a featherless bird was squeezed between the outline of her two ample breasts. I looked at the narcotic agent and stifled a laugh. His eyes were focused on the tiny yellow bird that appeared to be suffocating. I knew what he was thinking.

A close friend and fellow narcotics agent from the methamphetamine (meth) group and I decided to visit companies and farm supply stores selling chemicals and iodine to known meth cooks. We met with the owners of several farm supply stores selling multi-gallon containers of iodine. They assured us they would stop selling them to customers who weren't known to have a legitimate need.

The next day we arrived at a chemical company targeted by DEA for selling glassware and chemicals to known meth cooks.

"Brother, let me do the talking," I suggested to the other agent.

"Excuse me! Is the manager here?" I asked a group of young women sitting near the entrance.

"I'm the manager. Who are you?" responded a huge Hispanic woman.

"We are DEA," I replied with a grin.

The manager rose from her desk and approached us with a confident, businesslike stride. The tight white shirt with the yellow bird caught me by surprise. I glanced at the agent to see if he saw what I was looking at. He was squinting quizzically as he tried to identify the yellow object on the shirt.

"It's Titty Bird. It's Titty Bird," I told him after momentarily struggling to identify it for myself.

The manager smiled and held out her hand in greeting. I returned the handshake and the smile like a possum ready to eat roadkill.

"You're wearing a yellow "Titty bird" on your shirt," I said casually, unaware of my Freudian slip. The other girls in the office suddenly looked amazed by what I was saying. Most seemed to be giggling or stifling their laughter. A few of them seemed genuinely shocked. I was surprised to be getting so much attention. I noticed the other agent giving me a warning glance.

What had I said to the manager? I quickly scanned my memory of the incident, and it struck me. I had told Titty Bird when I meant to say Tweety Bird.

I tried to think of a way to save face and correct my error. "My wife loves the Titty bird on her t-shirt, too," I said. I quickly tried again, "My wife really likes Titty Bird a lot." To my growing horror, my tongue had developed a mind of its own. I could not say Tweety Bird to save my life.

The manager saw how embarrassed I was, and she was smiling from ear to ear. I looked at the agent standing next to me, mentally pleading for him to save me from my rebellious tongue. He stood there, showing his credentials, and waiting for me to say something. I showed the manager my DEA credentials again and slowly started over.

"Like I was saying, your Titty bird is beautiful," I managed to utter again. The manager said nothing but continued looking at me with a waning smile. *How had I managed to say it yet again?*

The other agent dropped his head in his hands and choked, literally choked, on the laughter that he was trying so hard to suppress.

"Are you okay?" I asked.

The manager was waiting for me to say why we were here at the chemical company. The other agent was staring at the floor, fighting to breathe. I was afraid he was having a heart attack.

"You want to go outside?" I asked with genuine concern. He nodded his head up and down to indicate that he did.

I quickly excused myself and apologized to the manager for the interruption. The agent was unable to say a word as we walked outside. He just kept shaking his head up and down as he gasped for breath.

"What happened?" he managed to say at last. "What's a Titty bird? You kept telling the manager you like her Titty bird. Your wife loves the Titty bird. I tried to tell you it's a Tweety Bird."

"I'm in trouble again," I admitted with a sigh. "My big fat tongue and nasty brain got stuck on her hooters."

By this time, the other agent had regained his composure. "We need to go back in and talk to the manager. Let me do the talking. I'll take care of it."

I'm going to lose my job for sexual harassment, I thought. I needed to keep my mouth shut when we went back to talk to the manager. She seemed to find humor in my embarrassment and didn't seem like the type to call DEA and file a sexual complaint incident on a DEA agent. I took comfort in that fact.

I eventually transferred out of the Diversion office and spent my final months before retirement back on the streets. My career would come to an end where it had begun, buying meth and heroin from dopers on the streets. It had come to feel like home, where I belonged and could do my best.

"It is as sport to a fool to do mischief: but a man of understanding hath wisdom."

(Proverbs 10:23, King James Version)

Retirement

They that Wait upon the LORD Shall Renew their Strength

After meeting the elderly Marine veteran, I felt deeply moved. I realized that many good men and women who had served their country in the military and law enforcement were alone and suffering. On a deeply spiritual level, I felt guided to contact the personnel office at the hospice.

"I would like to volunteer to visit military veterans and law enforcement officers living alone," I said.

The woman I spoke with sized me up with sad, hard eyes. "Do you understand that many of them are suffering from their illness and slowly dying without family?"

After 24 years of chasing bad guys, I finally retired from DEA. Yet again, I was left to ponder, as I had done in my youth, where my life would go from here. A few days later, I received a call from a former co-worker that had also retired from the Federal law enforcement community.

"Larry, you want to meet a World War II Marine veteran?" he asked. "The Marine veteran accidentally fell, hitting his head on the kitchen floor at home. He was living alone after his wife died. Do you want to see my friend? He's at the disability rehabilitation care facility (nursing home)."

"It would be an honor to see the World War II Marine Veteran," I said.

Soon after visiting the Marine, I received a call from Momma.

"Come on home," she said. "We're going to have a family reunion picnic at My Old Kentucky Home Park."

"Okay, Momma. I'm coming home to see you and everyone at the family reunion." It seemed only fitting that my retirement should be followed up with a trip back home.

After a good night's sleep back home, I awoke and stepped outside into the cool morning air. Later at the park, Daddy was busy, as I had always remembered him in my childhood, setting up the picnic tables and cooking equipment. My uncles arrived before long and started frying fish and some snapping turtle meat for family and friends coming for breakfast.

I was so excited; my family, relatives, friends, and stragglers would eat, sing, and dance throughout the day. They even had a karaoke machine. Wouldn't that be a hoot? I thanked God for bringing us together again.

After we were done eating, I asked Momma to dance with me. I grabbed Momma's hands as she reached out toward me. She smiled as we moved to the music, and I thought about how she loved us so much. The years of washing, sewing, cooking, and cleaning had made Momma's hands rough and callous, and she had done it all out of love for her family.

I looked into her bright blue eyes as we slowly danced. "I love you and Daddy so much."

"We love you, too, Lawrence Raymond."

I glanced around at the family, relatives, and friends sitting at the tables. They watched us warmly as though they had been touched by the heartwarming moment.

"Momma, everyone's staring at us," I spoke. She just smiled as we continued to dance. We did not know it would be our last dance together.

After visiting my family in Kentucky, I returned to California. I had three bottles of good Kentucky *Apple Pie* moonshine whiskey in my check-in luggage. When I arrived at the airport, I went to get my luggage at the baggage carousel. I noticed two DEA agents, close friends of mine, standing near the carousel. They were assigned to the airport narcotic group, my former group.

"Hey brother, how are you doing? It's great to see you," I said with a hearty greeting. "Man, I love my DEA retirement."

"Sir. I am a Federal Narcotics agent. I want to talk to you about your travel today," he said very seriously.

I laughed at the joke and smiled as though to say, "Good one, Buddy."

He kept his expression serious. "Sir. Can you consent for me to investigate your luggage?"

"What! Are you joking? We're buddies." I spoke.

"You know what is in my luggage," I added. "I always have moonshine Whiskey when I come back home. It is for our friends and retirement parties."

The other agent opened my luggage and quickly found three bottles full of reddish liquid. The agent searching my luggage immediately took one of the bottles and raised it over his head so everyone in the airport terminal area could see it.

"Sir. What is this?" he asked loudly.

"Are you joking? You know what it is." The objective of their apparent "joke" had become clear.

"Sir, I need to take this one bottle from you and test it for any illegal substance."

"Don't you mean taste it," I replied.

The agent grinned wickedly but said nothing.

"Look! I can't give you the bottle. I promised one bottle for an IRS agent, one for an NCIS agent, and the other for an FBI agent," I tried to explain.

He held the bottle just above eye level and studied the contents as though searching for the imaginary illegal substance.

"Brothers, you're embarrassing me in front of all these passengers picking up their luggage," I urged them.

"Thank you, sir, for the bottle. I will leave the other two bottles in your luggage," he said. I saw the two of them laughing as they walked away with the bottle.

"We look forward to seeing you again at the San Diego Airport," they shouted back.

I bet they did. I had never known how much my DEA brothers loved the moonshine.

About two years later, I was strongly encouraged by my former DEA co-workers to teach criminal justice courses at a university and a college located in Spain. I was hired as an adjunct professor teaching the military, their dependents, and law enforcement officers a criminal justice course.

The college in Spain allowed me to live and work, teaching criminal law courses to our military and their family members throughout Europe. I shared my DEA experiences with students majoring in Criminal Justice at a university and one of the European colleges.

As a young boy growing up in Kentucky, I could never have imagined everything that life would have in store for me. I found my retirement years to be quite full. In addition to teaching, I started a private investigation business and volunteered to visit military veterans, law enforcement agents, and police officers in hospice.

"But they that wait upon the LORD shall renew their strength; they shall mount up with wings as eagles; they shall run, and not be wery; and they shall walk, and not faint."

(Isaiah 40:31, King James Version)

Epilogue

Thoughts of Peace, and not of Evil, to Give you an Expected End

The most dangerous moments I encountered while working narcotics in the United States, Mexico, and at the American Embassy in Bogota, Colombia, were not physical threats to my life. The greatest threats I encountered were the ones to my soul. I was surrounded by temptation and had to learn to walk through corruption without becoming corrupt myself.

I saw evil in the eyes of some wicked men I arrested for narcotics trafficking. My trust in the military, law enforcement communities, and our government was challenged as they turned a blind eye to the justice I sought. It was difficult for me not to give up hope that someday our country could win the war on drugs and the war on crime. I hope it's not too late.

It was also one of my biggest challenges to maintaining faith in humanity. Without faith in God and Jesus Christ, society will have no hope.

The Road to Heaven, Leads Through Hell

"For I know the thoughts that I think toward you, saith the LORD, thoughts of peace,and not of evil, to give you an expected end."

(Jeremiah 29:11, King James Version)

DEA PRB #2023-12

Made in the USA
Columbia, SC
20 June 2023